The Supreme Court in the
Intimate Lives of Americans

The Supreme Court in the Intimate Lives of Americans

Birth, Sex, Marriage, Childrearing, and Death

Howard Ball

NEW YORK UNIVERSITY PRESS

New York and London

NEW YORK UNIVERSITY PRESS
New York and London
www.nyupress.org

First published in paperback in 2004

Library of Congress Cataloging-in-Publication Data
Ball, Howard, 1937–
The Supreme Court in the intimate lives of Americans :
birth, sex, marriage, childbearing, and death
p. cm.
Includes bibliographical references and index.
ISBN 0–8147–9862–4 (cloth : alk. paper) —
ISBN 0–8147–9863–2 (pbk : alk. paper)
1. Human reproduction—Law and legislation—United States—History.
2. Abortion—Law and legislation—United States—History.
3. Right to die—Law and legislation—United States—History.
4. United States—Supreme Court—History.   I. Title.
KF3760 .B35 2002   2002004198

New York University Press books are printed on acid-free paper,
and their binding materials are chosen for strength and durability.

Manufactured in the United States of America
c 10 9 8 7 6 5 4 3
p 10 9 8 7 6 5 4 3 2 1

For My Family,
Carol
Sue
Sheryl, Jay, Lila, and Nate
Melissa and Patrick
and
Stormin' Norman
Dirty Harry
Maggie
Sam
Charlie

Contents

Acknowledgments

A few words of thanks to some people who have been of great help to me in this and other projects I have taken on during my many years as researcher and writer about the U.S. Supreme Court, its personnel and its outputs. I have been blessed with some excellent editors over the years, especially Susan Rabiner, Jim West, Niko Pfund, and Mike Briggs. The manuscript personnel in the Manuscript Division of the Library of Congress (Madison Building) and Archivist John Jacob at Washington and Lee's Law Library have always been extremely helpful to me in my efforts to answer questions about the Court and its personnel.

I have had the friendship of a small number of persons throughout my career, men and women who have been sounding boards, reviewers, and, on occasion, coauthors. These people are Herb Rosenbaum, Hofstra University; Jim and Adele McComas, Virginia Tech University; Tom Lauth, University of Georgia; Phil Cooper, Wolfgang Mieder, and John Burke, University of Vermont; Bill Giles and Charles Lowery, Mississippi State University; Carol and Lee Teplin; Sam Conant; Irv and Gloria Altman, University of Utah; and Kate Green of the University of Southern Mississippi.

A special thanks to two bright Honors students at UVM, Leila Zayad and Beth Ryan, for their assistance. "Well behaved women rarely make history." Believe me when I say that these two women will make history.

There was a man who played an important part of my life, both professional and personal: Sid Neidell. I miss him every day. Finally, there is my family. I love you all and wish you the best. You all have been my strength over the years.

Thank you, all of you, for your help and your friendship.

Introduction

Storks do not, as Max Lerner observed many decades ago, deliver constitutional cases and the decisions that follow.[1] Nor do they "just 'happen,' as one might think if one were to look only at the cases decided by the Supreme Court as they appear in constitutional law casebooks and are discussed in academic commentary."[2]

First of all, the U.S. Supreme Court decides which cases it wishes to hear on the merits.[3] The Justices have total discretion in creating the Court's docket. Four Justices must vote to grant certiorari, called the "vote of four," in a particular case in order for it to be given plenary review.

There are legal, social, and political reasons that particular constitutional cases are brought to the U.S. Supreme Court at particular times in America's history. In the past four decades, litigation in defense of intimate personal, sexual associations against intrusive state actions came to the courts at a time when America was in the throes of a number of "revolutions."

The years between 1955 and the early 1970s were cacophonous ones. The nation saw and experienced on the evening news the emergence of the civil rights revolution, the anti–Vietnam War movement, the women's rights movement, the sexual revolution, and the gay liberation movement. Radicalized men and women, young and not so young, involved in one or more of these revolutions, confronted what seemed to them to be serious government intrusions into their personal lives.

Their personal liberties, they eventually argued in court, were protected from disturbing state actions by the Fourteenth Amendment's Equal Protection and Due Process Clauses. The Fifth Amendment's Due Process Clause protected them from invasive actions by agents of the national government.[4] They brought these legal arguments into America's courtrooms, directly challenging the legitimacy of government to proscribe their actions. There were, of course, the watershed civil rights cases heard and decided by the U.S. Supreme Court led by Chief Justice Earl Warren,[5] beginning with *Brown v*

1

Board of Education of Topeka, Kansas, 1954.[6] *Brown* toppled the pseudoracist 1896 Court opinion, *Plessy v Ferguson*,[7] a 7:1 decision validating the imposition—by government or by private persons—of separate, segregated facilities so long as the segregated facilities, from hospitals where people were born to cemeteries where they were buried, were equal.

Questions dealing with state restraints on matters of personal sexual privacy and bodily integrity began to be heard during the halcyon years of the Warren Court (1953–1969).[8] Some of the many questions raised and answered in this general issue area over the past forty years by different Supreme Court majorities were

Could Connecticut bar married couples from receiving birth control information and purchasing contraceptives?

Could Massachusetts prohibit a single person from acquiring birth control devices in order to prevent an unwanted pregnancy while engaging in sexual intercourse?

Could Florida prohibit two single persons of different races from having consensual sexual intercourse?

Could Virginia prohibit two persons of different races from marrying each other?

Could Texas and other states prohibit a woman from having an abortion?

Could parents prohibit grandparents from visiting their grandchildren?

Could Georgia make consensual homosexual[9] sodomy a crime punishable by up to ten years in prison?

Could life-support systems be withdrawn from a competent patient, thereby allowing the person to die? And what about a patient in a permanent vegetative state (PVS) existing on medical machines?

Could Washington State and New York State make physician-assisted suicide a felony offense?

The Warren Court began to answer some of these very complex legal, political, social, and, indeed, ethical questions. However, after 1969, the liberalizing, "revolutionary" Warren Court era ended.[10] Conservative U.S. Court of Appeals judge Warren Earl Burger replaced the empathetic Earl Warren as Chief Justice in 1969. William Hubbs Rehnquist (who had been appointed Associate Justice in 1971 by Republican President Richard M. Nixon) took over the center seat on the high bench when Burger retired at the end of the 1986 Term of the Court. (As the Court entered the twenty-first century, Rehnquist still presided as Chief Justice of the United States.)

The U.S. Supreme Court, in the first years of the twenty-first century, "is still a conservative court that also has become one of the most activist courts in American history," observed a critic.[11] This assertiveness of the Court majority is seen, clearly, in a host of cases involving the intimate lives of Americans. From questions of sexual intimacy, procreation, and birth or abortion to questions of death and dying, for the past four decades the Justices of the U.S. Supreme Court have been engaged in an examination of the most personal and intimate family relationships people can have. And the men and women on the Court have struggled mightily to understand and to decide these very complex issues.

In the chapters that follow, Court actions that have affected the disposition of intimate associations between couples and in families—both traditional and nontraditional associations—will be examined in greater detail. These chapters focus on the four major prongs associated with the courts and fundamental rights: marriage, procreation, family relationships, and the right to die.

Chapter 1 examines how various Supreme Court majorities, liberal and conservative, balanced the privacy rights of the individual with the interest of the state.

Chapter 2 examines marriage and marital privacy, both traditional and nontraditional (same sex). It examines the legal and ethical changes in the relationship between heterosexual married couples. There is an examination of the major problem of intimate violence, one that haunts the conscience of the society. Legislative efforts to deal with domestic violence, as well as the impact of U.S. Supreme Court decisions on the resolution of this problem, are discussed. Finally, there is an examination of the related question of same-sex marriage and a look at litigation that addresses this emerging issue.

Chapter 3 begins a discussion of the family. The concept "family" is a social construct; it is not an immutable, nonchanging one. Census data have shown that for the first time in American history, in the year 2000, "less than a quarter of the households in the United States are made up with married couples with their children."[12] From the traditional concept of the nuclear family, with the father as its head, and family privacy, the society's values and views have shifted to the notion that family consists of autonomous individuals who possess the "liberty" protections of the Due Process Clause.[13] Courts, too, have shifted and precedents have changed regarding the rights and liberties of all family members—both the immediate and extended varieties of family. The chapter concludes with an assessment of emergent relationships between husband and wife; between parents and children; and between parents, children, and grandparents.

Chapter 4 examines what courts have said about family planning in marriage. Discussed are questions answered by the Supreme Court that address the politically heated issue of abortion. What are the limits of state actions regarding the woman's right to choose to have an abortion? Does the boyfriend or husband of the pregnant woman have any rights in this matter? Does a woman have a right to have a "partial birth" abortion?

Chapter 5 examines what the U.S. Supreme Court has said about the rights parents have to raise and educate their children and whether or not members of the extended nuclear family, the grandparents, have protected liberty interests to visit with their grandchildren.

Chapter 6 discusses Court decisions that address the issue of death by choice. Especially troubling, poignant questions involving termination of life-support systems for a member of the family in a PVS, as well as the desire of a competent family member to commit (physician-assisted) suicide, are examined and the role of the U.S. Supreme Court is assessed.

The U.S. Supreme Court has made fundamental, substantive, and different value judgments about the meaning of a person's liberty interest as it relates to the beginning and the end of life—and all intimate associations that lie between birth and death.[14] These different value judgments are based on the Court majority's understanding of which of these intimate associations are "rooted" in the nation's history and traditions. How the Court's Justices have impacted intimate personal relationships are addressed in the seventh, final chapter.

Introducing the subject matter in each chapter is a brief vignette, most of them drawn from the papers of the Justices, illustrating the burdens of decision making and the fluidity of judicial choices. The titles of these sketches suggest the stresses, doubts, frustrations, and personal conflicts that are present as the Justices try to resolve exhausting questions about intimate personal relations:

- *"I am not talking very much like a lawyer,"* wrote Justice Lewis Powell to his law clerk in 1986 when the two of them were struggling with the issue of voluntary homosexual activity.

- *"I should like to suggest a substantial change for your consideration,"* wrote Justice William J. Brennan in 1965 to his colleague Justice William O. Douglas, after Douglas was assigned to write the opinion in the Connecticut contraceptive case.
- *"Something smells about this case,"* wrote Justice John P. Stevens in 1976 to his colleagues before he switched his vote in a case involving the legal definition of family.
- *"I will be God-damned,"* exclaimed Justice Brennan in 1972 to his colleague Justice Douglas after Chief Justice Warren E. Burger acted to delay the abortion cases.
- In 1971, Chief Justice Burger blurted out, in a letter to his colleagues about a child custody case: *"This is really a ridiculous case to be absorbing our time."*
- In 1976, a New Jersey Supreme Court justice confided to a reporter, about the "right to die" case before his court: *"This case should never have been started."*

Following these six stage-setting stories, is a discussion of how the Court became involved in the particular set of personal/intimate relations questions and how the Justices answered them. In each chapter there are "Case Studies" focusing on some of these important cases. These case studies are based, for the most part, on the private papers of the Justices, the secret conference session comments of the nine jurists, and the transcripts of oral arguments before the Justices in open Court. The case studies are presented in the effort to further illustrate the struggles, the passions, the uncertainties, and the doubts of the men and women of the high bench as they try to reach closure on these always troublesome, occasionally poignant constitutional questions.

U.S. Supreme Court decision making is a complex human dynamic. Answering the questions presented to them, the justices rely on their own values—and their understanding of the community's values. "We are very quiet here," wrote the great Associate Justice of the U.S. Supreme Court, Oliver W. Holmes, Jr., "but it is the quiet of a storm center." Without doubt, in this area of constitutional law—intimate family or personal rights versus state actions that proscribe them—Justice Holmes's observation is an understated truism.

Postscript, 2003

In January 2003 a Justice of the U.S. Supreme Court wrote me about this book. At one point in the note, the jurist said: "As you now know, you may have to issue a pocket-part supplement before too long." At that time it was public knowledge that the Court was going to hear and decide a case from Texas, *Lawrence v Texas*, involving two homosexuals who were charged and convicted of "deviate sexual intercourse, namely anal sex with a member of the same sex." Please consider the following paragraphs a "pocket part supplement" for one extremely controversial area of intimate human relations.

On June 26, 2003, the Supreme Court announced its decision in *Lawrence v Texas*. In a somewhat surprising 6:3 vote, the majority overturned the 1986 *Bowers v Hardwick* case. *Bowers* is discussed more fully in the following chapter. In that case, the Court majority concluded that consenting homosexuals did not have a fundamental liberty interest to engage in certain sexual actions (sodomy) and validated the Georgia statute prohibiting such sexual behavior.

Lawrence challenged a Texas statute that criminalized certain sexual acts. The Texas legislators singled out homosexual and lesbian partners who engaged in anal sex for punishment under the state's criminal statutes. However, in an opinion written by Justice Anthony Kennedy, the majority concluded that the petitioners were "entitled to respect for their private lives." While not willing to state that such sexual behavior was a "fundamental" liberty, the majority concluded that homosexuals' and lesbians' liberty interest under the Fourteenth Amendment's due process clause "gives them the full right to engage in their conduct without intervention of the government." The opinion then overturned the 1986 precedent: "[*Bowers*] demeans the lives of homosexual persons [and] ought not to remain binding precedent. *Bowers* should be and now is overruled."

A sixth justice, Sandra Day O'Connor (who voted to validate the Georgia statute in 1986), wrote a separate opinion arguing that the Texas statute was invalid because, by singling out only homosexuals, it conflicted with the equal protection clause of the Fourteenth Amendment.

Justice Antonin Scalia wrote the major dissent for himself, Chief Justice Rehnquist, and Justice Clarence Thomas. He maintained that the Texas statute reflected the values of the vast majority of Texans and that nothing in the Constitution prohibited a state from passing such morals legislation. He angrily claimed that the six-person majority had "signed on to the homosexual agenda" and had "taken sides in the cultural war" against the moral views of the great majority of Americans.

Clearly, the Court's role in the intimate lives of Americans is a very complex human dynamic one. Change is continuous in the Court. In *Lawrence*, five members of the Court have come to the conclusion that the Constitution's provisions "evolve" from generation to generation, thereby rejecting an "originalist" interpretation of the Constitution's language. The great "cobbler" of majorities on the Court, Justice William J. Brennan, must be smiling somewhere because of this change in the perspectives of some conservative jurists. But he would not be surprised at such a development.

1

"Fundamental" Rights versus State Interests
The Balancing Process

There is a fundamental right to marry, maintain a home, and a family. This is an area where we have the right to be left alone.
—Justice Tom C. Clark's remarks, in Conference Session,
Griswold v Connecticut, 1965[1]

The right to be "left alone" is not absolute. "I like my privacy as well as the next one," wrote Justice Hugo L. Black in his *Griswold*[2] dissent, "but I am nevertheless compelled to admit that government has a right to invade it unless prohibited by some specific constitutional prohibition." The Fourth Amendment, he reminded Americans for three decades, prohibited only "unreasonable" searches and seizures of persons, and their "houses, papers, and effects."[3]

Since *Griswold*, the "right of privacy" has been seen, legally, as a fundamental right all persons possess. Legislators, presidents, governors, attorneys general, judges, pressure groups, and the general public accept the premise and the promise of this fundamental right. However, all agree, the state can invade one's privacy if there are necessary and sufficient reasons for the intrusion. This, however, is the essence of the balancing dilemma faced by judges, from the local trial judge to the nine men and women who sit atop America's judicial system as Justices of the U.S. Supreme Court.

Because the "right to privacy," although labeled by Court majorities as a "fundamental" one, is not absolute, the U.S. Supreme Court has been intimately involved in resolving collisions between the individual and the state. In the past four decades, these clashes have involved issues that touch on the most private, the most intimate of personal relationships. This chapter examines how the Justices have employed the "balancing" process to resolve these intense encounters between individuals and the state.

I. "I Am Not Talking Very Much Like a Lawyer"

U.S. Supreme Court Justice Lewis F. Powell was in the throes of a legal and moral dilemma. It was early spring 1986. He and his law clerks were groping for a legal answer to the question: Does "the constitutional right of privacy give [a gay man] a fundamental right to engage in homosexual sodomy [with another consenting adult male]?"[4] The flip side of the issue was also a conundrum for the Justice: Does the State "have a legitimate interest in legislating a moral principle?" Certiorari[5] had been granted the previous Term. Briefs in No. 85-140, *Bowers v Hardwick* had been filed earlier in the 1985 Term of the Court; oral arguments were set for early April 1986.

The respondent, Michael Hardwick, a gay man[6] living in Atlanta, challenged the constitutionality of a Georgia statute that stated that "a person commits the offense of sodomy when he performs or submits to any sexual act involving the sex organs of one person and the mouth or anus of another." (If found guilty of the felony, the sentence was one to ten years in prison.) He sought a declaratory judgment from the federal district court that the statute was unconstitutional. After the U.S. District Court judge summarily ruled against him, the 11th Circuit Court of Appeals (CA11) reversed and sent the case back to the federal trial court for a trial on the merits. Georgia Attorney General Michael J. Bowers appealed to the U.S. Supreme Court and the Court took the case.

Lewis Powell, who, months before said to his law clerks, "we should not have taken this case," now had to answer the legal question before the Court. Although the statute's language encompassed sexual behavior by both heterosexual and homosexual couples, the state "practically concedes that the statute cannot apply to married couples," wrote Mike, one of Powell's three law clerks, in his Bench Memo of March 29, 1986.[7]

For Mike, *Bowers* "presents a fairly discrete legal issue: Is engaging in voluntary homosexual sodomy a *fundamental* right protected by the constitutional right of privacy?" Did the Georgia statute violate "the right of privacy found in the Fifth and Fourteenth Amendments' guarantees of protection against the deprivation of life, liberty, or property without due process of law?"[8]

He reminded Powell that, according to Supreme Court precedent, the standard for determining whether a right was *fundamental* meant that the justices "must look at the history and 'traditions and collective conscience of our people' to determine whether a [right] is 'so rooted' [there] as to be ranked as fundamental." He applied the "history and traditions" test and concluded that homosexual sodomy "does not fit within the right of privacy."

Although Hardwick's lawyer, Harvard Law School's Lawrence Tribe, argued that the right of privacy protected all "intimate sexual relations in the sanctity of the home,"[9] Mike suggested that the "Court's right of privacy cases have never recognized a broad-based right of sexual freedom." Only "traditional sexual relationships" have been protected by the Court: "Every one of the Court's right of privacy cases can be explained in terms of a concern for the fundamental right of [traditional] marital and family privacy." These cases dealt with "child rearing and child education, marital sexual privacy, the decision to marry, and the decision to have an abortion."

> The right-of-privacy cases are limited to marriage, family, and procreation [and] accurately reflect the basic values and traditions of our people. Personal sexual freedom is a newcomer among our national values, and may well be a temporary national mood that fades. I recommend reversal [of the CA11 decision].

On March 31, 1986, Powell wrote back. It was a somewhat personal note for, after talking about appropriate precedents in the case, he wrote:

> In view of my age, general background and convictions as to what is best for society, I think a good deal can be said for the validity of statutes that criminalize sodomy. If it becomes sufficiently wide-spread, civilization itself will be severely weakened as the perpetuation of the human race depends on normal sexual relations just as it is true in the animal world.

"As you can see, Mike," he added, *"I am not talking very much like a lawyer."* He feared that the justices would find themselves on a terrible slippery slope if the Court upheld the CA11 order. He said: "If sodomy is to be decriminalized on constitutional grounds, what about incest, bigamy, and adultery?"[10]

Justice Powell told his biographer that he never knowingly knew a homosexual in his entire life.[11] Ironically, the Justice did not know that, in the year he struggled with *Hardwick,* one of his law clerks was a gay man.[12] Another law clerk, that year, recalled that, according to his boss, Powell told his colleagues that he had "never met a homosexual."

> He made the same comment to one of his clerks, oblivious to the fact that this clerk (as well as others in the past) was gay. As Powell engaged him in presumably hypothetical discourse on gay sexual attraction, the clerk considered revealing his sexual orientation but ultimately chose instead merely to plead Hardwick's case with unusual emotion.[13]

As seen later in this chapter, *Bowers v Hardwick* expressed the majority's very traditional views of marriage, family, home, privacy, and liberty. As Mike reminded Powell: "The kind of marriage that our society has traditionally protected clearly is heterosexual, not homosexual. It would be 'bootstrapping' to say that marriage is protected because of our history and tradition, and then add that homosexual relationships are protected because they 'resemble marriage.' . . . Once you conclude [that], you would necessarily suggest that homosexuals have a right to adopt and raise children."

The *Bowers* insight touches on key issues this book will examine: marriage, sexual intimacy, procreation, family, homosexuality, personal privacy, the home, and liberty—and how the U.S. Supreme Court has participated in the dialogues. The conversations between Justice Powell and his law clerk also introduce the reader to the inevitable realities associated with judicial intervention into the general area of intimate associations.[14]

In America, as Alexis de Tocqueville observed almost two centuries ago, sooner or later all controversial public policy issues come before the U.S. Supreme Court. For over two hundred years America's existence as a sovereign nation has been framed by the language of the U.S. Constitution as interpreted by legislators, executives, judges, and, in many cases, *finally* by the Justices of the U.S. Supreme Court. As Justice Robert Jackson once wrote about the U.S. Supreme Court's "finality:" "We are not final because we are infallible, we are infallible only because we are final."[15]

When interpreting the Constitution's words in appropriate cases, most Justices of the U.S. Supreme Court have chosen one of two basic methodologies: "originalism" or the "evolving Constitution." Originalists such as Chief Justice Rehnquist and Justices Antonin Scalia and Clarence Thomas believe that interpretation of the Constitution must rest on the original intent of the men who wrote the words and/or the original meaning of the words. At bottom, there is an understanding that there are unchanging principles of governing in the covenant called the U.S. Constitution and the sole task of the Justices is to discover these enduring values when deciding cases before them.

Justices such as William J. Brennan, Jr., and Thurgood Marshall, on the other hand, believed that the U.S. Constitution must be seen as an evolving fundamental law of government. The task of the Justices, in cases that require them to ascertain the meaning of a constitutional phrase, is to interpret the words based on a contemporary understanding of their meaning. At bottom, these Justices believe that contemporary society should not be bound *solely* by eighteenth-century ideas and by outmoded, centuries-old language. As Justice Marshall sardonically recalled, if society were bound by the original words of the Constitution, he'd still be serving coffee to his masters.[16]

The Supreme Court Justices hear and try to resolve a variety of controversial social and political matters. Issues such as slavery, the extent of state powers, the general powers of the national government during war and economic depression, as well as disputes involving whether the Constitution protects a person's civil liberties and civil rights from governmental infringement. "In the past forty years [1960–2000] the courts have become forums for resolving social questions, and the docket of the Supreme Court has become defined by the most divisive issues. During the past fifteen years the line between law and politics has been increasingly hard to draw."[17]

A prime reason for the blurring of the line is that the U.S. Supreme Court has found itself confronted with many dozens of cases in which plaintiffs claim that their "fundamental rights," especially their "right of personal privacy," have been infringed in some manner by the state. The Justices of the Court, for the past four decades, have heard—and decided—cases that dealt with birth as well as death; sexual relations and abortion; the meaning of family; and the sanctity of the home.

Inevitably, in this process of deciding case outcomes, based on the majority's method of interpreting the Constitution, the Justices bring into the decisional equation and reach judgment based, in large measure, on their own values, prejudices, and biases. In a 1987 Memo to his colleagues Justice Antonin Scalia expressed his firm beliefs regarding the state of humankind: "It is my view that the unconscious operation of irrational sympathies and antipathies, including racial, upon jury decisions and (hence) prosecutorial decisions is real, acknowledged in the decisions of this court, and ineradicable."[18]

In the *Bowers* litigation, one sees that Justice Powell's own traditional belief about voluntary homosexual sodomy was determinative in his decision to validate the sodomy legislation. As he wrote to his clerk: "In view of my age, general background and convictions," Powell did not see any constitutional protection for that sexual act. "As you can see, Mike," he added, "*I am not talking very much like a lawyer*" (my emphasis).

Still another corollary axiom of U.S. Supreme Court decision making is "Who sits on the High Bench determines the outcome of controversial cases and controversies."[19] The presidential nomination of Justices of the U.S. Supreme Court—who must then be confirmed by the U.S. Senate—is one of the most significant of presidential powers. All Presidents want "their kind" of person appointed to the federal courts. A conservative President will want to nominate judges who share his conservative values, while a moderate or liberal President will want to nominate moderate or liberal judges.[20] Of course, once the jurist finds herself on the Court, she is there for life and can move in a direction different from the one imagined—and hoped for—by the appointing president.

When examining the Court's decisions in cases involving intimate personal and family relationships, there is a sharp demarcation between liberal and conservative judges, largely reflecting the positions of the Presidents who nominated them to the high bench. There is a significant correlation between the Court appointments by conservative Republican Presidents and the Court's decisions during and after these Presidents left office.

President Richard M. Nixon, 1969–1974, appointed Chief Justice Warren E. Burger and Justices Harry A. Blackmun, Lewis F. Powell, and William H. Rehnquist. President Gerald Ford, 1974–1977, appointed Justice John P. Stevens. Ronald Reagan, President from 1981 to 1989, appointed Chief Justice William Rehnquist and Justices Sandra Day O'Connor, Antonin Scalia, and Anthony Kennedy. George Bush, President from 1989 to 1993, appointed Justices David Souter and Clarence Thomas.

Of the ten new persons placed on the Court by Republican Presidents, at least seven of these reflected and continue to reflect the conservative values of the Presidents who appointed them.[21] Only Justices Blackmun, Stevens, and Souter have been disappointments to the Presidents who nominated them to serve on the Court.

An understanding of the Court's involvement in the intimate lives of Americans must be based, in large part, on such fundamental political realities. To a certain extent, Court majorities indirectly mirror the values and the history and traditions of the society that elected the President. More directly—if the President does a good job of screening potential Supreme Court justices—Court majorities tend to reflect the values of the President who nominated them. And if the President has a strong personal and party/policy commitment to the "sanctity of life" and to "traditional family values," then "his" Court will express such views in the opinions it writes.

II. The U.S. Supreme Court and "Fundamental" Rights

A careful reading of the U.S. Constitution will reveal that there is no right labeled "fundamental" in the document. However, the Court has determined that many of the rights found in the Constitution's Bill of Rights are so "fundamental" that if governmental agents infringe them, they violate the Constitution's command that no state shall "deprive any person of life, liberty, or property without due process of law."[22] Originally, the Bill of Rights—the first ten amendments to the U.S. Constitution, ratified in 1791—were added to the Constitution as restrictions on the actions of only the *national* government.[23] In the twentieth century, Court majorities gave themselves the arduous task of trying to determine which rights were so important to the maintenance of a democratic republic that if they were rejected or ignored by *any* government—state or national—fundamental fairness was lacking and liberty was endangered.

Case Study: *Palko v Connecticut*, (1937)[24]

Frank Palka, not Palko as the Clerk of the Supreme Court erroneously recorded, was a twenty-three-year-old aircraft riveter. He robbed a music store and killed two policemen who responded to the call for help.[25] Palko was tried for first-degree murder but the jury found him guilty of second-degree murder. A Connecticut statute allowed the state prosecutor to appeal the judgment of the trial court if there was "serious trial error" by the judge.

A new trial was held; Palko was found guilty of first-degree murder and sentenced to death by electrocution. Palko appealed the second conviction to the U.S. Supreme Court. His lawyers argued that the Fifth Amendment protection against double jeopardy was absorbed into the Fourteenth Amendment's "due process" clause. As such, the double jeopardy protection was applicable in Palko's case and the death sentence was invalid.

In an 8:1 opinion, written by highly respected Justice Benjamin Cardozo,[26] the Court validated his death sentence. Cardozo admitted that some segments of the Bill of Rights, such as the First Amendment's freedoms of speech, assembly, and religion, were so "fundamental" to society's notions of liberty and justice that they were absorbed into the language of Fourteenth Amendment's "due process" clause. "Of [those] freedoms one may say that [they are] the matrix, the indispensable condition, of nearly every other form of freedom."

Such judicially identified rights, Cardozo wrote, "represented the very essence of a scheme of ordered liberty, [they were] principles of justice *so rooted in the traditions and conscience of our people as to be ranked fundamental.*" However, the Fifth Amendment protection against double jeopardy, *in 1937*, was not deemed by the majority to be one of those fundamental "principles of justice." Connecticut's law allowing a second trial for Palko was constitutional; Palko was executed.

Palko was overturned in the 1969 case of *Benton v Maryland.*[27] A seven-person Court majority concluded that the double jeopardy protection in the Fifth Amendment was so "fundamental" that if Maryland ignored that "principle of justice," it was denying Benton due process of law. The majority, in an opinion written by Justice Thurgood Marshall, maintained that the double jeopardy protection's origins could be traced back to English common law and that the protection was so "deeply ingrained" in the American system of justice as to be labeled a "fundamental right."

This book examines how judges have grappled with new demands that certain personal, often very intimate and private decisions and actions are so "fundamental" that no government—national or state—can restrict, restrain, and/or punish those who practice them. Are all intimate and consensual associations considered fundamental rights, protected by the Constitution? Is personal and family *privacy* a fundamental right "rooted in the traditions and conscience" of the society?

Similarly, is personal autonomy—bodily integrity—a fundamental right, even when it extends to two homosexuals having intimate, consensual sexual relations? Or to a terminally ill patient who wants the assistance of her physician to commit suicide? If these are fundamental rights, are they absolute? Can government *never* constitutionally intrude and constrain a person's privacy and personal autonomy?

A number of traditional privacy-type personal liberty interests, for example, marriage and reproductive freedom, have been held by U.S. Supreme Court majorities to constitute "fundamental rights" protected by the Fourteenth Amendment's Due Process Clause. Other claims, such as sexual freedom for gays and lesbians and for physician-assisted suicide, have not been so designated as "fundamental" rights by the Justices. After an examination of the Court's actions dealing with such intimate issues, there will be an assessment of its contributions to the debates surrounding them.

III. The Liberty and Rights Protected by the Due Process Clause

The U.S. Supreme Court has interpreted the Due Process Clause in two basic ways: procedurally and substantively. It has been interpreted as a procedural demand that no person's life, liberty, or property be taken without, for example, a fair, open jury trial, with the assistance of counsel present at every stage of the justice process. Due process also has come to mean, procedurally, the unconstitutionality of the coerced confession, the unreasonable search and seizure of evidence, and cruel and unusual punishment. In essence, procedural due process is the protection of an individual's life and liberty against unreasonable governmental actions that jeopardize one's life and liberty in America's criminal and civil justice systems.[28]

Due process has also been given what scholars call a substantive meaning. Courts assumed the power to examine the *content* of challenged legislation in order to determine whether it was governmental action that infringed due process of law. This concept suggests a more comprehensive judicial perspective on the meaning of liberty—especially "economic" liberty in the late nineteenth century and the first four decades of the twentieth century—and, toward the middle of the twentieth century, a person's right to privacy.

For Court majorities from the 1880s through 1937, there was a substantive right of economic liberty that all persons had, workers as well as their employers. Any effort by government—whether state or national—to interfere with the right of workers and management to come to terms on hours and wages, for example, was a violation of their "liberty of contract" protected by the Due Process Clause.

Case Study: *Lochner v New York*, 198 U.S. 45, 1905

New York's legislators, in 1895, passed a health measure, the Bakeshop Act, limiting the hours of labor in bakeries across the state to ten hours a day (with a maximum of sixty hours weekly). At the time, it was not uncommon for bakery workers to put in one hundred-plus hours weekly.

The legislators, concerned about the health of these workers' long hours in very unsanitary workplaces, passed the legislation limiting the hours and calling for improved working conditions.

Joseph Lochner was the owner of a small bakery shop, the Home Bakery (employing five workers), in Utica, New York. He was fined $25 for allowing one of his workers to stay on the job for more than sixty hours. He appealed in the New York courts but the state judges validated the state law. Lochner's lawyers then appealed to the U.S. Supreme Court. Their argument: the New York State law deprived Lochner of "life, liberty, and property" protected in the Fourteenth Amendment's Due Process Clause to bargain over contract terms with his employees. Lochner's specific assertion was that his "liberty of contract" was restricted by the Bakeshop Act.

In a 5:4 decision, the Court agreed with Lochner and invalidated the New York statute. Justice Rufus Peckham wrote the opinion, stating that the state law "necessarily interfered with the right of contract between the employer and the employee." The "liberty" protected by the Fourteenth Amendment included the right to purchase and to sell labor. Any statute restricting this economic liberty was invalid "unless there are circumstances which exclude that right."

Justices John M. Harlan and Oliver Wendell Holmes wrote dissenting opinions. Holmes's dissent attacked the majority for incorporating into the Constitution their philosophic commitment to Social Darwinism: "A Constitution is not intended to embody a particular economic theory. It is made for people of fundamentally differing views."

In 1937, in *West Coast Hotel Company v Parrish*,[29] a different Court majority ushered in an era of almost unlimited Court deference to state and national laws that regulated economic activities. In the case, a five-person majority upheld a Washington State minimum wage law for women. Chief Justice Charles Evans Hughes, for the majority, wrote [of the freedom of contract between workers and management protected in *Lochner*]: "What is this freedom? The Constitution does not speak of freedom of contract." The state, he concluded, has the right to "preserve the strength and vigor" of women in "order to maintain their primary role as nurturing wives and mothers."

Two decades after *Lochner*, Supreme Court majorities substantively examined and overturned state statutes that restricted parental control over their children's education. In *Pierce v Society of Sisters*, 268 U.S. 510, 1925, the

Court invalidated a state statute that required all parents to enroll their children only in public schools. That same year, in *Meyer v Nebraska,* 262 U.S. 390, the Court invalidated a state law prohibiting the teaching of any foreign language at all to elementary school children. In both cases, the judgment was based on the Court's substantive review of the state law in light of the parents' "liberty" interest protected by the Fourteenth Amendment's Due Process Clause.[30]

In the last half of the twentieth century, substantive due process has evolved because of court examinations of new and controversial matters. Judges have confronted questions relating to the power of the state to restrict the autonomy of persons with respect to intimate personal associations. State and federal judges, especially the men and women who sit on the U.S. Supreme Court, have struggled to define the essential meaning and the scope of personal and family privacy and of the more general concept of personal autonomy in America's constitutional system.

The U.S. Supreme Court has regularly explored, defined, and pronounced, in majority opinions (*almost always* with accompanying concurring and dissenting opinions), its interpretation of these values. In doing so, the Court has had to continually revisit the meaning of the U.S. Constitution's Due Process Clause. Recently, in an important abortion rights decision, *Planned Parenthood v Casey,* 501 U.S. 503 (1992), the Court said that

> marriage, procreation, family relationships involving the most intimate and personal choices a person may make in a lifetime, choices essential to personal dignity and autonomy, are central to the liberty protected by the Fourteenth Amendment.

Note that these terms are part of the "traditionalist" Supreme Court vision of privacy. The liberty protected by the Due Process Clause includes "not merely the freedom from bodily restraint but also the right of the individual to contract, to engage in any of the common occupations of life, to acquire useful knowledge, to marry, establish a home, and bring up children."[31] Purely nonprocreational sexual behavior by consenting adults is not mentioned in *Casey* and other Court decisions because they are not perceived by the Court majority as falling four-square within the protection of the "liberty" clause of the Due Process Clause.[32]

In determining the breadth of the "liberty" protected by the Due Process Clause, judges have had to consider the status in society of three associated concepts: *intimacy, privacy,* and *personal autonomy.* For most people, *intimacy* has been defined as a very close personal relationship characterized by affection and love, whether heterosexual or homosexual. Intimate relatior.s generally are kept private or discreet. *Privacy* is therefore inseparable from intimacy. It is the right to be left alone and free from unauthorized governmental intrusion into a person's private, intimate life. But it is not an absolute right. Finally, all humans are seen, in religion and in science, as autonomous individuals. (*Autonomous* comes from the Greek words *auto* and *nomos,* and means self-governing.)[33]

As early as 1952, the Court, in *Rochin v California,*[34] said that a person's constitutional right to liberty protected by the Due Process Clause included the right to bodily integrity. Rochin was dragged by police to a local hospital to have his stomach emptied by forcibly administering an emetic. The procedure produced two morphine capsules that in turn led to Rochin's arrest and conviction. Overturning his conviction, the Court majority said that such state conduct "shocked the conscience" of the community and denied Rochin his "liberty" without due process of law.

Arguably, every person has the right to determine what shall be done to his/her own body. Every person has the liberty of *bodily integrity.* That liberty, it is argued, is a cornerstone of common law, statutes, and constitutional law. It has two components: (1) the right to *choose* how to live life, as well as (2) the right to *consent* to what is done to one's body by another person.[35]

The many troublesome questions associated with intimacy, privacy, personal autonomy, and bodily integrity are probably the most profound ones judges have been asked by plaintiffs to answer. Does an adult, mentally competent human being in America have a set of substantive, fundamental intimate privacy rights allowing her to take an action determined by her to be in her best interest—free from governmental interference? In struggling to answer essential questions involving intimacy, privacy, and personal autonomy, the Justices have drawn upon "mainstream" society's moral, religious, and legal principles.

In America's constitutional Republic, *all* governments are prohibited from intruding on one's right to privacy and personal autonomy unless there are presented, in court, justifications for the passage of the narrowly tailored legislation that restricts personal rights, showing "compelling" reasons for such action. In the late 1930s, the Court took notice of the fact that legislation allegedly depriving persons of their civil rights and liberties was different from legislation that regulated economic or social relationships.

Case Study: *U.S. v Carolene Products,* 1938, Footnote 4[36]

The "story of footnote 4 really began in 1933, with the rise in power of two men, Franklin Roosevelt and Adolf Hitler. [Chief Justice] Stone viewed the events taking place in Nazi Germany with great alarm. In 1938, he decided to offer the Supreme Court as a refuge for persecuted minorities. The morning of the oral argument in the case, April 6, 1938, Stone read in the *New York Times* that under Nazi rule in Austria, '2,000 Jewish physicians and surgeons have been removed from all hospitals.'"

In a letter to a friend, Stone wrote: "I have been deeply concerned about the increasing racial and religious intolerance which seems to bedevil the world, and which I greatly fear may be augmented in this country."[37]

The case selected for footnote 4 insertion involved the constitutionality of the Filled Milk Act of 1923, which forbade the shipment in interstate commerce of skimmed milk containing fat or oils. Stone worked closely with his Jewish law clerk, Louis Lusky, on the language of footnote 4 and then had the entire opinion reviewed by the other Justices.[38]

The Court majority, in the opinion written by Stone, concluded that the congressional statute was "reasonably related" to the legislative purpose. In footnote 4, Stone indicated that at least three sets of cases that come to the Court required more than passive judicial deference to the legislature's will.

There may be narrower scope for operation of the presumption of constitutionality [1] when legislation appears on its face to be within a specific prohibition of the Constitution, such as those of the first ten amendments.

Furthermore, he wrote,

[2] it is unnecessary to consider now whether legislation which restricts those political processes [voting] which can ordinarily be expected to bring about repeal of undesirable legislation, is to be subjected to *a more exacting judicial scrutiny* under the general prohibitions of the Fourteenth Amendment than are most other types of legislation. . . . [3] Nor need we enquire whether similar considerations enter into the review of statutes directed at particular religious, or national, or racial minorities; whether prejudice against discrete and insular minorities may be a special condition, which tends seriously to curtail the operation of those political processes ordinarily to be relied upon to protect minorities, and which may call for a *correspondingly more searching judicial inquiry.* [My emphasis.]

Chief Justice Charles Evans Hughes, after reading the footnote in the draft opinion circulated by Stone, immediately wrote Stone: "I am somewhat disturbed by your note 4 on page 6." Stone wrote an explanatory letter back:

> I wish to avoid the possibility of having what I have written in the body of the opinion about the presumption of constitutionality in the ordinary run of due process cases applied as a matter of course to these other more exceptional cases. For that reason it seemed to me desirable to file a caveat in the note, without, however, committing the Court to any proposition contained in it. [It reflects] the notion that the Court should be more alert to protect constitutional rights in those cases where there is danger that the ordinary political processes for the correction of undesirable legislation may not operate.[39]

The Chief, evidently, was placated by the Stone note and joined the Court's opinion.

This "more searching judicial inquiry" became, in the 1940s, the judicially molded concept of "strict scrutiny." It meant that laws restricting a person's fundamental civil rights or liberties or that discriminated against persons because of their race, religion, or ethnicity would be subjected to a much greater degree of judicial scrutiny than that afforded economic regulations such as the Filled Milk Act of 1923.

It must be underscored that application of the "strict scrutiny" standard did not mean a categorical rejection of the challenged state action by the reviewing court. The standard was, in reality, a "balancing" action by the courts. "Balancing is more like grocer's work—the judge's job is to place competing rights and interests on a scale and weight them against each other."[40] Judges and the justices of the U.S. Supreme Court had to weight a person's claim that "fundamental" rights had been violated by the state *against* the state's counterclaim that there were "compelling reasons" for that action.

The U.S. Supreme Court initially put into practice Stone's footnote 4 in *Korematsu v U.S.*, 323 U.S. 214 (1944). The case involved the constitutionality of national actions by the Congress, the President, and his wartime commanders that led to the incarceration of more than 110,000 Japanese, including 75,000 Japanese-American citizens. Fred Korematsu, a Japanese-American citizen attending the University of Washington, was convicted in federal court for violating Civilian Exclusion Order No. 24 (which prohibited Japanese from remaining in a restricted military area).

Justice Hugo Black, by 1944 recognized as a jurist strongly committed to the preservation of civil rights and liberties,[41] wrote the opinion for the Court majority—upholding Korematsu's conviction.

> It should be noted, to begin with, that all legal restrictions which curtail the civil rights of a single racial group are *immediately suspect.* That is not to say that all such restrictions are unconstitutional. *It is to say that courts must subject them to the most rigid scrutiny.* [My emphasis.]

For the Alabama native, military necessity during wartime validated a significant restriction (internment) on a racial groups civil rights and liberties. However, the *Korematsu* opinion held, for the first time as a matter of American constitutional law, that racial and other classifications based on religion or national origin were to be subjected to the most exacting strict scrutiny by judges. The burden was on the state to show a "compelling" interest that was reached by such legislation. If that burden was not met, then the legislation was to be invalidated by the judge.

As applied since then, the Court (by balancing the arguments of the petitioner against the counterclaims of the respondent) first has to determine whether the right alleged to have been violated by state action is a *fundamental* one protected by the Due Process Clause's "liberty" interest or by other clauses in the U.S. Constitution. If it is deemed "fundamental" by the Justices, they then strictly scrutinize the facts to determine whether or not there were "compelling" reasons for the restrictive state action. If the state does not present "compelling" reasons, its action is unconstitutional.

If, however, there are compelling reasons accepted by the Court, the justices must then determine whether the statute was narrowly drawn and not unconstitutionally vague or overbroad. If the Court concludes that the challenged state action was not "narrowly tailored," the Justices will declare it to be an unconstitutional violation of the plaintiff's "fundamental" rights. Only when, as seen in *Korematsu*, there are compelling reasons for a narrowly tailored, restrictive state action will such action be allowed.

These intimate privacy/personal autonomy issues come to the courts because the plaintiff claims that the infringed-upon right is a fundamental one protected by the "liberty" interest in the Due Process Clause. One's "liberty" interest is inherent in any due process argument put forward by a plaintiff in personal privacy litigation. The plaintiff's argument would conclude with the assertion that the governmental action deprived the plaintiff of liberty without due process of law. Generally, but not always, the plaintiff will emerge victorious based on U.S. Supreme Court determinations of what rights are fundamental. In a 1997 opinion, *Vacco v Quill,* 521 U.S. 793, Chief Justice Rehnquist summarized these fundamental, substantive personal rights:

> Due Process protects individual liberty against certain governmental actions regardless of the fairness of the procedures used to implement them. [It] also provides heightened protection against governmental interference with certain fundamental rights and liberty interests.
>
> In addition to specific freedoms protected by the Bill of Rights, the "liberty" specifically protected by the Due Process Clause includes the right to marry, to have children, to direct the education and upbringing of one's children, to marital privacy, to use contraception, to bodily integrity, and to abortion. We have also assumed and strongly suggested that the Due Process Clause protects the traditional right to refuse unwanted lifesaving medical treatment.

Throughout most of the twentieth century, but especially since the mid-1960s, the U.S. Supreme Court has heard cases and developed sets of guidelines regarding the scope of a person's intimate personal choices involving life and death. The Justices determine whether a claimed "liberty" interest protected by the Constitution is a "fundamental" one by drawing upon their own views and biases. Given these prejudices and values, they determine whether the "history and traditions" of society reflect the right claimed by the petitioner. In these activities, the rights claimed by homosexuals have not fared as well as traditional family privacy rights.

IV. Is There a Protected Liberty Interest for Persons Having Intimate Homosexual Relations?

Entering the twenty-first century, federal and state court judges, as reflected in Chief Justice Rehnquist's observations above, have acknowledged the fundamental, substantive "due process" rights of *heterosexual* persons, couples, and families. However, *homosexuals* have been treated quite differently by the U.S. Supreme Court when they claim that their intimate, private actions are also fundamental "liberty interests" protected by the Due Process Clause. In his concurring opinion in *Bowers*, Chief Justice Burger defined homosexual sodomy as "an offense of deeper malignity than rape," a "heinous act the very mention of which is a disgrace to human nature." Most saw this venomous statement as "indicative of our society's hostile attitude toward gays and lesbians."[42]

Ironically, *Bowers* "came to the Supreme Court as much by misadventure as by measured deliberation" wrote Justice White's biographer.[43] In early October 1985 the Court's review of petitions for certiorari included the petition from Georgia's Attorney General Bowers. In the Conference Session, all of the Justices voiced their views about homosexuality.[44] For Burger, "privacy was not the controlling issue." The state could punish sodomy in order to "protect our society's values." Brennan spoke next and maintained that one's "home is one's castle," citing the *Stanley v Georgia* precedent. Powell thought that such private consensual behavior should be "decriminalized," while Justice Sandra Day O'Connor maintained that "the right of privacy is not absolute and does not extend to private homosexual activity."

Seven of them, however, did not want to hear the case on the merits. There were only two votes to grant the petition (Justices White and Rehnquist). Chief Justice Burger said in the conference that he "would join three," but there was not a third vote to grant.)[45] A "vote of four" is needed to grant certiorari and so White asked to have the case relisted in order for him to prepare an opinion dissenting from the denial of certiorari.

On October 17, 1985, White circulated his draft dissent, hoping to get another Justice to join his dissent or, more substantively, to get the third vote to grant certiorari. That is what happened, much to the chagrin of a number of Justices. One of Justice Brennan's law clerks read the White dissent and suggested that his boss add his name to the White internal circulation. Brennan, who had voted to deny certiorari a few weeks earlier, "somewhat absentmindedly," quickly agreed and sent a Memo to his colleagues telling them of his change of mind.[46]

Justice Blackmun immediately hurried over to Brennan's chambers and demanded that Brennan retract his join. Blackmun feared that if the conservatives on the Court heard *Bowers* on the merits, "a majority would not only refuse to protect homosexual conduct but would also undermine [the abortion decisions] in the process."[47]

Brennan then changed his mind about his "join" and sent a short note to his colleagues informing them of his change of heart: "I was one of those voting to grant certiorari in this case. I have since relisted the case for a second look. I have decided to change my vote. I vote to deny."[48]

However, it was too late. As soon as Burger heard Brennan had changed his mind and voted to grant certiorari, Burger wrote his colleagues: "my tentative 'join three' is now a grant." And Thurgood Marshall, taking his cue from Brennan's precipitous "join" of White's internal dissent, provided the new third vote to grant certiorari. "He could not change his own vote, too, without looking as if he were in lockstep with Brennan!"[49]

Certiorari was granted on November 4, 1985. The case was argued before the Justices in late March 1986. Two months later the opinion came down. The pessimistic Justice Blackmun, as it turned out, was correct after all.

Case Study: *Bowers v Hardwick*, 478 U.S. 186 (1986)[50]

Michael Hardwick was charged with violating Georgia's sodomy statute. A police officer came to his house to serve an arrest warrant for Hardwick's failure to appear in court on a ticket issued to him earlier by the police. When there was no answer to the knock on the door, the officer opened the door, entered and observed Hardwick and his male friend engaging in oral sex in the bedroom. The officer then arrested the two men for violating Georgia's antisodomy statute. They were taken to jail and released the following morning.

The District Attorney chose not to prosecute him on the sodomy charge, and the charge was dropped. After consulting with a civil rights organization in Atlanta, Hardwick filed a federal civil rights action contesting the law's constitutionality. He argued that Georgia's sodomy law violated his "liberty" protected by the Fourteenth Amendment's Due Process Clause.

The Georgia Attorney General, Michael Bowers, argued against the motion and the U.S. district court judge dismissed Hardwick's motion to declare the act unconstitutional. In the CA11, a three-judge panel reversed, 2:1, on the ground that the Georgia statute violated Hardwick's fundamental right of personal privacy. Bowers immediately sought and received a grant of certiorari by the U.S. Supreme Court. On March 31, 1986, oral argument took place in the Supreme Court and the 5:4 decision validating the Georgia statute was announced on June 30, 1986.

In the Friday Conference Session after oral argument in the case, the initial vote was 5:4 to affirm the lower federal appellate court decision. However, over the next week Powell reconsidered his vote to overturn the statute.

And, in a Memo to his colleagues, he informed them of his change of heart and joined his brethren who had voted, in the minority, to validate the statute.

> At Conference last week, I [expressed the view that the statute violated the Eighth Amendment] rather than the view of four other Justices that there was a violation of a fundamental substantive constitutional right—as the lower court had held. . . . I write this memorandum today because upon further study, I conclude that my "bottom line" should be to reverse rather than affirm. . . . My more carefully considered view is that I will vote to reverse but will write separately to explain my view of this case generally.

Justice Blackmun, who had been assigned the task of writing the opinion for the Friday majority of five, now found he was writing one of two *dissents* in the case. Justice White, the writer for the dissenters on Friday, became the author of the *majority* opinion the following week.

White rejected Hardwick's argument that there was a fundamental right protecting consensual acts of homosexual sodomy committed in the privacy of the home. White's opinion differentiated this fact-situation from other, traditional, right of privacy cases involving "family, marriage, and procreation." Hardwick's argument that "any kind of private sexual conduct between consenting adults is constitutionally insulated from state proscription is unsupportable." To argue, as Hardwick's lawyer, Lawrence Tribe, did, that such homosexual activity is rooted in the "history and traditions" of American society or is implicit in the "concept of ordered liberty is, at best, facetious," wrote White.

A furious Justice Blackmun, a victim of the "fluidity of judicial choice,"[51] maintained that the case was "about the 'most comprehensive of rights and the right most valued by civilized men,' . . . the right to be left alone." Although he tried to persuade Powell to stay with the Friday majority, Powell could not do so.

He joined White's opinion, and he wrote a separate concurrence. In it, he maintained that, had Hardwick been charged and convicted for voluntary homosexual sodomy, which carried a maximum penalty of twenty years in prison, there would be arguable Eighth Amendment "cruel and unusual punishment" grounds for overturn of the conviction and the Georgia sodomy statute.

A postscript: In 1998, the Georgia Supreme Court, in the case of *Powell v State*,[52] overturned the antisodomy statute because it violated the Georgia Constitution.

There is nothing "fundamental" about claimed homosexual rights. Judges, asked to confront questions dealing with the intimate, private, and personal autonomy rights of homosexuals in American society, have not elevated them to that level. The right to personal privacy, to date, has been conferred by the Court when there is a traditional, historic, and clear connection to marriage or family or procreation. Because the Court decided that voluntary homosexual sodomy is not a historic part of the nation's social fabric, a state need show only a "reasonable" justification for the challenged restrictive legislation to pass muster.

For most of America's history, homosexual relationships have been seen as immoral and sinful. They were unnatural; they were not thought of as an aspect of a person's fundamental liberty interest protected by the Due Process Clause. Only in the 1940s did the perception change. For two decades, until the turbulent decade of the 1960s, homosexuality was viewed as abnormal, a mental illness. By the late 1960s, homosexuals came out of their closets to demand the same right of privacy and personal autonomy that heterosexuals had. The early 1970s saw some Americans acknowledge that homosexuality was a matter of private, voluntary choice.[53]

However, it was still viewed by elected officials and judges as a sexual relationship not rooted in America's religious and social tradition. Courts, including the U.S. Supreme Court, validated laws that prohibited private, consensual homosexual sex. Homosexual relations and same-sex marriage have not yet been considered fundamental rights of privacy, ones rooted in the traditions and history of American society and therefore protected by the "liberty" interest in the Due Process Clause.

During its 1995 Term, the U.S. Supreme Court examined a Colorado amendment to the state's Constitution that prohibited all governmental action protecting homosexual persons. It classified individuals on the basis of sexual orientation; it was challenged by gay groups as being in conflict with the Fourteenth Amendment's Equal Protection Clause.

Case Study: *Roy Romer, Governor v Richard Evans, et al.*, 1996[54]

A Colorado state constitutional amendment, "Amendment 2," was adopted in a 1992 statewide referendum. It came on the heels of a number of local ordinances passed in the cities of Aspen, Boulder, and the city and county of Denver. Each of the ordinances banned discrimination in many transactions and activities, including housing, employment, education, public accommodations, and health and welfare services.

Triggering the statewide firestorm of controversy that led to the introduction and passage of Amendment 2 was the protection all the ordinances afforded to persons discriminated against by reason of their sexual orientation.[55] The protesters included family-values and Christian fundamentalist groups; they were very successful in getting the referendum on the ballot and then winning on the merits.

Amendment 2 repealed those ordinances because they prohibited discrimination on the basis of "homosexual, lesbian, or bisexual orientation, conduct, practices, or relationships."[56] "It did more than repeal or rescind these provisions," wrote Justice Kennedy for the six-person majority.

> It prohibits all legislative, executive, or judicial action at any level of state or local government designed to protect the named class, a class we shall refer to as homosexual persons or gays and lesbians.[57]

Nine days after the vote, Richard Evans, eight other homosexual residents of the three cities, and a number of governmental leaders from the three cities, challenged the constitutionality of Amendment 2. They argued that enforcement of the amendment would subject them to immediate and substantial risk of discrimination on the basis of their sexual orientation. The amendment was in violation of the Fourteenth Amendment's Equal Protection Clause. Governor Roy Romer defended the amendment, asserting that "it would do no more than prevent lesbians and gay men from reaping special rights."[58]

The state trial court granted a preliminary injunction to stay enforcement of Amendment 2 and an appeal was taken to the Colorado Supreme Court. That court sustained the interim injunction and remanded the case to the trial court for further proceedings. The judges instructed the trial judge to apply the "strict scrutiny" standard because the amendment "infringed the fundamental right of gays and lesbians to participate in the political process." On remand, Colorado argued that it was narrowly tailored to serve compelling governmental interests, but the trial court, relying on precedents established in voting rights and discriminatory restructuring of government cases by the U.S. Supreme Court, found that none of the arguments "was sufficient. It enjoined enforcement of Amendment

2, and the Supreme Court of Colorado, in a second opinion, affirmed the ruling."

The U.S. Supreme Court granted certiorari and affirmed the judgment, "but on a rationale different from that adopted by the State Supreme Court." In remarks that greatly pleased the gay community, Justice Anthony Kennedy, the author of the majority opinion, said, in the opinion's first paragraph,

> One century ago, the first Justice Harlan admonished this Court that the Constitution "neither knows nor tolerates classes among citizens." Unheeded then, those words now are understood to state a commitment to the law's neutrality where the rights of persons are at stake. The Equal Protection Clause enforces this principle and today requires us to hold invalid a provision of Colorado's Constitution.

Colorado's fundamental premise was that, by removing protective classifications based on sexual orientation, "it put gays and lesbians in the same position as all other persons. . . . The measure does no more than deny homosexuals special rights." However, the Court majority found "this reading of the amendment's language implausible."

> Homosexuals, by state decree, are put in a solitary class with respect to transactions in both the private and governmental spheres. The amendment withdraws from homosexuals, but no others, specific legal protection from the injuries caused by discrimination, and it forbids reinstatement of these laws and policies. . . . Homosexuals are forbidden the safeguards against discrimination that others enjoy or may seek without constraint.

Kennedy and his five "joiners" concluded that the amendment failed to clear even the minimalist Fourteenth Amendment "rational relation to some legitimate end" standard. [It] fails, indeed defies, even this conventional [deferential judicial] inquiry." For the majority, the amendment "seems inexplicable by anything but animus toward the class it affects; it lacks a rational relationship to legitimate state interests."

Some observers have suggested that the *Romer* decision "may very well be the first step on the road to recognizing gays and lesbians as a suspect class.

However, *Romer* does not give any hints that this step is imminent."[59] Because of the hard and fast commitment by the Justices to their values concerning gays and lesbians, change in doctrine will not happen until new moderate Justices are appointed to the U.S. Supreme Court by a moderate President.

V. The Limits of Sexual Privacy

What was the scope of sexual privacy as seen by the U.S. Supreme Court when Michael Hardwick challenged Georgia's antisodomy statute? Eskridge[60] suggests the following hierarchical array of protected and unprotected sexual activities:

Protected:

Procreative marital sexual intercourse,[61]

Nonprocreative contraceptive use: marital sexual intercourse,[62]

Nonprocreative contraceptive use: non-marital sexual intercourse,[63]

Masturbation in one's home,[64]

Abortion.[65]

Unprotected:

Adultery,

Incest,

Rape,

Consensual oral sex,[66]

Prostitution.

This catalog has not changed since *Bowers*. Clearly, Court majorities have not accepted John Stuart Mill's libertarian argument that the state must leave people alone unless their conduct has third-party effects.[67] Equally clear is the fact that the Court majority entering the twenty-first century still maintains limits on the extent to which a person's sexual privacy is beyond the reach of the state. The extent of these limits will be explored in the following chapters.

VI. Summing Up

In a host of cases involving rights and liberties—the intimate associations that most people have and practice in the privacy of their home—U.S. Supreme Court justices have attempted to define which of them are "fundamental," for the most part constitutionally protected from state intrusion. Some have been labeled by the justices as fundamental; others, such as same-sex marriage and voluntary homosexual sexual relations, have not because the Court majority determined that the action in question was not rooted in the traditions and history of the society. To offer them the constitutional protections accorded the traditional intimate relations, Court majorities have argued, would lead to the end of a civilization based on Judeo-Christian tenets. Recall Powell's remark to his law clerk:

> If [homosexuality] becomes sufficiently wide-spread, *civilization itself* will be severely weakened as the perpetuation of the human race depends on normal sexual relations just as it is true in the animal world. [My emphasis.]

At the heart of these judicial deliberations lies the substantive concept of due process. In two places the U.S. Constitutions states, categorically, that no person's life, or liberty, or property may be taken without due process of law. We all have a liberty interest protected by the Fourteenth Amendment. But the question has been and remains whether that liberty interest is so fundamental that a law prohibiting a person from actualizing an intimate relationship must fall unless there is a compelling "reason of state" for the restriction. As the justices of the Supreme Court readily admit, in their private jottings to each other as well as in the published opinions they write, these are difficult and value-laden matters. This book is an effort to examine these struggles from the inside out, from the ruminations and doubts of the justices to the impact of their opinions on American society.

2

Marriage and Marital Privacy

I will do the laundry, if you pay all the bills.
I will raise the children, if you pay all the bills.
I will do the dishes while you go have a beer. . . .
Where is my John Wayne?
Where is my prairie son?
Where is my happy ending?
Where have all the cowboys gone?
—Lyrics by Paula Cole, Warner Brothers, 1996

The Supreme Court's decision in *Romer* was seen by many who supported same-sex marriage as the light that effectively obliterated the darkness of *Bowers*, allowing a state to make criminal such "malignant" behavior. *Romer* was viewed by these optimists as the judiciary's "demonstration of equal respect and concern for gay and lesbian people, and its positive language seriously undercuts the harsh anachronistic views by the 1986 majority opinion in *Bowers*."[1] However, as this chapter will suggest, marriage law and public policy actions in defense of traditional views of heterosexual marriage still hold sway as the United States enters the twenty-first century.

According to U.S. Supreme Court majorities, as well as Presidents, overwhelming majorities in Congress, and the general public, marriage remains a legal as well as a religious association of two individuals of the opposite sex. It is a "sacred" bond between a man and a woman—and *only* a man and a woman—legitimatized by government and sanctified by God. Given the Court's views about marriage and marital privacy, that only traditional heterosexual intimate relations are valid and that the right of privacy extends only to such couples, the exhilaration in the gay community following *Romer* was illusory.

Ironically, today there are a host of problems associated with marriage and marital privacy that confront American society. These include the dramatic increase in the number of divorces (and the precipitous drop in the number of traditional married couples with children—from 40 percent in 1970 to less than 25 percent in 2000), the number of children born out of wedlock, as well as the horror of domestic violence. Until *Lawrence v Texas*, 2003, issues associated with intimate homosexual relationships have been given short shrift by the U.S. Supreme Court and by public policy makers as they grapple with the complexities of traditional marriage and marital privacy.

Privacy, the right to be left alone, is inherently at the core of the marital relationship. The U.S. Supreme Court initially addressed legal, political, and, inevitably, ethical questions that focused on heterosexual marital privacy in the 1960s. The Warren Court majority crafted the idea that there were—in the interstices of a number of amendments in the Bill of Rights—"zones of privacy" where individuals, married and single, were free from governmental intrusion unless the government presented "compelling" reasons justifying such encroachment.

However, these "zones of privacy" were conferred only if there was a connection between the privacy right and traditional notions of marriage or procreation, that is, privacy was conferred on heterosexual sex partners.[2] The view of marital privacy held by Justice John M. Harlan II, voiced in *Poe v Ullman*, best expressed the Court's views on the subject—then and now: "The right of privacy most manifestly is not an absolute. Thus, I would not suggest that adultery, homosexuality, fornication, and incest are immune from criminal enquiry, however privately practiced."[3]

Who sits on the Court when cases are filed determines how the Justices will respond to the question of law the litigation raises. This was certainly true with the Court's initial venture into the marital privacy maelstrom.

I. "I Should Like to Suggest a Substantial Change for Your Consideration"

Justice William O. Douglas was a brilliant but brittle jurist. Almost all his colleagues disliked him.[4] Appointed by President Franklin D. Roosevelt, he sat on the Court for an as-yet- unmatched thirty-six-plus years, 1938 to 1975. In late March 1965, the Court heard oral argument in *Griswold v Connecticut*,[5] a case that questioned whether a state statute banning the circulation of birth control information was constitutional. The Warren Court, in its secret Conference Session, voted 7:2 (only Justices Black and Stewart dissented), to overturn the statute and Douglas was selected to write the majority opinion.

Douglas faced a conundrum. It was one Court writers for the majority face when having to justify a controversial Court decision: How to write a majority opinion if there existed "considerable diversity among the seven on just how to strike the statute."[6] The Term was rapidly drawing to its summer recess and Douglas, always the fast writer, quickly drafted an opinion and showed it to his colleague, Justice William J. Brennan, Jr.

Douglas's initial draft reflected what he believed was the majority's consensus view expressed in the Conference. He wrote that the Connecticut statute was unconstitutional because it invaded the First Amendment right of association. While "freedom of association" was not specifically spelled out in the First Amendment,[7] that amendment clearly suggested that a person had a fundamental right to associational freedom. "Nothing," he had said in the Conference, "was more personal than this [doctor-husband/wife] relationship and if it's on the periphery, it is [still] within First Amendment protection."

Brennan, recall, was one of the Court's major advocates of the idea that the Constitution was an evolving document, given specific meaning by Court majorities at particular times in the nation's history. Brennan's strategic response[8] was a lengthy letter that encouraged Douglas to broaden the justification and not pin the justification for the Court's action on the First Amendment argument alone. "I should like to suggest a substantial change in emphasis for your consideration," he wrote.

> Instead of expanding the First Amendment right of association to include marriage, why not say that what has been done for the First Amendment can also be done for some of the other fundamental Guarantees of the Bill of Rights. In other words, where fundamentals are concerned, the Bill of Rights guarantees are but expressions or examples of those rights, *to situations unanticipated by the Founders.* . . . The Connecticut statute would run afoul of the right of privacy created out of the Fourth Amendment, and the self-incrimination clause of the Fifth, together with the Third. Taken together, those Amendments indicate a fundamental concern with the sanctity of the home and the right of the individual to be let alone. It is plain that, in our civilization, the marital relationship above all else is endowed with privacy. With this change in emphasis, I think there is a better chance it will command a Court.

Douglas accepted all of Brennan's suggestions "without [being] offended," observed Brennan's law clerk.[9] The draft majority opinion he circulated (accepted by four others, with Justices Arthur Goldberg, Hardan, and White writing separately) stated that there was a constitutionally protected right of privacy, emanating from a number of amendments (the First, Third, Fourth, Fifth, and Ninth) in the Bill of Rights. The "specific guarantees in the Bill of Rights have penumbras formed by emanations from these guarantees that help give them life and substance. [These] guarantees create zones of privacy."[10]

The marital relationship was the essential focus of his opinion. Douglas, sort of an expert himself in this area (he was married four times in his life), wrote:

> We deal with a right of privacy older than the Bill of Rights—older than our political parties, older than our school system. Marriage is a coming together for better or for worse, hopefully enduring, and intimate to the degree of being sacred. It is an association that promotes a way of life, not causes; a harmony in living, not political faiths; a bilateral loyalty, not commercial or social projects. Yet it is for us as noble a purpose as any involved in our prior decisions.

Justice Black dissented, joined by Justice Stewart. He called his dissent in *Griswold* "the most difficult I have ever had to write. I found that law abhorrent, just viciously evil, but not unconstitutional."[11] However, he was ever fearful of justices "roaming at will" beyond the words of the Constitution in order to find another "substantive" meaning for the "liberty" interest in the Due Process Clause. Like Justice Holmes's dissenting voice in *Lochner*, Black did not believe that the Constitution's words should be given contemporary meaning by the Justices.[12]

This insight into the *Griswold* decision-making process illustrates the interactions that occur regularly in Supreme Court decision making. Majorities, especially when struggling with sensitive public policy matters such as marital intimacy, *always* manage to find ways—*always* consistent with the basic values brought with them to the Court—to justify their answer to the question of law raised in the litigation. In *Griswold*, Brennan's "suggestions" to Douglas became the law of the land, just as, in *Bowers*, Powell's ruminations and fears led to a different kind of Court opinion regarding the scope of one's expectation of intimate privacy.

Griswold and *Bowers* also make clear the reality that the marriage arrangement "incorporates legal issues, but also moral, religious, and ethical questions."[13] Marriage, as Justice Powell wrote to his law clerk during his personal struggle with the image of voluntary homosexual sodomy, is a sacred, holy, very unique social, religious, and immensely personal *heterosexual* relationship.

Other cases handed down by the Court emphasized that the fundamental right to marry deserves constitutional protection.[14] For critics of the Court, these cases also accentuated the perception that "American society is a heterocentric society, dominated and centered around a heterosexual viewpoint of marriage, family, sexual desires, and moral right. Homophobia[15] is an outgrowth of this heterocentric attitude."[16]

II. Heterosexual Marriage

Marriage law in the United States originated in the canon law of the Catholic Church.

> This law, evolving into the English common law, did not require an actual ceremony or religious sacrament. The United States common law adopted the canon and civil laws of England, as administered in the British ecclesiastical courts and patterned its marriage laws after the British model.[17]

In that model, marriage was seen as the major social institution promoting "family values." But it was also seen as a legal contract between two persons; one based on the general laws of the state regarding that relationship.

States have the constitutional power to regulate marriage, to set down in law the qualifications (for example, the legal age) of the contracting parties, the duties and obligations of the parties, and the grounds for the legal dissolution of the relationship, divorce.[18] "Under the marriage contract, the husband retained a limited property interest in his wife's body. He could demand sexual relations in exchange for providing shelter."

In the nineteenth and twentieth centuries, states codified this property right through the marital rape exemption. Under this exemption, the state was precluded, as a matter of law, from charging a husband with raping his wife since wives could not withhold consent to sexual relations. Husbands had unfettered access to their wives' bodies. The only charge available to the state for marital rape was battery in cases where excessive force was used to force submission.[19]

Additionally, the traditional obligations of husband and wife are not the same. Through the end of the twentieth century, in Anglo-Saxon common law, state statutes, and court decisions, the male partner was the powerful one of the duo. This was the case in law and in social, moral, and political relationships. The husband had the responsibility to provide a secure home, he participated in political debates and voted, he earned money to pay for food, and clothing, and other marital and family needs. The wife's obligation was to maintain the home, live in the home, engage in sexual relations with her husband, and raise the couple's legitimate children. She had few property rights and could not enter the professions.

In America, until the 1970s, men were granted immunity from prosecution to protect family privacy and to promote domestic harmony. Family law structures the familial relationship but also the power relationships and hierarchies within the family. Under common law, the concept of *coveture*, male dominance in the family, was the primary relationship. Under this concept, ideas of personal autonomy, bodily integrity, and privacy were illusory. Under coveture, the marriage vows extinguished a woman's existence and freedom. She was under the domination of the male partner. Intrafamily violence was invisible in the public sector, for such conduct was not cognizable in law.

By the 1970s, there was some "deliberate speed" detected in U.S. Supreme Court actions that addressed the constitutionality of the admittedly unequal husband-wife relationship. During its 1971 Term, the U.S. Supreme Court was asked to examine a mandatory provision of the Idaho probate code that gave preference to husbands over wives in the appointment as administrator of a decedents estate.

The case, *Reed v Reed*,[20] involved a minor, Richard Reed, who died intestate in March 1967. His parents were parties in this case. Richard's mother, Sally Reed, filed a petition with the probate court seeking appointment as administratrix of her son's estate (valued at less than $1,000). Cecil Reed, the boy's father, who was separated from his wife, filed a competing petition. The probate judge, after meeting with the couple, ordered that Cecil administer the estate. The judge reached that decision in light of Section 15-314 of the Idaho Code. It stated that in the event both the father and the mother (male and female) seek legal permission to administer the estate, "males must be preferred to females."

Sally Reed appealed the court order and a state district court held that Section 15-314 violated the Fourteenth Amendment's Equal Protection Clause and remanded the case back to the probate court judge to determine "which of the two parties" was better qualified to administer the boy's estate. That did not happen, for Cecil Reed immediately appealed the judgment to the Idaho Supreme Court. That court reversed the district court judgment and reinstated the original probate order. The preference given to males in the statute is "mandatory" and leaves no room for judicial discretion. On the equal protection issue, that court rejected Sally Reed's contention. It concluded "that the elimination of females from consideration is neither an illogical nor arbitrary method devised by the legislature to resolve an issue that would otherwise require a hearing as to the relative merits of the two or more petitioning relatives."

Sally Reed then took her appeal to the U.S. Supreme Court. For the unanimous Court, Chief Justice Burger concluded:

> [T]he arbitrary preference established in favor of males cannot stand in the face of the Fourteenth Amendment's command that no state deny the equal protection of the laws to any person within its jurisdiction. To give a mandatory preference to members of either sex ... is to make the very kind of arbitrary legislative choice forbidden by the Equal Protection Clause of the Fourteenth Amendment.... By providing dissimilar treatment for men and women who are thus similarly situated, the challenged section violates the Equal Protection Clause.

One year later, the Justices of the U.S. Supreme Court came within one vote of adding "sex" to the small list of "suspect" classifications enumerated in Justice Stone's *Carolene Products* footnote 4 (race, alienage, and national origin). Had the Court found that additional vote, then in all future cases involving allegations of discrimination based on sex or gender, judges must apply the "strict scrutiny" standard. In such a critical scrutiny, the government had to show a "compelling" justification for its state action or have it invalidated because it ran afoul of either the Fifth or the Fourteenth Amendments.

Frontiero v Richardson involved a married female Air Force officer, Sharron Frontiero, stationed in Alabama who sought increased benefits for her husband, Joseph Frontiero, as a "dependent" under 37 USC Sections 401, 403, and 10 USC Sections 1072 and 1076.[21] (Her husband was an Air Force veteran attending a local college.) These federal statutes provided that only spouses of male members of the military were "dependents." Spouses of female members of the military were not considered "dependent" unless they were, in fact, dependent for more than one-half of their support.

When her application was denied, the couple brought suit in a three-judge federal district court. The statutes, they claimed, "unreasonably discriminated on the basis of sex in violation of the Due Process Clause of the Fifth Amendment." Such discrimination was "inherently suspect and must therefore be subjected to close judicial scrutiny."

The three-judge court ruled, 2:1, against her constitutional claim and the couple took direct appeal to the U.S. Supreme Court. The Court noted probable jurisdiction, heard the case, and ruled, 8:1, that the discrimination deprived her of due process of law. Associate Justice Rehnquist was the sole dissenter. There were, all told, four opinions written to explain the Justices' positions in the case.

Justice William J. Brennan, Jr., joined by Justices William O. Douglas, Thurgood Marshall, and Byron White, concluded that the challenged federal statutes were "inherently *suspect* statutory classifications based on sex, [and] are so unjustifiably discriminatory as to violate the Due Process Clause of the Fifth Amendment." Justice Stewart wrote a separate concurrence, in which he concluded that the statutes "worked an invidious discrimination in violation of the Constitution."

Justice Powell also wrote a concurring opinion, joined by the Chief, Burger, and Justice Harry A. Blackmun. He refused to join Brennan's judgment because of the fact that the proposed Equal Rights Amendment had just been approved by the Congress and submitted to the states for ratification. He believed it was "premature, unnecessary [and] inappropriate" for the Court to decide whether sex was a suspect classification "at the very time" the states were debating and voting on the merits of the proposed constitutional amendment. To so act, as Brennan was willing to do, was to "weaken Democratic institutions" and "impair" the public's confidence "in the restraint of the Court."[22]

Brennan, writing for the liberal Court quartet, spoke directly to the reality of the traditional marital relationship:

> There can be no doubt that our Nation has had a long and unfortunate history of sex discrimination. Traditionally, such discrimination was rationalized by an attitude of "romantic paternalism" which ... put women not on a pedestal, but in a cage.... The position of women in [nineteenth-century

America] was, in many respects, comparable to that of blacks under the pre–Civil War slave codes.[23]

Sex, like race, and the other "immutable characteristics determined solely by the accident of birth," Brennan concluded, "frequently bears no relation to ability to perform or contribute to society." To discriminate against one person because of the sex or the race or national origin of that person, is to violate the command of the Due Process and Equal Protection Clauses. "We can only conclude that classifications based on sex, like classifications based upon race, alienage, or national origin, are inherently suspect and must therefore be subjected to strict judicial scrutiny. It is clear that the statutory scheme now before us is constitutionally invalid."

The Court never again came close to "reaching out"[24] to elevate sex to the "suspect classification" level. *Reed* and *Frontiero* show a Court movement away from the traditional discrimination against women and the Brennan opinion was appreciated by millions of women. Fran Harris, Chairperson of the U.S. Department of Defense's Defense Advisory Committee on Women in the Services, was extremely pleased with the outcome in *Frontiero.* Writing to Brennan, she said: "Thank you for a achieving a goal we have been working for years."[25]

Five years later, in *Orr v Orr,*[26] the Supreme Court continued to overturn state statutes that discriminated on the basis of the sex of the married couple. Alabama state alimony statutes required husbands, but not wives, to pay alimony upon divorce. An Alabama court ordered the husband, William Orr, to pay alimony, almost $1,300 monthly, to his former wife, Lillian Orr. After two years, she filed a petition in state court seeking to have William held in contempt for failing to maintain the alimony payments.

At the hearing he claimed that the Alabama statute, because it was gender-based, violated the Fourteenth Amendment's Equal Protection Clause. However, the presiding judge issued judgment for $5,524 and the state appellate courts affirmed. Orr then asked the U.S. Supreme Court to review the constitutional issue. Justice Brennan delivered the 6:3 opinion of the Court. Joining him were Justices Stewart, White, Marshall, Blackmun, and Stevens. (Justices Blackmun and Stevens also wrote concurring opinions, while Justice Powell and Justice Rehnquist, joined by Chief Justice Burger, wrote separate dissents).

The majority opinion concluded that the Alabama "gender-based distinction is gratuitous; without it the statutory scheme would only provide benefits to those men who are, in fact, similarly situated to the women the statute aids." Gender discriminations "carry the inherent risk of reinforcing stereotypes about the 'proper place' of women and their need for special protection. . . . The State cannot be permitted to classify on the basis of sex."[27]

May a wife, in the twenty-first century, be compelled to testify either for or against her husband, or a husband testify against his wife? In an 1839 civil case involving the settlement of an estate, the deceased husband's wife, Frances Stuffle, was asked to testify—before the U.S. Supreme Court in open session— that her late husband had accepted a bribe. Justice John McLean refused to allow her to take the stand:

> Public policy and established principles forbid it. This Rule is founded upon the deepest and soundest principles of our nature. To break down or impair the great principles which protect the sanctities of husband and wife would be to destroy the best solace of human existence.

One hundred years later, in *Funk v U.S.*,[28] the U.S. Supreme Court relented and ruled that a wife could testify in her husband's defense. However, a quarter of a century later, a unanimous Supreme Court, in an opinion written by Justice Hugo L. Black, ruled that a wife's testimony, however voluntary, violated the nineteenth-century "Stuffle" Rule. The wife had testified against her husband in a federal criminal trial. Thanks to her testimony, her husband, James Hawkins, was convicted under the Mann Act for transporting a woman from Arkansas to Oklahoma for immoral purposes (prostitution in Tulsa, Oklahoma). Said Black, who was an extremely homophobic southern father and husband,[29] the purpose of the rule against a spouse's testifying in court is "to foster family peace, not only for the benefit of husband, wife, and children, but for the benefit of the public as well. [The rule] has never been unreasonable and is not now."[30]

In 1980, the Court majority did a flip-flop on the issue. Otis Trammel, Jr., was convicted for importing heroin from Thailand into the United States. His wife, given immunity by federal prosecutors, testified against him at the trial. A unanimous Court, in an opinion written by Chief Justice Burger, rejected the old rule and allowed Trammel's conviction to stand. Adverse spousal testimony was permitted in American courts. Burger noted that the old Anglo-Saxon canon concerning this aspect of the marital relationship had "long since disappeared."[31] And in the Court's 1999 Term, the Justices denied certiorari in a case where a wife testified against her husband and the

Ninth Circuit U.S. Court of Appeals upheld the conviction, rejecting the husband's argument that his wife could not testify against him.[32]

The marital relationship was and remains the basis of the family unit in civilized society. To the chagrin of gay and lesbian couples, heterosexual marriage remains vital to the preservation of society's morals. Judges, including those who sit on the high bench, speak glowingly about marriage. The U.S. Supreme Court has "frequently reiterated and affirmed the fundamental right to marry—the autonomous right of each individual to decide whether to marry and to whom to marry."[33] In *Maynard v Hill*, for example, the U.S. Supreme Court said that "marriage [is] the most important relation in life, [is an institution] the maintenance of which in its purity the public is deeply interested,... it is the foundation of the family and of society, without which there would be neither civilization nor progress."[34]

More practically, "only marriages between a man and a woman receive [a multiplicity of] benefits and legal recognition" by the state. The benefits and rights bestowed on the married couple include at least the following: state and federal income tax advantages, social security survivor benefits, bereavement leave, sick leave for care of the other, assumption of a spouse's pension, public assistance, property rights, child custody awards, dower payments, rights relating to inheritance, the right to spousal support, and the right to change one's name.[35]

The Court has said that fathers who are in child support arrears cannot be denied the right to remarry.[36] Even prisoners, the Court has said, have a right to marry while they are incarcerated. Although the Justices stated that the "right to marry, like many other rights, is subject to substantial restrictions as a result of incarceration," nevertheless, "legitimate corrections goals" aside, they reasoned that even a prisoner's right to marry was constitutionally protected.[37]

Yet, paradoxically, in the twenty-first century, marriage is viewed, in employment matters, politics, and the law, as a legal, intimate association of two *equal* and *autonomous*, heterosexual individuals. Marriage is still society's essential legal and moral relationship; however, society's views about traditional marriage—and the reality of marriage when viewing data collected by the U.S. Census Bureau—have changed dramatically. A century earlier, couples married for life; there were few divorces. Today, data show that half of all marriages now end in divorce, one child in four is born out of wedlock, and traditional married heterosexual couples with children are a distinct minority cohort in America.[38]

Regulating marriage is one of the many responsibilities left to the states by the Tenth Amendment.[39] The U.S. Supreme Court has held that states can "reasonably" regulate marriage by prescribing who is allowed to marry, and how a marriage can legally be ended. A state cannot prohibit two persons from marrying each other without presenting a "compelling" reason for the restriction. In *Loving*, for example, the Court rejected a Virginia state law prohibiting interracial marriage because such state action violated the Fourteenth Amendment's Equal Protection Clause.

Richard Loving, a white Virginian, fell in love with Mildred Jetter, a black and Native American woman. They were married in the District of Columbia because Virginia law barred interracial marriage. Forced to live outside the state, they instituted a suit challenging the constitutionality of the Virginia antimiscegenation statute. The Supreme Court unanimously ruled that liberty and the freedom to marry is a fundamental right protected by the Fourteenth Amendment's Due Process Clause. Chief Justice Warren wrote: "These statutes deprive the Lovings of liberty without due process of law in violation of the Due Process Clause of the Fourteenth Amendment. The freedom to marry has long been recognized as one of the vital personal rights essential to the orderly pursuit of happiness by free men. . . . Under our Constitution, the freedom to marry or not marry, a person of another race resides with the individual and cannot be infringed by the state."[40]

The traditional *heterosexual* marital relationship, then and now, was considered a fundamental liberty interest protected from most state action by the Due Process Clause. The U.S. Supreme Court has regularly tied this fundamental right to other intimate activities associated with marriage, including contraception, procreation, raising children, and other family relationships.

Case Study: *Skinner v Oklahoma*, 1942[41]

In 1942, most states authorized eugenic sterilization of the feeble-minded or habitual criminals. In 1927, the U.S. Supreme Court, in an 8:1 opinion authored by the great Justice Oliver Wendell Holmes, concluded that Virginia has a right to sterilize feeble-minded persons. Rejecting the argument that Carrie Buck had a right to "full bodily integrity," Holmes validated the state's eugenics policy, stating that "three generations of imbeciles are enough."[42]

The other class of persons who faced the prospect of eugenic sterilization were criminals who had been convicted two or more times. Oklahoma's Habitual Criminal Sterilization Act provided that "habitual criminals," i.e., those who had been convicted for at least two felonies involving moral turpitude, could face, at the discretion of the prosecutor, sterilization (by vasectomy or salpingectomy). Crimes involving moral turpitude included larceny by fraud, but the state statute expressly exempted persons convicted of embezzlement.

Jack Skinner was convicted in 1926 of the crime of stealing chickens. In 1929, he was convicted for the crime of robbery, with firearms. In 1934, he was convicted a third time of robbery with firearms and sentenced to the Oklahoma penitentiary. He was there when, in 1935, the sterilization act was passed. In 1936, the state's Attorney General instituted proceedings against Skinner. Skinner claimed that the act was unconstitutional by reason of the Fourteenth Amendment. A jury trial was held; the only question for the jury was whether Skinner was healthy enough to undergo a vasectomy. The jury found that his health was fine and the medical procedure would not be a detriment to his general health. The judge issued the order for a vasectomy and the Oklahoma Supreme Court affirmed the judgment.

Skinner appealed to the U.S. Supreme Court. He argued that the state did not have a Tenth Amendment "police power" to sterilize him, that due process was denied him because, unlike the Virginia statute validated in *Buck v Bell,* Skinner had no opportunity at the trial to challenge the validity of the act. Finally he claimed that forced sterilization was "cruel and unusual punishment" prohibited by the Fourteenth Amendment. Oklahoma's Attorney General told the Justices that criminal tendencies were inherited and that the way to end crime was to sterilize all habitual criminals.

In the Conference Session after oral arguments, there was unanimity to reverse the sterilization order.[43] The Justices distinguished the Oklahoma statute from the West Virginia one that led to Carrie Buck's sterilization. As Douglas said in the meeting: "[M]oronic minds are different." Skinner's "civil rights are involved, and he has a right to protection of those rights."

Justice William O. Douglas wrote the opinion for a unanimous Court. (Chief Justice Stone and Justice Robert Jackson wrote concurring opinions.) The Court did not address any of the issues Skinner raised "for there is a feature of the Act which clearly condemns it. That is, its failure to meet the requirements of the equal protection clause of the Fourteenth Amendment." A store clerk who steals twenty dollars from his employer's cash register and a stranger who enters the store and steals the same amount are both guilty of felonies. If the latter repeats his act and is convicted three times, he may be sterilized. But the clerk is not subject to the pains and penalties of the Act no matter how large his embezzlements nor how frequent his convictions.[44]

For Douglas, the Oklahoma statute "runs afoul of the equal protection clause." Furthermore,

> We are dealing here with legislation which involves one of the basic civil rights of man. Marriage and procreation are fundamental to the very existence and survival of the race. . . . When the law lays an unequal hand on those who have committed intrinsically the same quality of offense and sterilizes one and not the other. it has made as invidious a discrimination as if it had selected a particular race or nationality for oppressive treatment.

In *Skinner*, a chicken thief's appeal led the Court to state that "marriage and procreation" are fundamental rights, protected by the Due Process and Equal Protection Clauses found in the Constitution's Fourteenth Amendment. Three decades later, Jack Skinner's behavior led another group of Supreme Court Justices to find, in the substance of the Due Process Clause, the "fundamental" right to marital privacy.[45]

III. Molecular Changes in the Definition and Reality of the Traditional Marital Relationship

Throughout most of America's social and legal history women were seen as the inferior partner in heterosexual marriage. Under common law, in accord with statutes, and with the U.S. Constitution, the male partner was the primary power holder in the marriage relationship. The role of the husband in Anglo-Saxon and American common law, as well as in American statutory and constitutional law has been, until recently, paramount. He was the master of the family and could punish his wife and his children.

Case Study: *Bradwell v Illinois*, 1872[46]

Myra Bradwell, a married woman born in Vermont but a citizen of Illinois, applied to the Illinois Supreme Court for a license to practice law. She also filed an affidavit indicating that she was born in Vermont and had been a citizen of the Green Mountain state for years prior to moving to Chicago. She maintained that she was entitled to the license to practice law because Vermont did not bar women from the practice of law and that Illinois had to give "full faith and credit" to Vermont's policy.

The Illinois bar admission statute required that a person who wanted to practice law had to obtain a license from two justices of the Illinois Supreme Court. Her application was refused because, under the existing decisions of State's Supreme Court, "the applicant as a married woman would be bound neither by her express contracts nor by those implied contracts which it is the policy of the law to create between attorney and client."

Myra Bradwell then filed a printed argument urging the court to grant her a license. The Illinois Supreme Court again concluded that the common law in the state was brought over, undisturbed, from England.

> It is to be remembered that female attorneys at law were unknown in England, and a proposition that a woman should enter the courts of Westminster Hall in that capacity, or as a barrister, would have created hardly less astonishment than one that she should ascend the bench of bishops, or be elected to a seat in the House of Commons.

The judges concluded their unanimous opinion, stating, "God designed the sexes to occupy different spheres of action, and that it belonged to men to make, apply, and execute the laws, was regarded as an axiomatic truth."

Bradwell appealed to the U.S. Supreme Court, and the Justices, with only a single dissent, affirmed the judgment of the Illinois Supreme Court. Justice Miller wrote the opinion for the majority. He concluded that Illinois violated no provision of the federal Constitution. The privileges and immunities clause "only guarantees privileges and immunities to citizens of other states" and Bradwell is a citizen of Illinois. The right to practice law in state courts, Miller stated, was not a privilege and immunity of U.S. citizenship. Finally, the Court concluded that the state's power to "prescribe the qualifications for admission to the bar of its own courts is unaffected by the Fourteenth Amendment."

Justice Bradley wrote a concurring opinion that expressed his views—and the views of the society at the time—about the role of women in nineteenth-century America:

The civil law, as well as nature herself, has always recognized a wide difference in the respective spheres and destinies of man and woman. Man is, or should be, woman's protector. The natural and proper timidity and delicacy which belongs to the female sex evidently unfits it for many of the occupations of civil life. . . . The domestic sphere is that which properly belongs to the domain and functions of womanhood. . . . The paramount destiny and mission of woman are to fulfill the noble and benign offices of wife and mother. This is the law of the Creator.

Obviously, ideas about marriage and the marital relationship have changed since *Bradwell.* The major case involving the issue of marital privacy came to the Justices during the liberal Warren Court era.

Late in the U.S. Supreme Court's 1964 Term, the Justices heard and decided the watershed case of *Griswold v Connecticut.*[47] An 1879 Connecticut statute made it a crime for any person to use any drug, article, or instrument to prevent conception. It had been challenged twice before but, in both cases, the Justices avoided a decision on the merits.[48]

However, "Dr. Buxton is back," wrote Earl Warren's law clerk, John Hart Ely, in November 1964, to his boss.[49] Dr. Buxton and Ms. Estelle Griswold were arrested, convicted, and fined one hundred dollars apiece for violating Section 54-196 of the Connecticut General Statutes (giving birth-control information to married couples at the Planned Parenthood clinic). The conviction was upheld by Connecticut's highest court, the Supreme Court of Errors.

They appealed to the U.S. Supreme Court, arguing that their First Amendment rights had been violated: They were deprived of the right to advocate birth control and, in Dr. Buxton's case, to practice medicine. Their clients, patients, were also unconstitutionally deprived of their liberty interest protected by the Due Process Clause of the Fourteenth Amendment.

Case Study: *Griswold v Connecticut,* 1965[50]

In the Conference Session after the oral arguments, there was a great deal of heat given off by the "nine scorpions."[51] While all of the brethren believed the Connecticut law was absolutely asinine, the tough question was whether it was unconstitutional. For seven justices, it was; for two others, it was not. The Chief always starts the discussion of the cases in these secret Conference Sessions.

Earl Warren began by stating that it was a hard case because there weren't too many choices. He ruled out overturn of the law on substantive due process and/or "privacy" grounds. It was not, he argued, an important federal question. The case did not involve a First Amendment "right of association" issue (between doctor and patient). Nor was the freedom of speech of Buxton and Griswold constrained, Warren maintained: "[T]hey were convicted for actions, not speech." Furthermore, "I cannot say that the State has no legitimate interest—that would lead me to trouble on abortions."

He was left with an argument based on the fact that wealthy women could get a prescription from a private physician for the contraceptive device while poor women had to go to the clinic to receive information and the device, which was the target of the state's law enforcement authorities. "Since it affects the rights of the poor, the act is not narrowly enough written. Marriage is the most confidential relationship in our society, the [law] has to be clear cut and it isn't."[52]

Hugo Black was the senior Justice and spoke next. He, too, was having great difficulty with the legal resolution of the case. For him, there was no First Amendment issue. Humorously, he said: "The right of a husband and wife to assemble in bed is a new [First Amendment] right of assembly to me!" He could not "find why it isn't within the state's power to act" as Connecticut did. Black's erstwhile friend, Justice William O. Douglas next spoke. He disagreed with Black: The right of association is more than a right of assembly, it is a right to join with, advocate with—the right to send children to a religious school. Nothing is more personal than the [marital] relationship—it's within the First Amendment protection."

Potter Stewart agreed with Black. For him, although the statute was "an incredibly silly law," there was no amendment in the Bill of Rights that prohibited Connecticut from passing such a statute. "So I'd have to affirm," he concluded. Justice Tom C. Clark added that the state cannot interfere with the right to marry. "There's a right to marry, maintain a home, and a family. This is an area where persons have a right to be left alone!"

Justice Arthur Goldberg, a recent addition to the Court (appointed by Democratic President John F. Kennedy in 1962), maintained that "there's no compelling state reason justifying the statute."

Douglas wrote the opinion for the majority, with help from Justice Brennan. His opinion concluded that the two had standing to raise the constitutional rights of persons with whom they had a professional relationship and that the Connecticut law was unconstitutional because it infringed on the constitutionally protected, but unenumerated, right to marital privacy.

That "right" was found in the emanations and penumbras of a number of the amendments in the Bill of Rights.

The Chief's law clerk adamantly rejected Douglas's reasoning and told his boss: "I do not think you should join his opinion. It concludes that the Constitution incorporates a general right to privacy.

> When one seizes upon a right which does not appear in the Constitution, that right can be given any shape and scope the person discussing it wishes to have. This opinion incorporates an approach to the Constitution so dangerous that you should not join it.

The three concurring opinions were written by Justices White, Goldberg, and Harlan. White called for the Court to use the "strict scrutiny" test to balance the rights of the individual against those of the state. In such a weighing of the arguments, the individual's liberty interest took precedence. He rejected Douglas's and Goldberg's justifications as versions of substantive due process.

Goldberg's was a more expansive opinion than was Douglas's. Joined by Warren[53] and Brennan, he argued that the Ninth Amendment was controlling. It said: "The enumeration in the Constitution, of certain rights, shall not be construed to deny or disparage others retained by the people." For Goldberg, "[L]iberty protects those personal rights that are fundamental, and is not confined to the specific terms of the Bill of Rights." The Ninth Amendment allows the incorporation of rights "so rooted in the traditions and conscience of our people as to be ranked fundamental."

Harlan rejected Douglas's penumbras and emanations argument. Instead, he based his judgment on the Due Process Clause's liberty interest. Connecticut had violated a basic value "implicit in the concept of ordered liberty" (*Palko*).

Justice Black dissented, joined by Justice Stewart. They believed that Connecticut violated no constitutional guarantee. The Court majority was accused of judicial usurpation of legislative powers. "Use of any such broad, unbounded judicial authority would make of this Court's members a day-to-day constitutional convention." This was, Black argued, a "great constitutional shift of power to the courts which will be bad for the courts and worse for the country."

While the Court, 7:2, reversed the state court decision, there was no consensus on the reasons for so acting. In so doing, as noted earlier, the Court majority "created by finding" in the Constitution's "penumbras and emanations" the right of marital privacy. As will be seen, this watershed decision led to other major decisions that impacted the very essence of the marital relationship and struck deep at a question Chief Justice Warren didn't want to tackle: abortion rights.

IV. The Dilemma of Intimate Violence and Congressional Passage of the Violence Against Women Act (VAWA), 1994

"Violence against women by intimate partners" is deeply embedded in our social fabric. It is "contextual. It denotes physical or psychological acts that are committed by one who is in a relationship with the victim."[54] Violence against women is partner violence; it most often occurs in the privacy of the marital relationship. Mothers, wives, girlfriends are beaten and, all too often, killed.

This remains a major dilemma, involving millions of women and children in America annually,[55] There is also, the Department of Justice recently reported, a "racial divide" in intimate partner violence cases. The number of African American victims fell between 1976 and 1998, while the number of white victims killed or injured rose in the same time period.[56]

Children in these situations are traumatized. Furthermore, there is a tragic "Catch-22" outcome: the state removes children from homes where the sole charge is violence against the *mother* by the male member of the family. Battered mothers are charged with "failure to protect" their children. The state severs the mother-child relationship, regardless of the mother's nonculpability.[57]

Underscoring the dilemma facing women and children, a recent study published in the *Journal of the American Medical Association* (JAMA) concluded that one in five adolescent girls, ages fourteen to eighteen, "become the victims of physical or sexual violence, or both, in a dating relationship." About 20 percent of the two thousand girls reported "that they had been hit, slapped, shoved, or forced into sexual activity by a dating partner."[58]

Even after the women's rights movement fully emerged in the late 1960s, there remains the dilemma of state inaction in the face of intimate violence against mothers, wives, girlfriends, and—equally unfortunate—against the children of the violent person. Additionally, there is the great reluctance of the Rehnquist Court to interpret the Fourteenth Amendment as a shield against intimate, private, violence in the face of state inaction.

Case Study: *Joshua DeShaney, a minor, by his guardian ad litem, et al.,*
v Winnebago County, Wisconsin Department of Social Services, et al.,
1988[59]

"Poor Joshua"[60] DeShaney was born in 1979. In 1980, his parents were divorced and the court awarded custody to Randy DeShaney, Joshua's natural
father. In March 1984, four-year-old Joshua was severely beaten by Randy,
causing permanent brain damage such that the youngster was expected to
spend the rest of his life in an institution for the profoundly retarded.
"Emergency brain surgery revealed a series of hemorrhages caused by trau-
matic injuries to the head inflicted over a long period of time." Randy De-
Shaney was subsequently tried and convicted of child abuse.

The boy and his natural mother brought a civil suit in U.S. District Court
under 42 USC 1983[61] against the Wisconsin county, its department of social
services (DSS), and a number of DSS employees. The complaint alleged that
the county and its DSS employees had deprived the boy of his "liberty interest in bodily integrity" without due process of law, in violation of the
Fourteenth Amendment's Due Process Clause. They did so because they
failed to intervene to protect him from the risk of deadly violence "of which
they knew or should have known."

The papers filed by the plaintiff indicated that the county received a report in January 1982 indicating that the youngster might be a victim of
child abuse. One year later the boy was hospitalized with multiple bruises
and abrasions. The DSS obtained an order from juvenile court that placed
him in temporary custody of the hospital.

On the recommendation of a county "child protection team," consisting
of a pediatrician, a psychologist, a police detective, the county's lawyer, several DSS case workers, and various hospital personnel, the juvenile court
dismissed the case and the boy was returned to the custody of his father.
This was done after Randy met with DSS personnel and agreed to take steps
that would lessen the danger of child abuse. During 1983, however, the boy
was hospitalized twice for "suspicious" head injuries, and a DSS case worker
who made monthly visits to the home recorded in her files her continuing
suspicion of child abuse. The DSS, however, took no action.

The U.S. District Court held that the DSS's failure to render protective
services to persons within its jurisdiction did not violate the Due Process
Clause. The judge summarily dismissed the case, without an evidentiary
hearing. The U.S. Court of Appeals, CA7, affirmed the district court dis-
missal. It held that the Fourteenth Amendment's Due Process Clause does

not require a state agency to protect its citizens from "private violence," the causal connection between the county and the boy "was too attenuated to establish a deprivation of constitutional rights actionable under Section 1983."

The mother appealed the CA7 decision to the U.S. Supreme Court. On certiorari, a divided Court affirmed. Chief Justice Rehnquist wrote the majority opinion, joined by Justices White, Stevens, O'Connor, Scalia, and Kennedy. Rehnquist's opinion concluded that the county had no duty under the Due Process Clause to protect the boy against his father's violence and therefore its failure to provide protection did not deprive him of his "liberty" interest in violation of the Fourteenth Amendment's Due Process Clause. First, the harms the boy suffered occurred in the privacy of his home, not while he was in state custody. Further, the state had no part in the creation of the dangers that the child faced. Finally, the county DSS personnel did not do anything to render the boy any more vulnerable to the danger that existed in his home.

Rehnquist noted that while

> the facts of this case are undeniably tragic, . . . nothing in the language of the Due Process Clause itself requires the State to protect the life, liberty, and property of its citizens against invasion by private actors. The Clause is phrased as a limitation on the State's power to act, not as a guarantee of certain minimal levels of safety and security. . . . History [does not] support such an expansive reading of the [Fourteenth Amendment]. . . . Its purpose was to protect the people from the State, not to ensure that the State protected them from each other.

Rehnquist rejected the DeShaneys' argument that because the DSS knew of the abusive behavior of the father and tried to protect him, there was a "special relationship" formed between the county agency and Joshua. This meant, the DeShaneys claimed, that the county had a duty to protect Joshua from his father's cruel behavior. Rehnquist rejected the DeShaneys' premise: "Because the state had *no* constitutional duty to protect Joshua against his father's violence, its failure to do so—though calamitous in hindsight—simply does not constitute a violation of the Due Process Clause." His concluding words followed:

> Judges and lawyers, like other humans, are moved by natural sympathy in a case like this to find a way for Joshua and his mother to receive adequate

compensation for the grievous harm inflicted upon them. But before yielding to that temptation, it is well to remember once again that the harm was inflicted not by the State of Wisconsin, but by Joshua's father.

Three brethren angrily dissented: Justices Brennan, Marshall, and Blackmun. In two dissenting opinions (written by Brennan and Blackmun) they maintained that the county had a constitutional duty to help the boy but that the county officials effectively confined the boy within his father's home. They believed that the boy and his mother should have been allowed, in an evidentiary, Section 1983, hearing, the opportunity to show that the county's failure to help the boy—after it knew what the father was doing to him—was an arbitrary and capricious decision, one that violated the Fourteenth Amendment.

"The Constitution imposes upon the State an affirmative duty to help Joshua DeShaney." And, indeed, Wisconsin's DSS personnel, implementing DSS's child-protection program, "actively intervened in Joshua's life and, by virtue of this intervention, acquired ever more certain knowledge that Joshua was in grave danger." For that reason, the dissenters

> would allow Joshua and his mother the opportunity to show that respondents' failure to help him arose, not from the sound exercise of judgment but from the kind of arbitrariness that in the past we have condemned.

The Rehnquist opinion "construes the Due Process Clause to permit a State to displace private sources of protection and then, at the critical moment, to shrug its shoulders and turn away from the harm that it has promised to try to prevent. [We] cannot agree that our Constitution is indifferent to such indifference, [we] respectfully dissent."

DeShaney, one critic observed, is a cruel reflection of a "cultural/legal system that has constructed an impenetrable wall of privacy that obscures intra-familial violence, marginalizes the survivors and shields the perpetrators from accountability."[62] In the case, the Supreme Court majority "made it eminently clear that violence within the home is a private matter—concerning only the abuser and the abused."[63]

The physical, medial, emotional, and economic costs of this horrible reality are extremely high. Congressional reports published in the four years prior to passage of the Violence Against Women Act (VAWA) enumerated, in ghastly detail, the personal and societal costs of violence against women by an intimate spouse. Justice Souter's dissent in the case that examined the constitutionality of parts of VAWA,[64] listed some of the congressional findings "with respect to domestic violence:"

- Three out of four women "will be victims of violent crime sometime during their life."
- "Violence is the leading cause of injuries to women ages 15 to 44."
- "As many as 50% of homeless women and children are fleeing domestic violence."
- "Battering is the single largest cause of injury to women in the U.S."
- "An estimated 4 million American women are battered each year by their husbands or partners."
- "Over 1 million women in the U.S. seek medical assistance each year for injuries sustained from their husbands or other partners."
- "Between 2,000 and 4,000 women die every year from domestic abuse."
- "Arrest rates may be as low as 1 for every 100 domestic assaults."
- "Partial estimates show that violent crime against women cost this country at least 3 billion—not million, but billion—dollars a year."
- "Estimates [are] that the U.S. spends $5 to $10 billion a year on the social costs of domestic violence."

With respect to rape,

- "Close to half a million high school women will be raped before they graduate."
- "125,000 college women can expect to be raped during one year."
- "Three quarters of women never go to the movies alone at night because of the fear of rape and nearly 50% do not use public transit alone after dark for the same reason."[65]

Because intimate violence, for centuries, has been perceived as private, governments have not been concerned about intervening on behalf of the battered spouse. Such state "nonfeasance and misfeasance contributes to the systemic abuse of women in the family."[66] The traditions, customs, and common law found in both British and American societies until literally the last decade of the twentieth century have left the battered wife—and very frequently, her children—at the mercy of the husband. Government, until the 1990s, utterly failed to protect mothers, wives, and lovers from intimate violence by the spouse or partner.

English laws permitting, legitimating, wife beating came to the American colonies

> through the incorporation of the Blackstonian concept of "subtle chastisement." Under this doctrine, the husband's right to beat his wife was limited only by the "same moderation that a man is allowed to correct his apprentices or children."[67]

Husbands were "permitted to inflict injury upon their wives so long as the resulting harm was not life threatening.

> Conduct that resulted in black eyes, welts, and split lips constituted no violation of law. . . . [Mississippi law, for example] held that husbands would not be prosecuted if they beat their wives with a stick no thicker than the diameter of their thumb. [This "rule of thumb"] in effect gave husbands the right to use physical force as a means to control their wives' behavior.[68]

"Subtle chastisement" law in America ended in 1870 and the situation for married women improved, but not very much.[69] The public policy lethargy accompanying centuries of "systemic inaction" by the states was shattered when, in June 1994, former pro-football athlete O. J. Simpson was arrested and charged with the murders of his former wife, Nicole Brown Simpson, and Ronald Goldman. A nation sat, in a hypnotic trance, in front of television screens to watch the sensational criminal trial that took place in California. The nation was forced into a shocked recognition of the persistence of wife beating in America. And the public became aware of the twin sources of oppression against women and children: the "sanctity" of the home and massive governmental inaction.

A number of states and the Congress were moved to pass legislation that had been under consideration for years. The Violence Against Women Act (VAWA) was passed by Congress in October 1994, five months after Simpson was accused of murdering his former wife by California prosecutors. VAWA was the consequence of four years of arduous research by congressional staffers. Based on two major congressional powers,[70] its purpose, as stated in the act, was to "free persons from crimes of violence committed because of gender or on the basis of gender, and due, at least in part to an animus based on the victim's gender."

VAWA "created a federal civil right to be free from crimes of violence motivated by gender." It embraced "the feminist characterization of violence against women as a form of sex discrimination, rather than merely a private, individual harm,"[71] a view of domestic violence long embedded in the American culture. As noted, there exists, even today, the "historic tendency to view violence against women as intrinsically private and therefore undeserving of legal redress, particularly in the federal courts."[72]

Criminal penalties for the commission of gender-motivated crimes of violence are enumerated in Title 18 USC Sections 2261, prohibition against interstate domestic violence; 2261A, prohibition against interstate stalking; and 2262, interstate violation of a protective order. Based on the power to regulate commerce, the VAWA makes criminal actions to injure a spouse or "intimate partner," to stalk "a member of that person's immediate family," and/or to violate a protection order received by a "spouse or intimate partner." The penalty for committing, or intending to commit any of the above actions was fine and imprisonment. The penalty was "for life or any term of years, if death of the victim results"; for not more than twenty years "if permanent disfigurement or life threatening bodily injury to the victim results"; for not more than ten years, if "serious bodily injury to the victim results or if the offender used a dangerous weapon during the offense"; and for not more than five years "in any other case, or both fined and imprisoned."

The civil remedies available to women who are abused is contained in 42 USC 13981C. A person "who commits a crime of violence motivated by gender and thus deprives another of the right to be free from [such a crime] shall be liable to the party injured, in an action for recovery of compensatory and punitive damages, injunctive and declaratory relief, and such other relief as a court may deem appropriate."

VAWA's criminal provisions have been challenged in federal courts. And they have been consistently upheld by the judges.[73] The primary reason for judicial validation is because interstate travel is involved. As one federal appeals court noted: "The criminal provision regulates the use of channels of interstate commerce. As a result, that violence against a spouse is a private or noncommercial activity, is of no moment."[74]

In 2000, the Supreme Court answered the other question of law: Was VAWA's civil remedy constitutional? (Unlike the criminal provisions of the law, the civil rights provision does not contain any explicit reference to the congressional power to regulate interstate commerce.)

Case Study: *U.S. v Morrison*, 1999[75]

Christy Brzonkala entered Virginia Polytechnic Institute (Virginia Tech) in the fall of 1994. She immediately met the two respondents, Antonio Morrison and James Crawford, Virginia Tech undergraduates and starting members of the university's football team. She alleged that within thirty minutes after meeting the two men in her dormitory, "they assaulted and repeatedly raped her."[76] After this horrid incident, Brzonkala became "severely emotionally distressed and depressed. She sought assistance from a university psychiatrist, who prescribed anti-depressant medication. Shortly after the rape Brzonkala stopped attending classes and withdrew from the university."

In early 1995, Brzonkala filed a complaint against Morrison and Crawford under the university's Sexual Assault Policy. Morrison was found guilty of sexual assault (but not Crawford) and the Judicial Committee sentenced him to immediate suspension for two semesters. In July 1995, Brzonkala—who was getting ready to return to school in the fall—found out that Morrison was going to challenge his conviction and suspension. The university then held a second hearing under its Abusive Conduct Policy, which was in force prior to the adoption of the Sexual Assault Policy. The committee found him guilty and reimposed the suspension. However, the description of his offense was changed from "sexual assault" to "using abusive language."

He appealed the punishment to the university's provost, who, in August 1995, set aside Morrison's punishment. Brzonkala found out about this decision from media stories and dropped out of the university because Morrison was back on campus again.

In December 1995, Brzonkala sued her rapists and the university in the U.S. District Court, Western District, Virginia. She alleged in her complaint that the two men's actions violated VAWA's Section 13981 and that the university's handling of her complaint violated Title IX of the 1972 Education Amendments. The two football players moved to dismiss the complaint, arguing that that section of VAWA was unconstitutional. The district court judge dismissed her claims against the university. The judge then held that Brzonkala's complaint stated a claim against the two men but dismissed the complaint because Congress lacked the authority to enact the section under either the Commerce Clause or Section 5 of the Fourteenth Amendment.

A divided CA4 panel reversed, 2:1, the district court, reinstating both claims. However, the CA4, sitting *en banc,* reversed the panel and upheld the district court judge's conclusions. "Because the Court of Appeals invalidated a federal statute on constitutional grounds, [the U.S. Supreme Court] granted certiorari."

During oral argument in January 2000, observers heard the five conservative justices level very tough questions at U.S. Solicitor General Seth P. Waxman (who was arguing on behalf of the validity of the VAWA). The congressional approach, said Justice Sandra Day O'Connor, "'would justify a federal remedy for alimony or child support!'" Justice Scalia "warned that 'the entire realm of criminal justice' might be co-opted by the federal government. Justice Anthony M. Kennedy similarly warned that the federal government could, under the Justice Department's theory, assert control over murder and robbery."[77]

On the other side, Justice Ruth B. Ginsburg challenged Morrison's lawyer to explain why Congress couldn't attack the problem of violence against women. "'But this isn't commerce. This is violence. This is interpersonal violence that is under the states' purview!'"[78]

Chief Justice Rehnquist delivered the opinion for the five-person majority (Justices O'Connor, Scalia, Kennedy, and Thomas joined Rehnquist's opinion). It validated the CA4 3-judge panel judgment that the civil remedies in VAWA could not be sustained under the Commerce Clause or Section 5, the "enforcement" section, of the Fourteenth Amendment.

Rehnquist first dealt with the use by Congress of its power to regulate commerce found in Article I, Section, Clause 3 of the Constitution. Basing his judgment on the Court's 1995 decision *U.S. v Lopez,*[79] Rehnquist wrote:

> Due respect for the decisions of a coordinate branch of Government demands that we invalidate a congressional enactment only upon a plain showing that Congress has exceeded its constitutional bounds.

For the majority, the civil sections of VAWA did not "regulate those activities having a substantial relation to interstate commerce."

Rehnquist greatly narrowed the scope of the congressional commerce power when he repeated the *Lopez* precedent: "Where economic activity substantially affects interstate commerce, legislation regulating that activity will be sustained." Regulating handguns was not an economic activity that substantially affected commerce; nor were "gender-motivated crimes of violence" economic activities substantially affecting commerce.

The Chief turned to the argument that Congress has the power to enforce the Fourteenth Amendment by passing appropriate legislation. Brzonkala's lawyers and the U.S. Solicitor General argued that there exists "pervasive bias in various state justice systems against victims of gender-motivated violence." This bias, they maintained, denies victims the equal protection of the laws

> and that Congress therefore acted appropriately in enacting a private civil remedy against the perpetrators of gender-motivated violence to both remedy the States' bias and deter future instances of discrimination in the state courts.

Citing nineteenth-century cases, the Rehnquist majority rejected that argument. Congressional attempts to regulate gender-motivated violence using Section 5 were invalid because the legislators were targeting private action and the Fourteenth Amendment is a limit on "state action." Any effort to regulate and to punish "purely private conduct [went] beyond the scope of [Congress's] Section 5 "'enforcement' power."

If Christy Brzonkala's "allegations here are true, no civilized system of justice could fail to provide her a remedy for the conduct of respondent Morrison," concluded Rehnquist. "But under our federal system that remedy must be provided by the Commonwealth of Virginia, and not by the United States."[80]

Justice David H. Souter wrote a dissent, joined by Justices Stevens, Ginsburg, and Breyer. For the New Hampshire native, Congress had the power, in the "commerce clause," to pass legislation concerning actions that had a substantial impact on interstate commerce. Congress and pressure groups had presented voluminous evidence showing the adverse impact on interstate commerce of gender-motivated criminal actions. Congressional reports presented data showing that such crimes of violence

> have a substantial adverse impact on interstate commerce, by deterring potential victims from traveling interstate, from engaging in employment in interstate business, and from transacting with business, and in places involved, in interstate commerce, by diminishing national productivity, increasing medical and other costs, and decreasing the supply of and demand for interstate products.

Souter maintained that the act "would have passed muster" anytime between 1941 and 1995 (when the Court handed down *Lopez*). And he went on to explain why the five-person majority moved away from existing precedents.

> *In the mind of the majority there is a new animating theory* that makes categorical formalism seem useful again, . . . useful in serving a conception of federalism [limiting national power] in favor of preserving a supposedly discernible, proper sphere of state authority to legislate or refrain from legislating as the individual states see fit.

In 1994, while the legislators were still *debating* VAWA, Chief Justice Rehnquist said that Congress "was increasingly federalizing crimes for symbolic reasons." Again, in 1998, in a speech to the American Law Institute, the Chief Justice singled out VAWA for criticism. It was one of "the more notable examples" of bad law: "Our system will look more and more like the French government, where even the most minor details are ordained by the national government in Paris."[81]

In the 2000 Term, the Chief had a case and the five votes necessary to invalidate the civil provisions of VAWA.[82] His "animating theory" of federal-state relationships was given precedential status in *Morrison*. Rehnquist's outlook led to "a convergence between the Court's focus on a Congress of limited powers and its newly found solicitude for state sovereignty."

By ruling that VAWA was not an appropriate exercise of Congress's power to enforce the equal protection guarantee of the Fourteenth Amendment, the Court emphasized that in the area of civil rights, no less than interstate commerce, congressional assertions of power were now to be scrutinized under a judicial microscope.[83]

Immediately, critics saw in Rehnquist's opinion a deference that took the nation "back to an era of 19th century racism."[84] U.S. Attorney General Janet Reno called *Morrison* a "deeply disappointing" decision. "Violence still devastates too many lives," she said.[85]

Senator Joe Biden (D-Del.), the sponsor of the 1994 VAWA, "said he would 'figure out a way to rewrite the law to allow rape victims to circumvent the ruling.' Asked if there were any changes that could be made to make federal rape lawsuits legal, he replied: 'Yes, two new justices.'"[86]

V. Same-Sex Marriage

There are opponents of the conventional, very traditional view of the history of marriage in Western society. "Contrary to [the immutability of heterosexual marriage imagery in history], same-sex relationships were widely recognized in Europe . . . and countries in Asia." It was not until 1793 that the English Parliament required a church ceremony and a license to "achieve a valid marital status," so that a "marriage could only be recognized by the government." Common law marriages in England and America were widely accepted and recognized by government through the nineteenth century. With the "increased mobility of society and a more structured system of government," there emerged in the late nineteenth and early twentieth centuries state regulation of marriages.[87]

Proponents of same-sex marriage, since the early 1970s, have made attempts to "expand the definition of marriage to include same-sex couples."[88] In a Minnesota state court case, two men were denied a marriage license because they were of the same sex.[89] The court validated the state statute and dismissed the plaintiffs' claim, relying on the traditional definition of marriage as a union of a man and a woman. The Court also stated that *Loving* involved the constitutionality of antimiscegenation statutes. Such state laws were deemed unconstitutional because they were marital restrictions based on race. There were no "compelling" reasons for such racially discriminatory laws.

The question that courts began to face in the 1990s was "whether [the liberty of interracial couples to marry] extended to marriage regardless of the parties' genders. Thirty years after the *Loving* decision, the same legal arguments are being used to expand the fundamental right to marriage to include same-sex couples."[90]

However, reasonable grounds for validating the states' sex-based marital restriction have consistently been found by judges. "The legalization of same-sex marriages, one of the more radical policy decisions facing the judiciary and legislature today, could have drastic consequences on modern society's traditional definition of marriage," said one critic of the idea.[91]

Another opponent of same-sex marriage, U.S. Court of Appeals judge (and legal scholar) Richard Posner, has written that "to permit persons of the same sex to marry is to be declaring that homosexuality is a desirable, even noble, condition in which to live. [However], this is not what most people believe."[92] To date, courts in America have concluded that same-sex marriages do not qualify as a "fundamental right" protected by the "liberty" interest in the Fourteenth Amendment's Due Process clause because same-sex marriage is not a relationship deeply rooted in the nation's history and traditions.

The Fourteenth Amendment cannot be used to validate same-sex marriage by invalidating state laws that prohibit such a relationship. In case law created by the U.S. Supreme Court, "suspect classes" are entitled to strict scrutiny by judges. If the state legislation allegedly discriminates on the basis of race, alienage, national origin, or religion, then—consistent with *Carolene Product's* footnote four, judges must apply the strict scrutiny standard. Was there a "compelling" interest presented by the state in defense of its discrimination? Was it a narrowly tailored statute (or was it too broad, or too vague)?

From cases such as *Bowers*, one can conclude that the U.S. Supreme Court as constituted at this time in America's history, would not place homosexuality in the "suspect class" category. Nor would the Court conclude that state laws prohibiting same-sex marriage are arbitrary and capricious and thus in violation of the Fourteenth Amendment's command that every person is entitled to the equal protection of the laws.

Legally, there is no "fundamental" right to same-sex marriage that prevents states from refusing to issue marriage licenses to such a couple. To uphold the same-sex marriage, the U.S. Supreme Court would have to set aside its views on homosexuality, as seen most notably in *Bowers*, and recognize a fundamental right to homosexual conduct. In his majority opinion in *Bowers*, Justice White was extremely leery about the court's finding such new "fundamental" rights: "The Court is most vulnerable and comes nearest to illegitimacy when it deals with judge-made constitutional law having little or no cognizable roots in the language or design of the Constitution."[93]

In December 1999, however, a state Supreme Court ruled that same-sex couples must be afforded the "benefits and protections" that heterosexual married couples receive.

Case Study: *Stan Baker, et al. v State of Vermont, et al.*, 1999[94]

Three same-sex couples residing in Vermont have lived together "in committed relationships for periods ranging from four to twenty five years."[95] Two of the couples have raised children together. Each couple applied for a marriage license from its town clerk; each was refused a license under the applicable state marriage laws. The six filed a lawsuit against the defendants—the State of Vermont, the towns of Milton and Shelburne, and the city of South Burlington. They sought a declaratory judgment that the refusal to issue marriage licenses to them violated the marriage statutes and the Vermont Constitution. They did not win in Vermont Superior Court and they took their appeal to the Vermont Supreme Court.

For the Vermont Supreme Court, the question of law was a "fundamental" one: "May the State of Vermont exclude same-sex couples from the benefits and protections that its laws provide to opposite-sex married couples?" It is a question, said Chief Justice Jeffrey L. Amestoy, that "arouses deeply-felt religious, moral, and political beliefs." Amestoy then wrote:

> We conclude that under the Common Benefits clause of the Vermont Constitution, which, in pertinent part, reads, "That government is, or ought to be instituted, for the common benefit, protection, and security of the people, nation, or community, and not for the particular emolument of any single person, family, or set of persons, who are a part only of that community,"[96] plaintiffs may not be deprived of the statutory benefits and protections afforded persons of the opposite sex who choose to marry. We hold that the State is constitutionally required to extend to same-sex couples the common benefits and protections that flow from marriage under Vermont law.[97]

The Vermont Supreme Court reversed the judgment of the Superior Court. "The effect of the [Superior] Court's decision is suspended, and jurisdiction is retained in this Court, to permit the Legislature to consider and enact legislation consistent with the [State] constitutional mandate described herein."[98]

Amestoy's judgment, based on the majority's interpretation of the Vermont Constitution, did not raise a federal question and was therefore not appealable to the U.S. Supreme Court. The Vermont legislators, in the months following the December 1999 *Baker* ruling, intensely debated the question. After rejecting any expansion of the marriage laws to include same-sex marriage, the legislators passed the civil unions bill (in the Vermont Senate by a 19 to 11 vote; the House vote was also close, 79 to 68). Governor Howard Dean (D) signed Act 60, the Civil Unions Act, on April 26, 2000; it became effective July 1, 2000. Since then, hundreds of same-sex couples have been joined in domestic partnerships. More than two-thirds of them came from out of state. The great majority of couples are female.

Public opinion polls, both national and state, continually record that three-quarters of the public strenuously oppose legal recognition of "civil unions" and same-sex marriage.[99]

Another argument put forward by proponents of same-sex marriage in the twenty-first century is the "*Loving* Analogy": Just as the race of a spouse was irrelevant to marriage after the *Loving* (1967) case, so the sex of a spouse is irrelevant to marriage today. However, only Vermont has partially accepted this hypothesis. In 2001, thirty-two states ban same-sex unions of any kind. The Congress, in response to litigation in Hawaii, strenuously defended traditional marriage by passing, in 1996, a very controversial piece of legislation, the Defense of Marriage Act.

VI. Congressional Passage of the Defense of Marriage Act (DOMA), 1996

If same-sex marriage were legalized in one of the states of the Union, then the U.S. Constitution's Full Faith and Credit Clause, the first clause in Article IV, could easily be interpreted to have such a marriage legally recognized in all the other states. It reads:

> Full faith and credit shall be given in each State to the public Acts, Records, and judicial Proceedings of every other State. And the Congress may by general laws prescribe the Manner in which such Acts, Records, and Proceedings shall be proved, and the Effect thereof.

That clause was put into the Constitution to "foster unity" among states that, until 1789, were sovereign entities. It was enacted to "safeguard [an] individual's legal rights in neighboring states, and to avoid the litigation of resolved disputes in other states."[100] The men in Philadelphia in the summer of 1787 literally lifted the clause verbatim from the Articles of Confederation, drafted in 1777. The thirteen states in the Confederation "wanted to retain their independence and sovereignty from federal rule, while still fulfilling their obligations to their sister states. They were well aware that failure to recognize the acts of their sister states would not further the life of the Confederation."[101]

Theoretically, the Full Faith and Credit Clause mandates that a same-sex marriage legally performed in one state be accepted as a legal and binding contract in all the other states. (In an early twentieth-century case, the U.S.

Supreme Court required the state of Mississippi to give full faith and credit to a Missouri judgment, even though that judgment validated a contract invalid in Mississippi.[102])

In 1993, the hypothetical issue became reality. Same-sex marriage "burst into the consciousness of the American public" because of litigation that began in Hawaii. Homosexual and lesbian plaintiffs were denied marriage licenses and went into the state courts to challenge this alleged discrimination. The case, *Nina Baehr, et al. v Lewin, Director, Hawaii Department of Health* (after 1994, it became *Baehr v Lawrence Miike*), was in the Hawaii courts from 1991 to 1999 and the Supreme Court of Hawaii reviewed Baehr's allegation at least three times.

Case Study: *Nina Baehr v Miike*, 1996, 1999[103]

When Nina Baehr and her partner, Genora Dancel, were denied an application for a marriage license in Hawaii, they, along with two other same-sex couples, went to court. Their requests were denied by the clerks because of Hawaii's marriage statutes, HRS Section 572-1 to Section 572-15,[104] which defined marriage as a "legal union between a man and a woman." They filed a complaint for a declaratory judgment on May 1, 1991. They sued

> on grounds that requiring parties to a marriage to be of different sexes was sex discrimination under the Hawaii State Constitution and was a denial of a fundamental right in violation of due process, equal protection and privacy.[105]

The circuit court entered its order in October 1991 against the couples. They appealed to the Hawaii Supreme Court. That court ruled that same-sex couples could marry unless the state could show a "compelling" justification for denying the plaintiffs the right to marry. The Supreme Court remanded the case back to the circuit court for further proceedings in May 1993.

In December 1996, the circuit court ruled in favor of the gay and lesbian plaintiffs. The state had not shown a compelling interest for the marriage statutes. It concluded that the sex-based classification in the statute was unconstitutional because it was in violation of the Equal Protection Clause in Article I, Section 5 of the Hawaii Constitution. (That clause in part states that "no person shall be denied the equal protection of the laws because of race, religion, sex, or ancestry.") The order also enjoined any official from denying Baehr, Dancel, and their coplaintiffs a marriage license because they were of the same sex, and that costs should be awarded against Miike and in favor of the plaintiffs.

In 1997, Hawaii's legislators, paralleling the actions of Congress a year earlier, passed an amendment to the Hawaii Constitution. Section 23 was the proposed addition to Article 1 of the Constitution. It read: "The legislature shall have the power to reserve marriage to opposite-sex couples [which is what HRS Section 572-1 stated]." Hawaii's voters, in November 1998, overwhelmingly ratified it. Baehr, Dancel, and their coplaintiffs again appealed; this time they tried to challenge the constitutionality of the constitutional amendment itself.

The Hawaii Supreme Court, in December 1999, concluded that "in light of the marriage amendment," the marriage statute "must be given full force and effect." The summary decision of the Hawaii Supreme Court concluded: "Inasmuch as HRS Section 572-1 is now a valid statute, the relief sought by the plaintiffs is unavailable. The marriage amendment has rendered the plaintiffs' complaint moot.

> IT IS HEREBY ORDERED that the judgment of the circuit court be reversed and that the case be remanded for entry of judgment in favor of Miike and against the plaintiffs. IT IS FURTHER ORDERED that the circuit court shall not enter costs or attorneys' fees against the plaintiffs.

As Nina Baehr's challenge to Hawaii's definition of marriage was taking place, in February 1998 an Alaskan trial court declared that the State of Alaska must show a "compelling state interest" in justifying the statutory definition of marriage as "a civil contract entered into by one man and one woman."[106]

Fearing a Hawaii court decision that would validate same-sex marriage, opponents of same-sex marriage in the 104th Congress successfully introduced and quickly passed the Defense of Marriage Act of 1996 (DOMA).[107] In its entirety, based on the use of Congress's power in the Full Faith and Credit Clause, the act states:

> No State, territory, or possession of the United States, or Indian Tribe, shall be required to give effect to any public act, record, or judicial proceeding of any other State, territory, possession, or tribe respecting a relationship between persons of the same sex that is treated as a marriage under the laws

of such other State, territory, possession, or tribe, or a right or claim arising from such relationship. In determining the meaning of any Act of Congress, or any ruling, regulation, or interpretation of the various administrative bureaus and agencies of the United States, the word "marriage" means only a legal union between one man and one woman as husband and wife, and the word "spouse" refers only to a person of the opposite sex who is a husband or wife.

The vote in Congress was a reflection of the overwhelming legislative support for the concept of the traditional heterosexual marriage—and only such a marriage. The Senate voted 85 to 14 in favor of DOMA; the House vote was 342 to 67.

President Bill Clinton, when he signed the DOMA at 12:50 A.M. on September 21, 1996, uttered the most understated ironic line of 1996: "*We need to do things to strengthen the American family.*" He contrasted DOMA with the *Romer* decision: "This is a separate issue. This goes to the heart of what marriage is."[108]

Clearly, the DOMA is something of a historic event; it is the first time that Congress has sought to use its powers under the Full Faith and Credit Clause to limit, not expand, the clause's reach. DOMA's constitutionality has not yet been addressed.[109]

While same-sex marriage is still prohibited in America, in the past twenty years a number of states and private employers have recognized the right of homosexual couples to create legal partnerships. This enables the homosexual couple to acquire rights and benefits that have traditionally been conferred only on married couples.[110] This arrangement "is a legal status granted by municipal governments to allow homosexuals to acquire employment benefits"[111] and other rights that benefit couples "in managing their financial affairs, planning for the future, and providing homosexuals with some external validation."[112]

In an opinion cheered by gay and lesbian groups, the U.S. Supreme Court, in the 1998 case of *Joseph Oncale v Sundowner Offshore Services, Inc.*,[113] unanimously concluded that federal laws that ban sexual harassment apply to situations in which the harasser and the victim are of the same sex.

Joseph Oncale was a twenty-one-year-old roustabout working on an offshore oil rig in 1991. His boss and two coworkers, all males, sexually taunted and abused him. "You know you got a cute little ass, and I'm going to get you," his supervisor once remarked to Oncale. One time, the three men grabbed Joe in the shower and shoved a bar of soap between his buttocks.

He complained to the Sundowner administrators about the harassment, which also included threats of rape.[114] They did not respond and, after the shower incident, Oncale quit his job.

He then brought a 1964 Civil Rights Act, Title VII discrimination suit against the company. The lower federal court threw out his suit. Title VII was written, the judge reasoned, to protect women from harassment by males. The U.S. Supreme Court unanimously overturned the lower court decision.

Justice Scalia wrote the opinion for a unanimous Court: "We see no justification for a categorical rule excluding same-sex harassment claims from the coverage of Title VII." He did, however, warn lower court judges to make sure they did not "mistake ordinary socializing in the workplace—such as male-on-male horseplay or intersexual flirtation—for discriminatory conditions of employment."[115]

"Civil Rights law will no longer unfairly exclude same-sex sexual harassment and this fact will benefit all American workers," said Elisabeth Birch of the Human Rights Campaign. Kathy Rogers of the NOW Inc. Fund said that the ruling "once and for all places sexual harassment law squarely in the mainstream of anti-discrimination law."[116]

VII. Summing Up

Given judicial, legislative, and executive rejection of same-sex marriage, the natural question is "What is necessary to support the recognition of a new 'fundamental' right?"[117] It would take a very significant change in public attitudes and in the public policies that follow public opinion before same-sex marriage was accepted as a practice "rooted" in the history and traditions of the society. While some inroad has been made, for example, Vermont's passage of its "civil unions" bill, fundamental change regarding the ideal of marriage in America is not at hand.

The realities of marriage and of family relationships, as seen in the following chapter, are light years ahead of public perceptions—and U.S. Supreme Court precedents.

3

The "Rhapsody of the Unitary Family"[1]

The basic unit of society [is] parents and their offspring. . . . This "nuclear" family is the basic building block of our society and it is a rational place to draw a line.
—Chief Justice Warren Burger's comments, sent in a Memo to the Conference, November 22, 1976[2]

The concept of the traditional family, that is, the "natural reproductive unit" of mom, pop, and the children all living under one roof, is not an immutable one. It is a social construct that varies from culture to culture and, over time, the definition changes within a culture. In American society, the idea of such a family was "forged in the early years of the Industrial Revolution."[3] One hundred years later, the idea of family is again going through significant change; it is an alteration that concerns many persons and institutions, including a majority of the Justices of the U.S. Supreme Court sitting in 2001.

In mid-June 2001, the Southern Baptist Convention met in New Orleans. While almost 500 mew churches joined the organization, and the nearly 42,000 churches in the organization recorded a near-record number of baptisms, 415,000, the annual convention ended on a "somber note." The traditional "nuclear family" is in severe trouble, the members concluded. It is "suffering high rates of divorce [four in ten marriages end in divorce], out-of-wedlock pregnancies and fathers' absence from the home, trends that the speakers said the 16-million-member denomination must work to remedy. [Southern Baptists must] save the family! Only 'strong, committed, Christ-centered families' can attract people to evangelical Christianity."[4]

George Murdock was the anthropologist who, in 1949, created the "nuclear family" metaphor. He wrote: "[N]uclear families are combined, like atoms in a molecule, into larger aggregates. [It is] the type of family recognized *to the exclusion of all others.*"[5] Certainly the vast majority of judges and Justices of the U.S. Supreme Court have accepted the metaphor and have judged cases in accordance with this traditional value.

Acceptance has led to the presence of a colossal paradox in the law. When U.S. Supreme Court Justices hear, read, discuss, and decide cases that involve family, it is the traditional ideal of family and home they have in mind. Most of the Justices had and have an almost blind reverence for the state of marriage. Justice White's biographer, for example, wrote that White "had a profound, almost preconstitutional respect for the marriage relationship and the family unit."[6]

But it is a "make-believe" perception of family, wrote a frustrated Justice Brennan in 1989.[7] In this fictional scenario, the husband is the breadwinner, the wife is the sex object and nurturer, and the children have no rights apart from those provided them by the master of the house. That this "Father Knows Best" imagery is no longer the dominant pattern of American households, and has not been for a generation, has been, tragically, overlooked by a majority of the Justices.[8] This bias arises naturally because Court majorities have proffered the "fundamental" right of family privacy when there is a clear connection between privacy and marriage (and family)—and procreation—between a man and a woman.[9]

For the most part, given the primacy of Court doctrine in our social, political, and legal systems, the law has not yet fully recognized the reality of family diversity in twenty-first century America. One scholar has listed no fewer than thirteen kinds of American "family" living arrangements—gay and lesbian and straight:

1. single parent with children
2. single without children
3. married, without children
4. married, with biological children
5. blended family, with biological, step-, adopted, and/or foster-children,
6. married, with an extended family
7. grandparents, with grandchildren
8. unmarried heterosexual couples, without children
9. unmarried lesbian couples, without children

10. unmarried gay couples, without children
11. unmarried heterosexual couples, with children
12. unmarried lesbian/gay couples, with children
13. unmarried couples, with extended families.[10]

Although unmarried heterosexual couples, with or without children, have been granted limited marital rights by the courts since the 1970s, unmarried gay and lesbian couples, with or without children, have not been as fortunate. In 2001, there were more than four million gay and lesbian couples living in the equivalent of domestic spousal relationships, raising about four million children from one or both partners' previous marriages or children who have been adopted. For these nontraditional families, the legal structure and judicial precedents are "incredibly unsupportive and often obstructive." The law does not recognize the existence of such couples; there has been very modest change in family law to deal with this reality.[11]

Until the U.S. Supreme Court acknowledges the diverse reality of the social construct known as "the family," there will remain a major "reality" gap between its judicial decisions and social reality.

I. "Something Smells about This Case"

President Lyndon B. Johnson (D-Texas) appointed Justice Thurgood Marshall to the U.S. Supreme Court in 1967. Marshall was the first African American to serve on the Court. Prior to his appointment, he was the chief counsel for the NAACP's Legal and Educational Fund (1938–1961), a judge on the CC2 (1962–1965), and U.S. Solicitor General (1965–1967).

Marshall was a tireless advocate for the less fortunate—they were his "constant companions."[12] They stood behind him when he sat on the Court, a Court he constantly sought to make aware of the grim realities of life for millions of "other" Americans. He was not very successful in enlightening his conservative colleagues.

During the 1977 Term, the case of *Inez Moore v East Cleveland, Ohio*,[13] clearly illustrated the dilemma Marshall constantly faced when dealing with his colleagues. *Moore* involved the question of how far a municipality could constitutionally intrude into the privacy rights of an "extended" family. East Cleveland, Ohio, a suburb of Cleveland, had a zoning ordinance that limited residential occupancy to single families, with "single family" defined as husband and wife and their unmarried children, or a grandparent, *one* child as parent, and the children of *only* that one parent.

Inez Moore, a resident of the town, had her two divorced sons, and *their* two sons living with her in her house—in violation of the ordinance. In January 1973, she was cited for violating the single-family ordinance because the two youngsters were cousins, not brothers. Either she had to leave the house or one of her grandchildren had to leave; either way the citation threatened to disrupt the relationship of an extended family living under one roof, a family in which the grandmother was the person holding it together. Inez Moore defended her family and challenged the constitutionality of the zoning ordinance in federal court, arguing that her privacy and associational rights were violated by implementation of this law. She lost her case and appealed to the U.S. Supreme Court.

The Court heard the case in its 1976 Term and, after oral arguments, voted 5:4 to validate the zoning ordinance. Justice Stewart was assigned the task of writing the opinion for the Court. However, given the occasionally fluid nature of judicial decision making, in *Moore* there was a change of mind by one justice that led, months later, to a final vote, 5:4 to *invalidate* the East Cleveland ordinance. Justice John Paul Stevens changed his mind.

Marshall tried and initially failed to get the majority to understand the importance of allowing people like Inez Moore to do what millions of poor people—mostly African American and other disadvantaged minorities— did to survive in an affluent America. "I cannot agree that the norms of middle-class suburban life set the standards of constitutional law for all people at all times," Marshall asserted in his draft dissent in the case.[14]

Justice Marshall was furious with the majority, led by Chief Justice Burger, and including Justices Rehnquist, Stewart, White, and John P. Stevens. In December 1976, Potter Stewart had been assigned the task of writing the majority opinion in *Moore* upholding the ordinance. Stewart's draft opinion initially reflected Burger's views. In a Memo to the brethren dated November 22, 1976, the Chief Justice contended that "the basic unit of society [is] parents and their offspring. . . . This 'nuclear' family is the basic building block of our society and it is a rational place to draw a line."

The following day Marshall wrote Burger disagreeing with his understanding of what a family was in American society.

I have seen too many situations where a strong grandparent literally held the family together, and was responsible for the education and upbringing of decent, law-abiding youngsters, to agree as a matter of constitutional law that the "nuclear family" is "the basic building block of our society." That is a middle class norm that government has no business foisting on those to whom economic or psychological necessity dictates otherwise.

Justice Stevens was the only one of the five in the majority who was truly perplexed by and uncomfortable with the case from the very beginning. In the Conference Session a few days after oral arguments, he told the brethren that "something smells about this case." But, at the time, he couldn't find any "Court handle [to overthrow the ordinance] except substantive due process—and I won't go for that."

After reading Marshall's draft dissenting opinion, however, and considering other Memos from him, as well as the draft dissents of Blackmun, Brennan, and Powell, Stevens wrote the brethren a Memo on April 12, 1977. In it, he informed them that he had changed his mind and was joining the quartet who viewed the ordinance as unconstitutional.

Brennan shared Marshall's disdain for Burger's views about the family. He had told the Chief, in November 1976, that the Burger "nuclear family" concept

seems to me to be completely out of touch with the reality of a vast number of relationships in our society, including my own as a youngster growing up. . . . In urban areas a grouping such as the Moores' remains an economic necessity. . . . I cannot believe that the Constitution embraces purely and simply an affluent suburban concept of what is a family.

Brennan immediately assigned the opinion to Justice Powell. On May 31, 1977, Powell read the judgment of the majority of the Court in *Moore*. It was one of only a few times in his twenty-four-years on the Court that Marshall had the pleasant experience of seeing one of his passionate draft dissents against the insensitivity of the Court majority transformed into a majority decision.

The Court's *Moore* deliberations, like the other snapshots of judicial behavior, is another example of the fluidity of choice when the Justices confront very difficult issues of personal and family intimacy versus the powers of government. It also illuminates the persistence of ideological cliques on the U.S. Supreme Court. These blocs of Justices held (and currently hold) opposing and inapposite views of the family, family privacy, and of the scope of the Constitution's protection of "fundamental" rights.

The ideal of the nuclear family, with its right to privacy in the home, was complicated a great deal in the late 1960s when the Court created an expansive perspective on privacy rights that centers on the idea of the family as a collection of *autonomous individuals*. Since then legislatures and courts have taken actions to protect women from battering and children from physical and mental abuse by the husband/father. Supreme Court majorities, from the late 1960s on, have maintained that a woman, whether or not married, and including minor daughters in the nuclear family, has a personal right to choose to have an abortion.

The concept of family has changed from a hierarchical, paternal, and holistic one, to associations of autonomous individuals (husband and wife; parents and children). This redirection has heightened the value dilemma for some of the Justices. It has come under fire from a quartet of sitting conservative Justices who would like nothing better than to return to an earlier time.

II. Who Is Family?

Who is considered family with respect to entitlement to family privacy protection? Family law contains "contrived" family ties, for example, marriage and adoption. Natural ties "are those of consanguinity," that is, blood ties between parent and child.

> The legally conceived family presumptively is, or has been, a reproductive unit. The primary tie is the heterosexual affiliation of husband and wife, which gives the family its form. Theirs is a connection considered basic to family and state, therefore historically mandated to be permanent, exclusive, and stable.[15]

However, there are at present more than a dozen categories that the U.S. Census Bureau employed to identify "family" in the 2000 census. In 2001, there are more than 2.2 million single fathers who are primary custodians of children under the age of eighteen, a 62 percent increase since 1990. Single-father household units make up 2.1 percent of American households, and single-mother households make up 7.2 percent of all households in

2001.[16] And the number of unmarried couples "nearly doubled in the 1990's, to 5.5 million from 3.2 million."

Clearly, as the 2000 census data reveal, fewer than a quarter of American households are traditional nuclear families, married couples living with their children. Most people, then, are living in some other arrangement outside the boundaries of the social contract.[17]

More and more, the public is made aware of these "other" families and told that the traditional nuclear family is in a very distinct minority in America. For example, on one Sunday in June 2001, the *New York Times* published the following: "Life With Father Isn't What It Used to Be" in its "Style" section,[18] and "Single Dads Wage Revolution, One Bedtime Story at a Time" on the front page.[19] The number of single-dad households increased by more than half between 1990 and 2000. There were 1.3 million such households in 1990; in 2000, 2 million. "More than 900,000 of these single fathers were divorced; nearly 700,000 had never been married; 350,000 were married to an absent spouse and 88,000 were widowed."[20] And an op-ed piece by law professor Catharine MacKinnon criticized a sexist U.S. Supreme Court opinion that came down earlier in the week, *Tuan Anh Ngoyan v Immigration and Naturalization Service.*[21]

Newsweek magazine, in May 2000, ran an extended story entitled "Unmarried, With Children." It presented a number of vignettes illustrating for the general reader just who are some of the 48 percent of unmarried American "family" householders in 2000. Included in the story were

- unmarried women, living alone, who adopted children and had natural children (percentage of parents who never married was 45% in 2000);
- same-sex lesbian householders with children (percentage of same-sex female householders with kids was almost 20% in 2000);
- engaged, but not married, single householders (9 percent of all householders in 1999); and
- kids living with a single female parent earning under $12,500 (41% in 1999).[22]

Although there is this diversity of family categories used by the Census Bureau for more than a generation, cities and towns, reflecting a commitment to the values associated with the traditional nuclear family, have continuously used zoning ordinances to restrict residency. The *Moore* case was an example of this form of state action. A case that came from the affluent village of Belle Terre, in Suffolk County, New York, led to a decision that is a still-viable precedent in this area of constitutional law.

Case Study: *Village of Belle Terre v. Bruce Boraas*, 1974[23]

Village of Belle Terre v Bruce Boraas, et al., was a case from Suffolk County, New York, that raised the question of the scope of the right to privacy. It involved the specific issue of privacy of a place and, again, Marshall disagreed with the Court majority and with the senior liberal justice William O. Douglas, who was the author of the majority opinion in *Belle Terre*.

Belle Terre is located on Long Island's north shore. There are about 220 homes inhabited by 700 people. Its total land area is less than one square mile. It restricted land use to one-family dwellings excluding lodging houses, boarding houses, fraternity houses, or multiple-dwelling houses. The word "family" as used in the ordinance means "one or more persons related by blood, adoption, or marriage, living and cooking together as a single housekeeping unit, exclusive of household servants. A number of persons but not exceeding two (2) living and cooking together as a single housekeeping unit though not related by blood, adoption, or marriage shall be deemed to constitute a family."

Bruce Boraas was a co-owner of a building in the village who rented it to six unrelated university students. The owners were cited for violating the ordinance and Boraas brought an action in federal court. He argued that the local ordinance was in violation of the First and Fourteenth Amendments' rights of association and privacy. The federal district court held the ordinance to be constitutional but the CC2 overturned, ruling that there was a constitutional violation. The village then appealed to the Supreme Court.

For Douglas and seven others, the ordinance was viewed as a piece of economic and social legislation and was upheld because there was shown to be a *reasonable*, "not an arbitrary," relationship between the ordinance and a "state objective." (Belle Terre officials claimed the law was passed to keep "transients" out of their community and the Court majority concluded that that was a reasonable goal of the local government.)

Douglas waxed eloquent about the family. Family privacy means

[a] quiet place where yards are wide, people few, and motor vehicle [restrictions] are legitimate guidelines in a land-use project addressed to family needs. . . . The police power is not confined to elimination of filth,

stench, and unhealthy places. It is ample to lay out zones where family values, youth values, and the blessings of quiet seclusion and clean air make the area a sanctuary for people.

In the Conference,[24] Chief Justice Burger intoned: "Permanent residents of the town are entitled to preserving the kind of community they want." Justice Powell argued that "for me, residential zoning is the guts of zoning and the family is the single most important unit. I would not denigrate the family as the CA2 did." Blackmun said: "[T]he preservation of the family enclave is a legitimate zoning objective."

Marshall disagreed with the views of the rest of Court on a number of grounds, including the standard that should be used by the Justices in deciding the case. For him, because the "disputed classification burdens the students' fundamental rights of association and privacy guaranteed by the First and Fourteenth Amendments, . . . the application of *strict scrutiny* is therefore required."

Marshall agreed with his brethren that creating zoning ordinances was an important function of local governments and that some "deference should be given to governmental judgments concerning proper land-use allocation. . . . *But deference does not mean abdication*" when a zoning ordinance clashes with a fundamental constitutional right like the right of privacy. And, in *Belle Terre*, that was exactly what had occurred: The village had "infringed upon fundamental constitutional rights" (my emphasis).

> Zoning authorities cannot validly consider who those persons are [who reside in dwellings], what they believe, or how they choose to live, whether they are Negro or white, Catholic or Jew, Republican or Democrat, married or unmarried.

Because no village-zoning ordinance can "unnecessarily burden appellees' First Amendment freedom of association and their constitutionally guaranteed right to privacy," he dissented. "[There is] the freedom to choose one's associates. . . . [And] the freedom of association is often inextricably entwined with the constitutionally guaranteed right of privacy," he argued. Belle Terre, New York, officials went beyond legitimate zoning goals and unconstitutionally "undert[ook] to regulate the way people choose to associate with each other within the privacy of their own homes."

One resident of Belle Terre, New York, appreciated Marshall's lonely dissent. Louise Strassenburg, of Buena Vista Road, wrote the Justice a letter on

April 2, 1974, thanking him and giving Marshall more information about the six college kids who were forced out of the house. She lived three houses down the street from them and found that they "did nothing to destroy the tranquility and tidiness of this village. Quite the contrary. They were an asset. I was never disturbed or aware that there was any noise from the house—and it was certainly much less than caused by the parties given by my own three daughters." The zoning ordinance was written, she said, by "outright bigots" who did not like college students, Blacks, or Hispanics.[25] As she requested, Marshall made copies of her letter for his brethren.

Family is still seen by judges as the traditional nuclear unit, even though the data tell another story. As *Belle Terre* indicates, even moderate to liberal Justices of the Court are loath to interpose themselves between the local prejudices of town officials and the reality of diverse households. Cases such as *Belle Terre* also underscore the theoretical—and real—clashes between opposing constitutional principles: the individual's right of privacy and the state's Tenth Amendment responsibilities to legislate to protect the general public's morals, health, welfare, and well-being.

III. Family Privacy Rights versus State Interests

In the nineteenth century there were two separated spheres of life: the private life (the family) and the public, civic life (the state). As noted earlier, family life was largely shielded from intrusion by the state: the husband/father had a fundamental immunity for most actions he took as the master of his private domain. His immunity prevented the state from intruding on the purely private activities of the traditional family. But that shield could and did protect the man when he abused his wife and/or his children. It also "observed and fostered" sexual inequality and exploitation by the male over the female and the children in the household, placing them in dangerous situations that led to battered women and children and female subordination.[26]

This dilemma was seen clearly by those who "viewed 'privacy' as essential to the concept of family while simultaneously conceding the more modern notion that privacy can conceal, even foster, situations dangerous to the individuals who [constitute] the family unit." For these persons, the goal is to "balance family privacy with protection for family members."[27]

Through *Griswold*, the state generally entered the area of family law only to restrict "unnatural" and, implicitly, immoral family relationships, ones that challenged the image and the ideal of the traditional nuclear family. A classic nineteenth-century case involving the Mormon practice of plural marriage by men, polygamy, illustrates this axiom.

Case Study: *Reynolds v U.S.*, 1878[28]

Reynolds came to the U.S. Supreme Court from the Utah Territory, where Mormons, after years of travel across the United States, had settled into their "promised land." They created the State of Deseret in the Western territories of the United States before the Civil War. For decades afterward there had been clashes between Union forces and the Mormons. During the presidency of Ulysses S. Grant, an effort was made to end the Mormon religious practice of polygamy. Grant appointed James B. McKean to be chief judge of the Utah Territorial Supreme Court and General J. Wilson Shaffer, to be territorial governor. Both were ordered to end the practice of polygamy.

McKean's U.S. marshals arrested hundreds of Mormons for violating a federal antibigamy law. The statute stated that "every person having a husband or wife living, who marries another, whether married or single, in a Territory, or other place over which the United States have exclusive jurisdiction, is guilty of bigamy, and shall be punished by a fine of not more than $500, and by imprisonment for a term of not more than five years."

The Mormons challenged the federal statute by setting up a test case. Brigham Young, who was the head of the Mormon Church, had his secretary, George Reynolds, arrested. After his conviction in the territorial district court and a failed appeal to the Utah Territorial Supreme Court, Reynolds and the Mormons asked the U.S. Supreme Court to hear the case. The Justices agreed and the case was argued in mid-November 1878.

The church's argument in support of the religious practice was based on the First Amendment, which barred Congress from passing any law "prohibiting the free exercise of religion." For the Mormons, plural marriage was an integral part of their religion. Further, they maintained that plural marriage was consistent with traditional "family values." The government countered with arguments that polygamy threatened the "public peace" and was destructive to America's social fabric, the nuclear family. Mormonism as practiced was, argued the federal government, a "moral menace" to conventional society.

The U.S. Supreme Court, in a unanimous 9:0 opinion, upheld the federal statute. "We think it may safely be said there never has been a time in any State of the Union when polygamy has not been an offence against society, cognizable by the civil courts and punishable with more or less severity."

Chief Justice Morrison R. Waite concluded that the federal government could punish criminal activity regardless of its religious foundation. Religious practices that "impaired the public safety" were not protected by the First Amendment. A "wall of separation between church and state existed," Waite wrote, and the Mormon actions breached that barrier.

The family privacy argument began to crumble in the latter decades of the twentieth century. Data showed, behind the veil of marital and family privacy, serious abuses of women and children. Family law had to change to deal with this no-longer-invisible problem.[29]

Traditional family law, however, continues to structure family relationships. It still generally validates the traditional power relationships and hierarchies in the family, to the detriment of women and children.[30] For some critics, family law is a series of legal exemptions "from the everyday rules that would apply to interactions among people in a non-family context, complemented by the imposition of a set of special family obligations."[31]

An "extraordinary" family law case came to the U.S. Supreme Court during its 1989 Term. It illustrates the continued vitality of traditional nuclear family values and the bifurcation of judicial views, based on the differing values of the Justices.

Case Study: *Michael H. v Gerald D.*, 1989

This case is one that could happen only in sunny California, a state well ahead of society's moral curve. The facts, said one scholar, "read like an excerpt from *Valley of the Dolls*."[32] Justice Scalia, who wrote the judgment of the Court admitted as much: "The facts of this case are, we must hope, extraordinary."

Under the California law challenged in the case, a child born to a married woman living with her husband is presumed to be a child of the marriage. Cal. Evid. Code Ann. § 621. The presumption of legitimacy may be rebutted only by the husband or wife, and then only in limited circumstances.

> The instant appeal presents the claim that this presumption infringes upon the due process rights of a man who wishes to establish his paternity of a child born to the wife of another man, and the claim that it infringes upon

the constitutional right of the child to maintain a relationship with her natural father.

The child's mother, Carole D., an internationally renowned supermodel, married Gerald D., a top executive in a French oil company in May 1976 in Las Vegas, Nevada. They established a home in Playa del Rey, California. In the summer of 1978, Carole became involved in an adulterous love affair with her next-door neighbor, Michael D. In September 1980, she conceived a child, Victoria D., who was born on May 11, 1981. Gerald was listed as the father on the birth certificate and always held Victoria out to the world as his daughter. Soon after giving birth, however, Carole told Michael that she believed he might be the father.

In 1982, Michael H. filed a civil action in the Superior Court of California to establish his paternity and right to visitation. From August 1983 to May 1984, Carole and Victoria lived with Michael. During this time, including three months residence in St. Thomas, U.S. Virgin Islands, Michael held Victoria out as *his* daughter, and he and Carole signed a stipulation that he was the child's natural father. (During this time blood tests were done on the trio, which showed a 98.07 percent probability that Michael *was* Victoria's dad.)

However, Carole left Michael in May 1984 and instructed her attorneys not to file the stipulation. In June 1984, Carole and Victoria moved back in with Gerald. In October 1984, Gerald, who had intervened in the Superior Court action, moved for summary judgment on the ground that there were no triable issues of fact as to the child's paternity.

This assertion was based on an obscure California statute[33] providing that (1) *a child of a married woman cohabiting with her husband is presumed to be a child of the marriage where the husband is not impotent or sterile,* and (2) the presumption may be rebutted by blood tests, but only if a motion for such tests is made, within two years from the date of the child's birth, by (a) the wife, if the natural father has filed an affidavit acknowledging paternity, or (b) the husband.

In 1985, having found sufficient evidence that the mother and her husband had been cohabiting at the child's conception and birth and that the husband was neither sterile nor impotent, the Superior Court granted the husband's motion for summary judgment. It rejected challenges by the putative father and the child to the constitutionality of the statute. The Superior Court also denied motions by Michael and the child for continued visitation pending an appeal, under a second California statute, which provided that reasonable visitation rights may be granted to any person, other than a parent, having an interest in the child's welfare.

The California Court of Appeal, Second District, affirmed. It held that (1) the conclusive presumption statute did not violate Michael's rights under the Due Process Clause of the Federal Constitution's Fourteenth Amendment, (2) the statute did not violate the child's rights under the Fourteenth Amendment's Equal Protection Clause, and (3) the Superior Court determined not only that Gerald was the child's presumed father but that Michael was not entitled to any visitation rights under the second statute. The Court of Appeal denied petitions for rehearing by the putative father and the child, and the Supreme Court of California denied discretionary review.

On appeal, the United States Supreme Court affirmed. Although unable to agree on an opinion, five members of the Court agreed that the conclusive presumption statute did not infringe on the due process rights of Michael or the child, or on the child's equal protection rights. Justice Scalia wrote the "judgment" of the Court, with Justices O'Connor and Kennedy concurring in part. Justice Stevens concurred with the judgment but not with Scalia's reasoning. Justice Brennan, who wrote the dissent, led the four dissenters. Justices Marshall and Blackmun joined him. Justice White wrote a separate dissent.

A law clerk who worked in Justice Blackmun's chambers that year has written that the case was used by Scalia to attack the broad interpretation given to substantive due process by the liberals on the Court led by Justice Brennan. Scalia wanted to limit the scope of substantive due process to what Justice White had said in *Bowers*: Due process protects *only* rights "so rooted in the traditions and conscience of our people so as to be ranked as fundamental."[34]

Scalia tackled the question of law by first looking at Michael's claim: "At the outset, it is necessary to clarify what he sought and what he was denied. California law, like nature itself, makes no provision for dual fatherhood. Michael was seeking to be declared the father of Victoria." He contends

as a matter of substantive due process that, because he has established a parental relationship with Victoria, protection of Gerald's and Carole's marital union is an insufficient state interest to support termination of that relationship. This argument is, of course, predicated on the assertion that Michael has a constitutionally protected liberty interest in his relationship with Victoria.

Scalia, the intellectually intimidating opponent of Brennan, rejected Michael's argument that he and Victoria be "treated as a protected family unit under the historic practices of our society, or whether on any other basis it has been accorded special protection. We think it *impossible* to find that it has. In fact, quite to the contrary, our traditions have protected the marital family (Gerald, Carole, and the child they acknowledge to be theirs) against the sort of claim Michael asserts."

"What counts" in this case, concluded Scalia, "is whether the States in fact award substantive parental rights to the natural father of a child conceived within, and born into, an extant marital union that wishes to embrace the child. *We are not aware of a single case, old or new, that has done so.* This is not the stuff of which fundamental rights qualifying as liberty interests are made."

Justice Brennan dissented. He condemned Scalia's very narrow view of history. "*Today's rhapsody on the 'unitary family' is out of tune,*" wrote Brennan. Such a "make-believe" view held by the plurality

> ignores the kind of society in which our Constitution exists. We are not an assimilative, homogeneous society, but a facilitative, pluralistic one, in which we must be willing to abide someone else's unfamiliar or even repellent practice because the same tolerant impulse protects our own idiosyncrasies. . . . In a community such as ours, "liberty" must include the freedom not to conform. The plurality today squashes this freedom by *requiring specific approval from history* before protecting anything in the name of liberty.

"When and if the Court awakes to reality, it will find a world very different from the one it expects," was Brennan's last thought on the matter.

Clearly, the Court division in *Michael H.* reflected the methodological and ideological breach between justices. On one side were Justices, like Brennan, who held an expansive view of constitutional interpretation. This perspective enabled Brennan and his allies to acknowledge the reality of family and family privacy in contemporary America.

On the other side, Scalia and his conservative colleagues were ever fearful of the Brennan-type of judge-made law where, through expansive interpretation of "fundamental" rights, the "liberty" interest of families would constantly change. Scalia's methodology and ideology would limit the meaning of the "liberty" interest in the Due Process Clause to the "history and traditions and conscience of the society." As he wrote: "to avoid the danger of 'arbitrary' judicial decision making, the Court should 'always' conduct its inquiry into tradition in the narrowest possible manner." To follow Brennan's approach was to employ an "ad hoc" and "standardless" methodology.[35]

IV. Family Privacy Rights versus Personal Autonomy and Other Constitutional Rights

Privacy, family and individual, suggests a private realm of thought and action largely immune from intrusive state action. They reflect racial, ethnic, and class perspectives held by the white majority in America that has the ability to incorporate its values into law. Is a family's right to privacy so absolute that another constitutionally protected right, for example, the First Amendment's free press guarantee, must be treated as inferior?

Case Study: *Time, Inc. v Hill*, 1967

Time, Inc. v Hill was a case concerning a 1955 *Life* magazine photographic article about a Broadway play, *The Desperate Hours*.[36] The play was the fictionalized story of a family's ordeal when trapped in its home by three escaped convicts. The playwright took dramatic license by adding particularly violent scenes that never occurred. The magazine story, however, claimed that the photographic essay was a reenactment by the actors of the actual events experienced by the Hill family in 1952. Cast members of the Broadway play were taken to the actual home owned by the Hill family in 1952. (The Hills moved to Connecticut from Pennsylvania after their nineteen-hour ordeal.) The actors, including Melvyn Douglas, reenacted scenes from the play in that setting, without the knowledge of the Hills.

The article was inaccurate in a number of spots, which was deeply disturbing to the Hill family. Under a New York statute, James J. Hill, a businessman and his family of four, with former Vice-President Richard M. Nixon acting as family counsel, sued Time, Incorporated, for invasion of privacy.

New York gave statutory protection to a family's right of privacy. Under the statute, any person or organization who used a name, picture, or portrait of any person "for advertising purposes, or for the purposes of trade," without written permission was subject to legal action. The law allowed a privacy action by "newsworthy" people or events in case of "material and substantial falsification by the press." Hill alleged that the *Life* essay falsely represented that the play reflected the actual family experience. The New York courts awarded Hill and his family $30,000.

It was argued before the U.S. Supreme Court in April 1966, and, in Conference, the Justices voted in favor of the Hill family, 6:3. Chief Justice Warren did not see the Court's affirmation of the award to Hill as a threat to a free press. However, Justice Hugo L. Black argued that it was exactly that. Newspapers, he argued, "have the right to report and criticize plays. This is nothing but a statute prohibiting the press from publishing certain things."[37] His views were shared by Justices Douglas and White.

Justice Abe Fortas was given the task of drafting the majority opinion for the Court. He quickly circulated a twenty-page draft that blasted the press:

> The facts of this case are unavoidably distressing. Needless, heedless, wanton injury of the sort inflicted by *Life's* picture story is not an essential instrument of responsible journalism. The deliberate, callous invasion of the Hills' right to be let alone—this appropriation of a family's right not to be molested or to have its name exploited and its quiet existence invaded—cannot be defended on the ground that it is within the purview of a constitutional guarantee to protect the free exchange of ideas and opinions. This is exploitation, undertaken to titillate and excite, for commercial purposes.

This was an opinion that fully and aggressively affirmed the right of the nuclear family to be let alone by the press. For Fortas, the right to family privacy far surpassed the First Amendment right of freedom of the press. For Black, the state could violate *anyone's* home, so long as the invasion was consistent with the commands of the Fourth Amendment's "search and seizure" clause.[38]

Black initially attacked the Fortas majority opinion, as he did every opinion he read in chambers—in the margins. He marked up every one of the twenty pages circulated by Fortas. This habit began when Black joined the Court in 1937 and ended when he left the high bench in September 1971.[39]

Some of his observations written in the margins of the Fortas draft follow. "The right to be let alone is a popular idea but not embodied in any constitutional provision." "Justice Brandeis never even intimated, much less asserted, that he was elevating the right of privacy to a constitutional plane on a level with the First Amendment." "Peeping Tom is not in the Constitution!" This draft is "the worst First Amendment opinion since [1952]."

Fortas's acerbic opinion was not to become the opinion of the Court. Justices Fortas and White fought with each other over the interpretations given the statute by various New York State courts. In addition, because Fortas's majority opinion was circulated a week before the scheduled summer recess, Black asked for the summer to write his dissent. "I'll need all summer to write a dissent. It'll be the best of my life," he told his colleagues in the Court's Conference Session.[40]

Black's request led to an order from the Court setting the case for reargument in October 1966. The parties were asked to write additional briefs that would provide the Justices with additional information about the statute's legislative and judicial history. It also gave Black the time to develop a strong dissent.

Justice Black worked hard over the summer drafting his dissent in the *Time* case. The diary of his wife, Elizabeth, reflected her husband's Herculean effort to turn the votes around through his writing:

August 12. Hot. Whew. 100°+. Hugo has been working until around 1:30 every night. He is working on this case he is so interested in. It's one that Abe Fortas got out about a week before the Court adjourned. Hugo told them he was going to write a dissent this summer, so they agreed to get it reargued this fall.

September 9. Hugo wanted to go to the office this morning. . . . He wanted to talk to his clerks about the Time case dissent.

October 20. He got the Court on his Time Magazine case! How he has worked. Abe and the Chief [were the] only ones against him.[41]

Justice Black, the absolute defender of the First Amendment and the other civil liberties and rights in the Bill of Rights,[42] circulated his own sixteen-page Memorandum to the other Justices in late September. If the Court went along with the Fortas arguments, Black maintained that it would have a "chilling" effect on the press. Publishers and editors would be fearful of publishing a story if there were

doubt as to the complete accuracy of the newsworthy facts. . . . After mature reflection I am unable to recall any prior case in this Court that offers a greater threat to freedom of speech and press than this one does, either in the tone and temper of the Court's opinion or in its resulting holding and ruling.

In the Conference Session after the reargument, a few Justices did a flip-flop: From 6:3 affirmation of the state court judgment favoring the Hills, the justices now voted 7:2 for *reversal* of the monetary award to the Hills. In the end, only the "Super Chief" and Justice Fortas still voted to affirm. Black, as the senior justice in the majority, assigned the writing of the majority opinion to his colleague Justice Brennan.

The *new* majority's opinion was based on an earlier Warren Court opinion, *New York Times v Sullivan,* 1964, also authored by Justice Brennan. That case involved a number of Alabama state officials who sued the *New York Times* for printing false comments in an ad paid for by Martin Luther King's Southern Christian Leadership Conference (SCLC). The 1964 Court held that public officials could not collect damages for defamation unless they could prove that the information was published with "actual malice," that is, the publisher *knew* the information was false or acted with "reckless disregard" of whether or not it was false. This quickly became known as the "Sullivan" standard.

In *Time v Hill,* the majority opinion, written by Justice Brennan, extended the *Sullivan* standard to cases where non-public-figure plaintiffs allege that their privacy was invaded by "false reports of matters of public interest." The subject of the *Life* photo essay, said Brennan, "the opening of a new play linked to an actual incident is a matter of public interest."

In a civil action based on a story involving such an incident, Brennan wrote, Hill must prove that the *Life* magazine editors "knowingly" published a false story. The Court sent the case back to the state court to determine whether there was actual malice evidenced by the press. Using the *Sullivan* standard as guide, the state courts dismissed the suit.

In 1968, *Eisenstadt v Baird* was a watershed legal event[43] that moved the judges away from the notion of family as a shielded space, safe from invasion by the state and its agents. Unlike *Griswold,* which continued the myth of family as a hierarchical, protected cohort, *Eisenstadt* established the notion that the family was not holistic; instead, it was an association of autonomous individuals, each with certain "liberty" interests protected by the Constitution's Due Process Clause.

The decision distinguished family privacy from individual-based constitutional privacy rights. It extended the right of privacy beyond the family to its individual components: men, women, and minors all had individually defined privacy rights.

The case came to the Court because Sheriff Thomas Eisenstadt arrested birth control advocate Bill Baird on the Boston University campus. Baird had been seen giving sample birth control vaginal cream to a young un-married co-ed who attended his lecture on birth control. Lower courts in-validated the arrest and conviction and the sheriff's legal counsel brought an appeal to the U.S. Supreme Court.

In the mid-November 1971 Conference Session after the Justices heard oral arguments in the case, the Chief Justice, who traditionally starts the dis-cussion, passed because, Warren Burger said, "I can't discover what the issue is."[44] Before he passed, however, he clearly expressed his dislike and disdain for Baird:

> Eisenstadt [*sic*] is what in times past [was] called an "officious intermeddler," a "common busybody," a "quack medicine man and a mountebank" who dispensed medicinal materials. He was the "casual street-corner peddler."[45]

Case Study: *Eisenstadt v Baird,* 1971

Massachusetts law[46] made it a felony for any person to distribute contra-ceptives to any unmarried person. Only registered doctors and nurses could distribute contraceptives but only to married couples. Bill Baird was not a physician and he distributed Emko Vaginal Foam to an unmarried woman after he his talk at Boston University.

After oral argument the seven-person Conference met on November 19 to discuss the case. (Both Justices Black and Harlan retired in September 1971 and their replacements, Justices Powell and Rehnquist, had not yet joined the Court.) Voting to affirm but for different constitutional reasons were Douglas (on First Amendment free speech grounds), and a small co-hort led by Brennan, including Justices Stewart, Marshall, and a hesitant Harry Blackmun. Brennan differed from Douglas, saying that "this [case] is in the *penumbra* of *Griswold.*"

Voting to reverse the lower federal court was Justice White. Chief Justice Burger initially passed. A few days later, Burger wrote to Douglas and Bren-nan that "my vote is a questionable reverse with a note 'could affirm-de-pends on how written.'"

In a 6:1 vote, the U.S. Supreme Court invalidated the Massachusetts statute. Associate Justice Brennan wrote the majority opinion. Justice White joined the majority; Chief Justice Warren Burger was the sole dissenter in the case. Said Brennan:

> If under *Griswold* the distribution of contraceptives to married persons cannot be prohibited, a ban on distribution to unmarried persons would be equally impermissible. . . . If the right of privacy means anything, it is the right of the *individual,* married or single, to be free from unwarranted governmental intrusion into matters so fundamentally affecting a person as the decision whether to bear or beget a child. [My emphasis.]

Brennan concluded that the distinction between married couples and single persons violated the Fourteenth Amendment's Equal Protection Clause. Contrary to the state's argument, the majority did not view the state statute as a legitimate health measure because of discrimination and because it was "over-broad."

The Chief Justice disagreed, arguing that the law was a legitimate health measure well within the state's Tenth Amendment's "police powers." This watershed decision was hailed by women's advocates and condemned by conservative opponents. All saw that the decision opened up a new avenue for plaintiffs to attack other restraints on a woman's rights, especially the right of a woman to choose to have an abortion.

Griswold had "set the stage for a change in the appreciation of the intersection of family and privacy by vastly increasing the span of privacy rights."[47] *Eisenstadt* stands apart, for it "expanded the application of the privacy doctrine beyond the family."[48] Brennan said it clearly: marriage is "*but an association of two individuals each with a separate intellectual and emotional makeup.*" An individual has the "fundamental right to be free, except in very limited circumstances, from unwanted governmental intrusions into one's privacy."

Eisenstadt freed the decision to have children from the sanctity of family privacy, protected from any interfering state action or control. After 1968 and especially after *Roe v Wade* was handed down in 1972,[49] the decisions to have a child or not ultimately rested with the woman—whether married or single. It was no longer a matter to be decided in the safety of the home nor could the state interfere with a woman's right to choose.

V. Summing Up

Eisenstadt liberated the individual (the wife and the daughter) from the traditional notion of the hierarchical, patriarchal family. The traditional family unit lost its privacy and its legal sanctity. The decision to use birth control devices and to have an abortion is the woman's alone, not the family's, i.e., the husband's. From this freedom to choose to control her body, the natural next step is to end inequality, exploitation, female subordination, and battering by the abusive male.

4

Motherhood or Not, That Is Her Decision

Did you ever stop to think—once they get rid of innocent babies—
the old people are next. I have never been so disgusted.
—Letter, Clara Jones, Valley Station, Kentucky,
to Justice Hugo L. Black[1]

Abortion rights of women was one of a number of demands of
the women's rights movement that emerged in the 1960s. It had emerged as
an explosive public policy controversy during the time that Republican
President Richard Nixon (1969–1974) appointed four new Justices to the
Court. It was Nixon's hope that they would reverse many of the Warren
Court's decisions that were the foundation for the revolution in civil rights
and liberties, especially the recently judicially crafted privacy right. (Just a
few years earlier, Nixon personally tasted defeat when the Court ruled in
favor of Time magazine.)

Eisenstadt freed the decision to have children from the sanctity of family
privacy, protected from any interfering state action or control. Marriage,
Brennan had written, is *"but an association of two individuals each with a
separate intellectual and emotional makeup."* After 1968 and especially after
Roe v Wade was handed down in 1973,[2] the decision to have a child or not
ultimately rested with the woman—whether married or single. It was no
longer a matter to be decided in the safety of the home nor could the state
interfere with a woman's right to choose. Women as well as men have "separate intellectual and emotional makeups." That conclusion led inexorably
to the Court's having to answer the next question: Did a woman have the
right to choose to have an abortion?

I. "I Will Be God-damned!"[3]

During the turbulent month of May 1972, just before the U.S. Supreme Court issued an order calling for reargument of the abortion cases the following Term before the full Court, the inside-the-Court passions and bitterness of some of the Justices could not be contained. In a scribbled note to Justice Douglas, Justice Brennan wrote:

> I will be God-damned! At lunch today Potter [Stewart] expressed his outrage at the high-handed way things are going, particularly the assumption that a single justice if CJ can order things his own way, and that he can hold up for nine [justices] anything he chooses, even if the rest of us are ready to bring down, 4:3's for example. He also resents the CJ's confidence that he has Powell and Rehnquist in his pocket.

Justice Douglas, too, was beside himself with anger over the Chief's "manipulations" in the abortion cases. The Court had reached a 4:3 decision to invalidate the two challenged state abortion statutes. Blackmun drafted two opinions for the majority overturning the statutes.

However, Chief Justice Burger was able to persuade his friend Blackmun to request additional arguments before the nine-man Court the following October. This would enable the two new Nixon appointees, Justices Powell and Rehnquist, to participate in the deliberations and the decisions in the Texas and Georgia abortion cases.

On June 1, 1972, Douglas wrote a note to the Chief with copies to the others. "If the vote of the conference is to reargue, then I will file a dissent telling what is happening to us and the tragedy it entails."[4] At the same time, Douglas sent Brennan a secret draft of his dissent. Brennan was shocked at Douglas's vituperation.

In Douglas's draft dissent, he drew attention to the Chief's manipulations from the time the abortion cases first came to the Court. For example, he pointed out that Burger, although in the voting minority in the post–oral argument Conference, nevertheless assigned the opinion to Blackmun. This was an action, wrote Douglas, that

> no Chief Justice in my time would have taken. . . . When, however, the minority seeks to control the assignment, there is a destructive force at work in the Court. *When a Chief Justice tries to bend the Court to his will by*

manipulating assignments, the integrity of the institution is imperiled. (This was one of the portions "pencilled-out" by Brennan.)

The plea that the cases be reargued is merely strategy by a minority somehow to suppress the majority view with the hope that exigencies of time will change the result. That might be achieved of course by death or conceivably retirement. But that kind of strategy dilutes the integrity of the Court *and makes the decisions here depend on the manipulative skills of a Chief Justice.* (This was another Brennan "pencilled-out" segment.)

Brennan's response to this broadside was direct: Don't make this dissent public. "If anything is to be made public (and I have serious reservations on that score), I hope the pencilled out portions can be omitted." An angry Douglas modified his draft dissent five more times and then circulated it to the others. It was met with undiluted anger by the Chief, who wrote a five-page retort. Burger said, in part,

> Your unprecedented proposed dissenting statement seems to imply bad faith if positions are not firm, fixed, and final when a Conference adjourns.... The record, which I re-examined in detail after the surprising statements of your dissent, shows that I have never undertaken to assign from a minority position. Thus there is not the slightest basis for your statement. I would be interested in having you identify the cases in which you think that happened.

Douglas, after speaking with Blackmun, withdrew his dissent and requested that all the circulated copies be returned to him. Further compounding the anger and stress within the Court, someone leaked the Douglas draft dissent to the *Washington Post.* Some thought that Douglas had leaked the draft to publicize the split in the Court over the abortion issue. Douglas had to write, in longhand, a response to the allegation. It was addressed to the Chief, with a copy to the Conference. His wife, Cathy, he wrote, "told me over the phone that the *Washington Post* today carries a nasty story about the Abortion Cases, my memo to the conference, etc., etc."

> I am upset and appalled. I have never quoted a word concerning the cases, or my memo, to anyone outside the court. I have no idea where the writer got the story. We have our differences; but so far as I am concerned they are wholly internal; and if revealed, they are mirrored in opinions filed, never in "leaks" to the press.
> With affectionate regards.

Weeks later a sullen Douglas wrote the Chief: "That chapter in the abortion cases is for me gone and forgotten."

This vignette captures the clash of wills between the Justices of the U.S. Supreme Court. Ideological differences among the brethren are dramatically highlighted, and the fur begins to fly in controversial cases involving family, marriage, and the issue of abortion rights. *Roe*, in this sense, is no different from *Bowers*, *Griswold*, and *Eisenstadt*.

Early in these tense months (that stretched into years), Chief Justice Burger wrote to Douglas: "The abortion issues, like obscenity and others, *are problems of extraordinary difficulty and we will need our best effort to achieve a reasonably satisfactory result.*" As this chapter will suggest, it has been impossible for the Justices to coalesce to achieve a "satisfactory result" in the abortion rights cases.

II. Not Having Children: Abortion as Personal Right

The abortion controversy has fiercely engaged millions of persons since the late 1960s. Soon after *Eisenstadt*, the Supreme Court found itself in the middle of the political thicket of abortion rights. Court opinions and files "indicate that no justice ever supported a woman's right to [choose to have an abortion] as uncompromisingly as Justice Thurgood Marshall did."[5] He, of all the Justices who sat on the Court and heard and decided abortion decisions, knew about "the circumstances of life of pregnant women in our pockets of rural poverty, or in the worst of our urban ghettos." He was the only one of 108 men and women who have sat on the Court

> who had defended and worked with so many poor women that he actually knew how they suffered financially, were pained emotionally, often became psychological wrecks over knowledge that another baby was on the way.[6]

In *U.S. v Vuitch*, a 1971 case heard the Term before the *Roe* case was brought to the Supreme Court, the Court initially entered the abortion quagmire. The case came to the Justices from the District of Columbia and it questioned the constitutionality of a local statute that made it a crime to perform an abortion except where "necessary for the preservation of the mother's life or health." The trial judge focused on the vagueness of the word "health" in the statute and concluded that it was "so vague in its interpretation and the practice under the act that there is no indication whether it includes varying degrees of mental as well as physical health."

In the Conference Session after oral argument, a wide range of views spilled out. This was, after all, the first occasion the Court had to discuss the issue of abortion and woman's rights. Chief Justice Burger, as usual, spoke first. For him, there was jurisdiction and, on the merits, "he would reverse. The statute was not vague and I *reject the argument that a woman has an absolute right to decide what happens to her own body.*"[7] The senior Associate Justice, Black, agreed with the Chief on all counts. He "could not go along with the woman's claim of a constitutional right to use her body as she pleases." Brennan did not think the Court had jurisdiction. Douglas disagreed with his friend. He said:

> I think some abortion laws can be constitutional. But I agree that this one is vague—the definition of what is meant by "health" must be very broad today. Does this statute sufficiently notify the doctor [as to] what that means?

In the end, two different five-person majorities joined the opinion written by Black. On Part I of his opinion, whether the Court had jurisdiction, four joined Black; they were the Chief, and Justices Douglas, Stewart, and White. Four dissented: Justices Harlan, Blackmun, Brennan, and Marshall.

Part II of Black's opinion, on the merits of the case, four others joined to reverse and remand the lower federal court ruling. They were the Chief, and Justices White, Harlan, and Blackmun. Two concurred, Justices Brennan and Marshall. Two dissented: Justices Douglas and Stewart.

The Court managed to avoid *the* question: Could a state regulate the abortion process at all? Instead, the opinion set aside the lower federal court ruling that the act was unconstitutional for vagueness and sent the case back on remand to the federal court. Black's opinion, handed down in April 1971, noted that the term "health" was clear enough to cover psychological and well as physical health of pregnant women.

However, in another one of the many Court blunders that show that it is all too human, the Court made another contretemps. Justices Black and Harlan had retired in September 1971, just weeks before the Court was to reassemble in Washington, DC, for its new Term. There was no way the President, Richard M. Nixon, facing a Democratic Senate that had recently voted down two persons nominated by him to replace Justice Abe Fortas, was going to quickly move two nominees through the "advice and consent" process.[8]

And so the Chief appointed a small committee of Justices, Harry Blackmun and Potter Stewart, to screen and schedule oral argument in the cases coming to the seven-person Court. Their task was seemingly not a difficult one: schedule "only relatively uncontroversial cases for argument."[9] However, they scheduled oral arguments for *Roe* and *Doe.* "It was a serious mistake," said Blackmun two decades later. "We did a poor job. . . . We should have deferred them until we had a full Court."[10] This oversight led the Justices into a yearlong maelstrom that left scars that healed very, very slowly.

The Court could not avoid deciding the question pressure groups on both sides of the issue had raised. The answer the Court came up with has been the basis of continuing litigation ever since; its decisions in these two cases have been condemned and applauded in presidential elections since then. And there have come to Washington, DC, every year since 1973, on the anniversary of the *Roe* opinion announcement, right-to-life groups to voice their grievous opposition as well as pro-choice groups to celebrate the decision.

Case Study: *Roe v Wade*, 1973[11]

Roe and *Doe* were granted certiorari during the Court's 1970 Term. As with all contemporary controversial cases that come to the Supreme Court, there were many briefs *amicus curiae* filed. The pro-choice briefs, filed by groups of medical experts (such as the American College of Obstetricians and Gynecologists)as well as civil rights and civil liberties groups, and groups such as Planned Parenthood and the American Public Health Association, were more numerous than the pro-life briefs.[12]

The medical briefs emphasized two points: the associational rights that exist between a patient and her doctor as well as the woman's right to privacy, to be left alone, with her doctor, to make a very difficult choice. These were rights that were denied in the challenged Texas and Georgia antiabortion statutes. The doctors from the Mayo Clinic, for example, argued in an *amicus curiae* brief that the state laws "unfairly discriminate against physicians and deny physicians equal protection of the laws."

The pro-life briefs, such as the one submitted from Americans United For Life, argued that the unborn has the constitutional right to life, a life guaranteed in the Fourteenth Amendment's Due Process and Equal

Protection Clauses. The unborn child is a person, it is human, it is living, and it has "being," quoting from a Supreme Court opinion, *Levy v Louisiana*.[13] That person's rights have to be balanced against those of the woman and, on balance, the child's life outweighs the right of a woman to choose to have an abortion.

Roe involved the constitutionality of a nineteenth-century Texas statute that prohibited all abortions except those for the specific purpose of saving the mother's life. In *Doe*, a more contemporary state antiabortion statute was challenged. The Georgia statute allowed abortions (1) if the woman's life was endangered, or (2) if the fetus was likely to be born with serious mental or physical defect, or (3) if the pregnancy was due to rape.

The Georgia statute also mandated procedural safeguards that had to be met if there was to be a legal abortion. The procedure had to be done in an accredited hospital; the doctor had to use approved procedures; and the need for the procedure had to have been validated by two other doctors.

The woman in the Texas case was not allowed to have the abortion because her life was not in danger; the woman in Georgia was not able to have a legal abortion because none of the three substantive conditions were met in her case. In *Roe*, a three-judge federal district court declared the Texas statute unconstitutional as vague and overbroad, and because it infringed in the woman's Ninth and Fourteenth Amendment rights. It did not enjoin the state from enforcement of the law, and Roe appealed to the U.S. Supreme Court. In *Doe*, another three-judge federal district court granted declaratory relief to Doe; however, although the three substantive bases for having an abortion were invalidated, the three procedural requirements were deemed constitutional by the federal judges. Doe appealed the ruling to the U.S. Supreme Court.

After oral arguments, the Justices met in Conference to discuss and vote on the cases. Burger started the discussion by noting that while the Texas statute was obsolete, it was constitutional, as was the Georgia statute.[14] All the brethren but White, including Burger's best man, Harry Blackmun, emphatically disagreed with the Chief, arguing that there was a constitutional right of privacy that extended to the woman's right to have an abortion. Burger's switch to the majority angered Douglas a great deal. As the senior Associate Justice, he would have made the assignment if Burger had not changed his vote and would have given it to himself or to Brennan and it would have been written with the "privacy" argument as the rationale . Instead, Burger's tactics resulted in the assignment being given to Blackmun, who based his judgment that the statutes were unconstitutional on other, less precedentially impactful, grounds.

Burger counted on Blackmun's inordinate slowness in the drafting and circulating of the majority opinion. If he ran true to form, Blackmun's circulation would be a "hurried one" and it would come toward the end of the Term. Its lateness would give the Chief the opportunity to have it reargued so that the two new Nixon appointees, Powell and Rehnquist, could participate. This could result in enough votes to support Burger's original view that the state statutes were constitutional.

For Brennan, and for Marshall, the strategy in these two abortion cases was to build a bridge from *Griswold* and *Eisenstadt* to *Roe* and *Doe*. There was a right to privacy that protected a woman's right to choose to have a baby or have an abortion. The cases were assigned to Blackmun in mid-November, but as Burger and the rest had anticipated, he did not circulate a draft until May 18, 1972, six months later and little more than one month away from the adjournment of the Term of the Court.

Furthermore, Blackmun's draft opinion distressed Douglas, Brennan, and Marshall because it was based on his observation that the law was unconstitutionally vague and overbroad, thus denying a medical doctor his Fourteenth Amendment "Equal Protection" right to carry out his professional obligations and duties. (Blackmun's draft opinion in the Georgia abortion case, however, was based on the individual privacy rights claim.)

Brennan wrote Blackmun a letter, with copies to the conference, saying that

> a majority of us feel the Constitution required the invalidation of abortion statutes save to the extent they required that an abortion be performed by a licensed physician within some time limit after conception. Your circulation invalidates the Texas statute only on the vagueness ground.

Despite this admonishment, Blackmun's second circulation, in early June, produced no change in the reasoning for the overturn of the statutes. The three liberal Justices concluded that this was the best they could hope to get from their fourth, and decisive, vote on the issue of abortion.

Burger then asked Blackmun to consider carrying the cases over to the following Term, where a full Court would participate in the discussion and the vote. Blackmun agreed, much to the chagrin and anger of Brennan, Douglas, Stewart, and Marshall. Blackmun wrote a letter to the brethren, saying that he was "not yet certain about the details." He wrote his colleagues that

> I have now concluded, somewhat reluctantly, that re-argument in both cases at an early date would perhaps be advisable.... I believe, ... the country deserves the conclusion of a nine-man, not a seven-man, court, whatever the ultimate decision may be.

During the summer, Justice Blackmun retreated to Minnesota, and to the Mayo Clinic, where he was resident counsel between 1950 and 1959. He continued to reflect on the abortion issue. He brought with him the many memos that had been circulated, including the critically important Brennan letters that argued that the Court had to rest its decision in *Roe* and *Doe* on the core constitutional issue of the right to privacy.

After reargument, on October 11, 1972, the colleagues met in Conference again and discussed the cases. By this time, Potter Stewart had joined with Brennan, Marshall, and Douglas, in asserting the primacy of the woman's right of privacy. So, too, did Blackmun, who said that "he'd be willing to bypass vagueness and put the Texas and Georgia cases together." And, to the surprise and dismay of Burger's faction, the new Justice, Lewis Powell, joined them. Douglas's notes state: "L.P. basically in accord with HAB!"

Justice Powell amazed many at the time. When his papers were opened to scholars in the late 1990s, there was even greater amazement when it was discovered that Powell helped Blackmun a great deal in shaping the final decisions for the Court majority in *Roe* and *Doe*.[15] With the help of Larry Hammond, one of his law clerks that year, Powell sent private Memo after private Memo to Blackmun to clarify the language and the reasoning in the opinions. As Hammond told his boss:

> I do believe that a well-reasoned opinion can be reached [by Blackmun] without placing the Court in the position of deciding as a super-legislature whether it will permit abortions at any specific time.[16]

William Rehnquist, however, viewed the statutes as constitutional and joined White in making that argument. With Powell in the Brennan camp, that meant that there were now six justices who saw the Texas and Georgia statutes as unconstitutional: Harry Blackmun (on First Amendment "vagueness" grounds) and the rest (Brennan, Stewart, Douglas, Powell, and

Marshall) on privacy grounds. Burger, who had passed, now joined the majority and immediately assigned the opinions, again, to Harry Blackmun—even though he was clearly expressing the minority rationale for the statutes' overturn. Douglas was, again, affronted by Burger's maneuvers.

Blackmun surprised the brethren on two counts. First of all, he had his opinions drafted in short order and, second, after the summer's period of reflection and additional notes from Brennan, Powell, and Marshall, his rationale for overturn was no longer vagueness. Instead, Blackmun switched to the privacy argument. His opinions were circulated in mid-November 1972. One of the first responses came from Rehnquist. He wrote: "Although I am still in significant disagreement with parts of them, I have to take my hat off to you for marshaling as well as I think could be done the arguments on your side."

In December 1972, Blackmun received important input from Powell, Marshall, and Brennan. Powell raised a fundamental question: Should the Court allow the woman absolute discretion to make an abortion decision anytime in the first trimester or should the woman's right to choose be unfettered until "viability," that is, the time when the baby can live outside the womb. (All in the majority agreed that after either the first trimester or viability, the state would be able to legislate to protect the fetus.) "I have wondered," wrote Powell, "whether drawing the line at 'viability'—if we conclude to designate a particular point of time—would not be more defensible in logic and biologically than perhaps any other single time."

Blackmun's response was a Memo to the Conference dated December 11, 1972. He did not mention Powell by name.

> One of the members of the Conference has asked whether my choice of the end of the first trimester, as the point beyond which a state may appropriately regulate abortion practices, is critical. He asks whether the point of viability might not be a better choice. The inquiry is a valid one and deserves serious consideration.

The following day Marshall responded with a "Dear Harry" letter. There was always the element of "balancing" in these very difficult and controversial cases before the Court. He told Harry that

> at some point the State's interest in preserving the potential life of the unborn child overrides any individual interests of the woman. I would be disturbed if that point were set before viability.

Marshall suggested to Harry that

> if the opinion stated explicitly that, between the end of the first trimester
> and viability, state regulations directed at health and safety alone were per-
> missible, I believe that those concerns would be adequately met.

Justice Brennan replied a day after Marshall. He was less supportive of
the "viability" time line. Viability, he wrote,

> is a concept that focuses upon the fetus rather than the woman. . . . I think
> our designation of such a "cut-off" point should be articulated in such a
> way as to coincide with the reasons for creating such a "cut-off" point (e.g.,
> "the danger to the health of a woman who undergoes an abortion tends to
> increase as the period of the pregnancy advances, or where abortions be-
> come medically more complex).

Douglas also answered the Blackmun letter. "I favor the first trimester,
rather than viability," he told Blackmun on December 11, 1972.

Blackmun, however, incorporated *both* the fetal viability and the
trimester "cut-off" time frames for the fetus and the mother. By January
1973, only some two months after the brethren met to discuss and vote on
the reargued cases, Blackmun's opinions were ready for announcement. In
the end, the Court voted 7:2 to invalidate both state laws (with White and
Rehnquist the only dissenters). Blackmun's opinion stated:

> With respect to the State's important and legitimate interest in the health of
> the mother, the "compelling" point, in the light of present medical knowl-
> edge, is at approximately the end of the first trimester. . . . With respect to
> the State's important and legitimate interest in potential life, the "com-
> pelling" point is at viability. This is so because the fetus then presumably
> has the capability of meaningful life outside the mother's womb. . . . *The
> right of privacy is broad enough to encompass a woman's decision whether or
> not to terminate her pregnancy.*

Blackmun's decision for the Court majority established the right of privacy
in this area and, relying on Brennan's, Powell's, and Marshall's comments
and thoughts, concluded that until the fetus is viable, the woman has a great
deal of freedom to choose, without restrictions by the state. Only in the
third trimester does the state's interest in preserving the life of the unborn

child become a "compelling" one and the government can pass legislation that severely limits or prohibits abortions at this point in the pregnancy.

After *Roe* came down, there were significant changes in abortion statutes in most of the states. A few liberalized the state's abortion policy. However, most of the changes in state laws

> sought to limit the impact of *Roe*. . . . In addition, ten states passed laws or resolutions pledging to ban or severely restrict abortions, and fifteen others left their pre-*Roe* laws on the books, in anticipation of *Roe*'s being eventually overturned.[17]

A short time after *Roe*, with Douglas no longer on the Court (replaced by John P. Stevens, the only Ford appointee to the Court), there was movement within the Court toward restricting the *Roe* opinion.

III. After Roe, What Are the Limits of "State Actions" That Regulate the Abortion Procedure?

Both the states and the federal Congress passed a variety of statutes that attempted to restrict a woman from using public funds or facilities to get an abortion. In 1976, the Hyde Amendment was passed. It was an amendment introduced by conservative Congressman Henry J. Hyde (R-Ill.) and attached to the Labor-HEW appropriations bill of 1977. It prohibited the use of federal funds "to pay for abortions or to promote or encourage abortions." After modifications, the amendment read: "None of the funds contained in this Act shall be used to perform abortions except where the life of the mother would be endangered if the fetus were carried to term."

Maher v Roe was one of three 1977 decisions of the Court that answered the abortion-funding-limitation question. The Justices, in a 6:3 vote, upheld such state restrictions on a woman's right to get an abortion. (The two other cases were *Beal v Roe* [from Pennsylvania] and *Poelker v Doe* [from Missouri].) It was a devastating decision for the pro-choice Justices, Marshall, Brennan, and Blackmun. These men clearly—sadly—saw the terrible impact of the majority decisions of the Court on impoverished women.

Connecticut passed a state regulation that prohibited the funding of abortions through the Medicaid monies received from the national government that were not medically or psychologically necessary for the health of the mother. Two indigent women (one an unmarried mother of three and the other a sixteen-year-old high school student) challenged its constitutionality. The federal district court ruled in favor of the women and the CA2 remanded the case back to the district court, stating that the federal law allowed but did not require Medicaid funding for abortions. After the federal judge ruled, again, against the state, Edward Maher, Connecticut's Commissioner of Social Services, appealed to the U.S. Supreme Court.

Justice Lewis Powell wrote the opinion for the six-person majority in the three cases. He wrote that the Constitution "imposes no obligation on the States to pay the pregnancy-related expenses of indigent women, or indeed to pay any of the medical expenses of indigents." The Equal Protection Clause of the Fourteenth Amendment was not violated if Connecticut decided to use federal funds to pay for childbirth but not for nontherapeutic abortions.

In *Maher*, Powell wrote: "This case involves no discrimination against a suspect class. . . . This Court has never held that financial need alone identifies a suspect class for purposes of equal protection analysis." And, under the rational relationship test, Powell concluded that the Connecticut

> funding scheme satisfies this standard [for the state has a "strong interest in protecting the potential life of the fetus"] . . . while indigency may make it difficult—and in some cases, perhaps, impossible—for some women to have abortions,

Powell concluded that the Connecticut statute "neither created nor in any way affected" the decision not to have an abortion. In effect, then, Powell's opinion maintained that both the rich and the poor have an equal right to get a privately funded abortion.

The dissenters were outraged at the insensitivity of Powell and the majority. These statutes, they argued, involved the "most vicious attacks yet devised" by the "ethically bankrupt" opponents of *Roe* to "circumvent the commands of the Constitution and impose their moral choices upon the rest of society." These restrictions fall "upon those among us least able to help or defend themselves." As Powell "well knows, these regulations inevitably will have the practical impact of preventing nearly all poor women from obtaining safe and legal abortions." Justice Marshall, in his draft dissent, pointed out that the practical consequence of Powell's decision was the birth of unwanted children to desperately poor women. "An unwanted child may be disruptive and destructive of the life of any woman, but the impact is felt most by those too poor to ameliorate those effects."

The conservative Court majority expressed a haughty and cavalier attitude in all of the cases. In *Harris v McRae*,[18] for example, Justice Stewart, for the majority wrote:

> Although government may not place obstacles in the path of a woman's exercise of her freedom of choice, it need not remove those not of its own creation. Indigency falls in the latter category.

These conservative opinions, ironically, did not stem the tide of criticism against the *Roe* precedent. Abortion became an issue, a very controversial one, in the presidential campaigns of 1980, 1984, and 1988. All three elections were won by conservative Republican candidates (Ronald Reagan in 1980 and 1984, and George Bush in 1988) who argued on behalf of the rights of the unborn and against the right of a woman to freely choose to have an abortion.

By the time *Webster v Reproductive Health Services,* was heard by the Court during its 1989 Term, there had been significant changes in the Court's personnel. Only three Justices remained from the seven-person 1973 *Roe* majority: Marshall, Blackmun, and Brennan. The two dissenters in *Roe*, Rehnquist and White, had been joined by the conservative Reagan appointees. Justice Stewart had been replaced by Sandra Day O'Connor (1981);[19] federal appeals judge Antonin Scalia had taken Rehnquist's Associate Justice seat when Rehnquist was made Chief Justice (replacing Burger in 1986); and, a year later, Lewis Powell had been replaced by another Republican conservative appointee, federal appeals court judge Anthony Kennedy.

The Court's first female Justice, Sandra Day O'Connor, a legislator and state judge from Arizona, was instantly critical of the *Roe* precedent. In the 1983 case of *Akron v Akron Center for Reproductive Health,* in which the Court majority invalidated portions of an Ohio city ordinance that restricted a woman's right to an abortion, she was one of three dissenting Justices (along with Rehnquist and White). She wrote that Blackmun's trimester approach was unworkable and that the framework created in *Roe* "is clearly on a collision course with itself." For her, the important question for the Court to raise in any abortion rights litigation was whether the state regulation placed an "*undue burden*" on a woman's right to an abortion.

When *Webster* was heard in 1989, given the Court's lineup, everyone thought that the case would be the vehicle the Court majority would use to overturn *Roe*. (In the Conference Session where the Justices voted to grant certiorari in *Webster*, six Justices voted to grant. The three who voted to deny certiorari were the pro-choice jurists: Justices Brennan, Blackmun, and Marshall. They feared that the majority would bury *Roe*. For example, Marshall's law clerk wrote his boss: "Taking *Webster* would pose a great threat that the majority on the Court would overrule or dramatically limit *Roe*."[20]

The CA8 had invalidated a number of provisions in Missouri's 1986 very restrictive abortion statute, and William Webster, the Missouri Attorney General, appealed to the U.S. Supreme Court. The provisions invalidated by the federal appeals court: (1) Life begins with the act of conception itself and that "unborn children have a protectable interest in life, health, and well-being." (2) Medical doctors, before performing an abortion on a woman more than twenty weeks pregnant, were required to test the fetus's "gestational age, weight, and lung maturity." (3) No public employee or public medical facility could be involved with a nontherapeutic abortion. (4) No public funds could be used to "encourage or counsel" women about the value of an abortion.

Case Study: *Webster v Reproductive Health Services,* 1989

Webster became a cause célèbre when the Court announced that it would hear oral arguments and decide the issue on the merits. An unprecedented number of organized groups (seventy-eight) filed briefs *amicus curiae* with the Court in *Webster*: forty-six sided with the appellant, the State of Missouri (including the U.S. Solicitor General's brief); thirty-two on behalf of the appellee, Reproductive Health Services.[21]

The Court narrowly, 5:4, overturned the lower federal court decision and restored the four contested provisions of the Missouri abortion statute. *Webster*, much like other controversial cases brought into a fragmented Court, led to the writing of five separate opinions. There was a great deal of fur flying in the discussions, and the printed opinions revealed the depth of the Court's differences.

Justice Blackmun was

livid as he read Chief Justice Rehnquist's May 25, 1989 draft opinion in *Webster*. If it came down as the opinion of the Court, he felt it would undo his own *Roe v Wade* opinion, which he labeled (in a 1986 speech) "a landmark in the progress of the emancipation of women."[22]

In record time, he drafted his dissent in response to the Rehnquist draft. "The simple truth," he wrote,

> is that *Roe* no longer survives. . . . The majority discards a landmark case of the last generation, and casts into darkness the hopes and visions of every woman in this country who had come to believe that the Constitution guaranteed her the right to exercise some control over her unique ability to have children.[23]

The two *Roe* dissenters (Rehnquist and White), Blackmun intoned, had finally prevailed because of the new personnel on the Court in 1989, all conservative Reagan appointees (O'Connor, Scalia, and Kennedy).

While the Rehnquist majority overturned the judgment of the lower federal appellate court, Rehnquist did not have the votes to overturn *Roe*. Only four Justices voted to overturn: Rehnquist, White, Scalia, and Kennedy. While weakened seriously, *Roe* was not overturned in *Webster*, although Harry Blackmun, *Roe*'s author, was less than sanguine about its future: "For today, at least, the women of this Nation still retain the liberty to control their destinies. But the signs [of overturn] are evident and very ominous, and a chill wind blows."

In stating the preference for "reasonable" state abortion regulations, the Rehnquist opinion narrowed the impact of *Roe*. Missouri could specify medical procedures, effective in the second trimester, in order to protect the unborn fetus. The liberty of a woman to choose to have an abortion was no longer a "fundamental" right. A state did not have to show a "compelling" state interest in passing a narrowly tailored bill. However, because he lacked O'Connor's vote, Rehnquist could not overturn *Roe*. And so he wrote that "to the extent indicated in our opinion, we would modify and narrow *Roe* and succeeding cases."

Justice Scalia's concurrence was scathing, calling O'Connor cowardly for not "joining" Rehnquist. *Roe* should have been overturned. Because O'Connor was cowardly, "*Roe* must be disassembled door-jamb by door-jamb, and never entirely brought down, no matter how wrong it may be."

An equally angry Justice Stevens, on May 30, 1989, wrote a stinging letter to the Chief. Calling Rehnquist's draft opinion "untenable," "gratuitous,"

and "without any attempt to explain or justify your new standard," Stevens
held the opinion up to ridicule:

> A requirement that the pregnant woman must be able to stand on her head
> for fifteen minutes before she can have an abortion . . . would satisfy your
> test. . . . As you know, I am not in favor of overruling *Roe v Wade,* but If the
> deed is to be done I would rather see the Court give the case a decent *bur-*
> *ial instead of tossing it out the window of a fast-moving caboose.*[24]

In a ringing defense of the *Roe* trimester framework, Blackmun's draft
dissent argued that the 1973 framework

> simply defines and limits the right of privacy in the abortion context to ac-
> commodate, not destroy, a state's legitimate interest in protecting the health
> of pregnant women and in preserving potential human life.

His dissent, joined by Marshall and Brennan, was a fierce, emotive defense
of *Roe* by its longtime bitterly attacked—and shot at—author. For them,
Missouri's "viability testing" requirement was a "patently irrational" one. It
was "an arbitrary imposition of risk, and expense, furthering no discernible
interest except to make the procurement of an abortion as arduous and as
difficult as possible."

The result in *Webster* was the rejection of the abortion choice as a "fundamental" right of privacy possessed by all women—certainly up to the
point of fetal viability. Rehnquist and his group, instead, argued that there
was a less essential "liberty" interest woman had, implicit in the Due Process
Clause, that gave them certain freedom to act. However, their choices were
subject to reasonable governmental regulations.[25]

Justices Marshall, Brennan, and Blackmun, joined separately by
Stevens, dissented from the affirming of the constitutionality of the Missouri regulations as well as from the view that *Roe* was no longer viable
precedent.

Many scholars and pro-choice advocates saw *Webster*'s impact direly: "The
right to have an abortion ceased to be a fundamental right."[26] The opinion
left the country anxiously awaiting the next round in *Roe*'s deconstruction
by the very conservative Supreme Court. The decision in effect encouraged
states to pass restrictive antiabortion laws. State lawmakers knew that there
was at least a five-person majority that either saw a weak—no longer fun-

damental—personal "liberty" interest outweighed by the authority of the state or that state laws did not impose an "undue burden" on a woman's right to have an abortion.

In 1991, the Court heard the case of *Rust v Sullivan.* The case involved the constitutionality of a number of Reagan administration amendments to Title X of the Public Health Service Act. Written in 1970, Title X of the public law authorized the government to provide financial grants to clinical organizations that engaged in family planning projects.

The 1988 amendments, in a major change from the funding guidelines in place since 1970, prohibited funds from going to any project where the organization counseled pregnant women about abortions (or either distributed materials about the abortion procedure or was physically associated with or attached to a facility that did the abortion procedure). Such organizations were forbidden to lobby for state or federal laws that would liberalize the availability of abortions.

Dr. Irving Rust, a medical doctor who was the recipient of Title X funds, immediately challenged the constitutionality of the federal amendments. His argument was that the new legislation deprived individuals and groups of their First and Fourteenth Amendments' freedoms of speech and association if they supported a woman's right to reproductive choice. The lower federal courts upheld the amendments and Rust appealed to the Supreme Court.

A sharply divided Court ruled, 5:4, that the amendments did not violate the Constitution and that the Reagan administration officials in the Department of Health and Human Services (HHS) did not unconstitutionally abuse administrative discretion. Nor was the woman's liberty interest, found in the Due Process Clause, "impermissibly burdened" by the administrative restrictions on free speech and association. Chief Justice Rehnquist once again wrote the majority opinion for the Court.

Justice Blackmun wrote the dissenting opinion. For him, joined by Marshall, with Justices Stevens and O'Connor joining parts, the Court, by validating the 1988 amendments, for the first time has "upheld viewpoint-based suppression of free speech simply because that suppression was a condition upon the acceptance of public funds." The majority opinion was another attack on the *Roe* precedent:

> *Roe* and its progeny are not so much about a medical procedure as they are about a woman's fundamental right to self-determination. [They] serve to vindicate the idea that "liberty," if it means anything, must entail freedom

from governmental domination in making the most intimate and personal of decisions.

In *Rust*, Justice O'Connor, once again, parted company with Rehnquist. She dissented in part from his decision affirming the lower federal courts' decisions upholding the 1988 changes in the law, joining Blackmun's opinion regarding the amendments' denying women and their doctors freedom of speech.

IV. After Roe, What Are a Husband's Rights?

During the December 13, 1972, Conference discussion of the *Roe* and *Doe* abortion cases argued earlier that week, Chief Justice Burger asked: "Is there the possible need to deal with whether husbands as such or parents of 'minors' have rights in this [abortion] area?"[27] His erstwhile friend, Justice Blackmun, wrote a Memo to the Conference about a week later: "The Chief has expressed concern about the rights of the father. . . . I am somewhat reluctant to try to cover [this] point in cases where the father's rights, if any, are not at issue."[28] This question, however, came up to the Court a few years after *Roe* came down.

During the 1976 Term, the Justices examined the traditional notion of the right of the husband to be notified and to give his consent to his wife's wish to have an abortion. In *Planned Parenthood of Central Missouri v Danforth*[29] the state's requirement of the written consent of a woman's husband before she could obtain an abortion was challenged by the birth control organization. The state argued that "marriage is an institution" and any substantive change in the family required a joint decision by both wife and husband.

For the U.S. Supreme Court, Justice Blackmun invalidated the Missouri statute. No state can "delegate to a spouse a veto power which the state itself is absolutely and totally prohibited from exercising during the first trimester of pregnancy." While aware of the "deep and proper concern and interest" a husband has in his wife's pregnancy, and while the Court "appreciated the importance of the marital relationship in our society," nevertheless

[w]e cannot hold that the State has the constitutional authority to give the spouse unilaterally the ability to prohibit the wife from terminating her pregnancy, when the State itself lacks that right.[30]

Privacy lies with the individual, not in the "marital institution," concluded the Court. "When a woman, with the approval of her physician but without the approval of her husband, decides to terminate her pregnancy, it could be said that she is acting unilaterally." However, Blackmun wrote, when the couple disagrees on the decision to terminate, "the balance weighs in her favor."[31]

During the 1992 Term of the Court, the *Danforth* doctrine was extended in the Court's penultimate abortion rights case to this time. A strange-looking Court majority of five invalidated a Pennsylvania statute requiring that a physician could not perform an abortion of a married woman unless the doctor first received a signed statement from her that she had notified her husband that she was about to undergo an abortion.[32] All the other challenged sections of the statute were validated.

The key player in this case, *Planned Parenthood of Southeastern Pennsylvania v Casey*, as in so many other controversial 5:4 cases was Justice Sandra Day O'Connor. She seldom dissents; in the 1999 Term of the Court (1999–2000), she "wrote only one dissenting opinion, approaching Justice William Brennan's record of zero dissents in 1967 at the height of the Warren era."[33] According to a former law clerk of O'Connor's, in *Casey* the Justice "was most offended by the provisions of the Pennsylvania law requiring wives to notify their husbands before having an abortion."

> Having decided to strike that down, she was amenable to Souter's suggestion that they write an opinion that would preserve the core of *Roe*. She and Souter then approached Kennedy, who agreed to adopt O'Connor's "undue burden" standard as the new test for evaluating all abortion restrictions.[34]

O'Connor and Kennedy, joined by Justice David Souter, the Bush administration's "stealth" candidate who took Brennan's seat in 1990, all took part in writing a unique joint opinion that, with the two votes of Blackmun and Stevens, upheld the *Roe* precedent. A Court insider said that when the trio circulated their joint opinion, "it was as if a neutron bomb exploded."[35] Shock and anger by the conservatives was accompanied by the tempered joy of the pro-choice Justices, especially Justice Blackmun. As one observer commented, "[T]he story of *Casey*—and Rehnquist's failure to find five votes to overturn *Roe*—is one of the most extraordinary in the annals of the modern Supreme Court."[36]

Case Study: *Planned Parenthood of Southeastern Pennsylvania v Casey,*
1992

Pennsylvania in 1988 and 1989 had passed a number of prohibitive amendments to its abortion law. They called for (1) a doctor to inform a woman contemplating an abortion about "fetal development," (2) women to give their formal consent or, if a minor, to get the consent of the parents, (3) a waiting period of one full day before the abortion procedure could take place, (4) spousal notification, (5) antiabortion counseling, and (6) the establishment of certain reporting procedures that all doctors had to follow when performing abortion procedures.

The Court was wildly divided over *Casey.* There was the Blackmun/Stevens cohort, who continued to argue for the viability of the *Roe* trimester framework. Blackmun voted to strike down all the challenged Pennsylvania amendments as violative of *Roe;* Stevens would have validated some and struck down others in light of the *Roe* judging framework. There was the conservative Rehnquist quartet—consisting of the Chief, and Justices White, Scalia, and the recently appointed, controversial Clarence Thomas. They voted to validate all the Pennsylvania abortion law amendments and insisted that *Roe* be directly overturned. (They would come up one vote shy of a majority.)

Finally, there was the position of the newly emergent moderately conservative trio of Justices O'Connor, Kennedy, and Souter. They argued that most of the Pennsylvania amendments were constitutional because there was no "undue burden" placed upon the woman by the state. Evidently Souter had proposed that the three jurists meet secretly "to explore the possibility of an opinion that would preserve the core of *Roe.*"[37] They met and with the help of only a few of their law clerks, drafted and then announced their joint decision to their surprised colleagues.

The exception was the husband-notification segment of the statute. Such a requirement, they wrote, was likely to

> impose a substantial obstacle [such that significant numbers of wives would not obtain abortions] as surely as if the Commonwealth had outlawed abortion in all cases. [Further, the husband's interest in the life of the child carried by his wife did not permit the state] to empower him with this troubling degree of authority over his wife. A husband has no enforceable right to require a wife to advise him before she exercises her personal choices.

While Rehnquist took the news without any apparent rancor, Scalia was so angry with Kennedy that he "walked over to Kennedy's nearby house in McLean, Virginia, to upbraid him."[38] The "essential holding of *Roe*," Souter, Kennedy, and O'Connor asserted, "should be retained and once again reaffirmed." The woman's right to terminate her pregnancy before viability is the "most central principle in *Roe v Wade*. It is a rule of law and component of liberty we cannot renounce." They concluded that the Pennsylvania statute did not "unduly burden" women seeking an abortion in the state.

Harry Blackmun, in *Casey*, applauded what he labeled the trio's opinion as

> an act of personal courage and constitutional principle. . . . In brief, five members of the Court today recognize that "the Constitution protects a woman's right to terminate her pregnancy in its early stages."

For Blackmun, O'Connor's "undue burden" standard required the Court to apply the standard of "strict scrutiny" when judging the validity of abortion regulations. That was fine with him, even though it clearly moved away from *Roe*'s trimester framework—which was at the heart of the *Roe* precedent.

Blackmun was still extremely pensive and certainly not sanguine about the future of *Roe*. He wrote:

> I remain steadfast in my belief that the right to reproductive choice is entitled to the full protection afforded by this Court before *Webster*. I fear for the darkness as four Justices anxiously await the single vote necessary to extinguish the light.[39]

Comments from pro-choice and pro-life advocates summarized the reaction to *Casey*. "George Bush's Court has left *Roe v Wade* an empty shell that is one Justice Thomas away from being destroyed," said Kate Michelman, president of the National Abortion Rights Action League (NARAL). Patricia Ireland, president of the National Organization for Women, simply said that "*Roe* is dead."[40]

Randall Terry, however, the founder of the pro-life group, Operation Rescue, denounced the trio of Republican presidential appointees, Justice O'Connor, Kennedy, and Souter. "Three Reagan/Bush appointees stabbed the pro-life movement in the back." And Gary Bauer, a candidate for the

Republican Party's presidential nomination in 2000 but, in 1992, President of the conservative National Research Council, condemned "the emergence on the Court of a Wimp Bloc who are quickly becoming an embarrassment to the presidents who appointed them."[41]

Only an overturn of the 1989 abortion decision or the appointment of pro-choice justices to replace retired conservatives, could restore *Roe* to its full potency as constitutional precedent in the area of abortion. (Given the results of the 2000 presidential election, the first decade of the twenty-first century will prove to be very decisive years for women.)

The year *Casey* came down, 1992, however, saw the conservative Republican incumbent President, George Bush, defeated in the presidential election by the moderate Democratic presidential candidate, Arkansas Governor Bill Clinton, a vocal supporter of a woman's right of freedom of reproductive choice. Furthermore, with his appointment of two abortion rights supporters, Ruth Bader Ginsburg in 1993 (replacing retired Byron White, who was a perennial opponent of *Roe*) and Stephen Breyer in 1994 (replacing retired Justice Harry Blackmun), the threat of a direct overturn of *Roe* subsided. Clinton's reelection in 1996 guaranteed continued support of the reproductive rights of women—at least from the executive.

Because of Justice O'Connor's switch, joined by Justice Kennedy (but only in *Casey*), in the 1992 case, *Roe* was not overturned—but its impact has been greatly blunted by the conservative Court majority.

> By adopting the vague "undue burden" language, O'Connor gave herself lots of discretion to decide, from case to case, whether or not she considered a particular abortion decision permissible.[42]

Things change. After the closest and most controversial presidential election in American history, the 2000 election between the Republican Texas Governor George W. Bush and the incumbent Democratic Vice-President Al Gore, the extremely conservative Bush (son of former President George Bush, 1989–1993), was sworn into office on January 20, 2001.[43]

> If a vacancy arises on the Court (there has not been one since 1994) while President Bush is in office, he will nominate "his kind" of person to sit on the Court, one who shares the president's values. Bush himself during the fall campaign suggested just whom that person might look like: an Antonin Scalia or a Clarence Thomas.[44]

V. When a Minor Daughter Wants to Terminate Her Pregnancy

In 1989, the year *Webster* came down, one million teenagers became pregnant; about 50 percent had an abortion—and more than 60 percent of these girls consulted with at least one parent before making their decision.[45] A question associated with such data came to the Court a few years after *Roe* came down. Must a pregnant minor daughter be required by the state to receive the written consent of her parents before she can undergo an abortion? In 2003, at least thirty-one states had such a regulation; with one exception, Utah, all had a judicial bypass section.

A section of the Missouri statutes challenged in the 1977 *Danforth* litigation had no judicial bypass provision. Unless the doctor certified that the abortion on the minor was necessary to preserve the life of the mother, without parental consent there could not be an abortion.

The federal district court judge found that there was "a compelling basis" for such a requirement: "Safeguarding the authority of the family relationship."[46] In the Court's majority opinion, Blackmun wrote that that section of the law was unconstitutional: There is no justification for giving a "third party a veto over the decision of a physician and his patient to abort the patient's pregnancy."[47] The Court said, in *Danforth*: "Any independent interest the parent may have in the termination of the minor daughter's pregnancy is no more weighty than the right of privacy of the competent minor mature enough to have become pregnant."

Courts have held that competent teenagers who are pregnant need not tell their parents about their decision to have an abortion. These decisions have established a conflict between the reproductive rights of a teenager versus the right of the parents to direct the upbringing of their children. *Danforth* clearly "illustrates the erosion of the parent-child relationship that was so central to earlier [Court] notions of the family and demonstrates how promoting the individual right to privacy comes at the expense of parents and family."[48] Parents, wrote critics of the opinion, "are reduced to third parties and in the name of their child's privacy become minor participants, at best, in the decision regarding abortion."[49]

In the *Belotti* decision of the Court,[50] the Justices examined the constitutionality of a Massachusetts law that required parental consent before a minor daughter could undergo an abortion. It differed from the Missouri statute in that the law provided for parental bypass: If the parents refused to consent to their child's proposed abortion, *only then* could she go to court for a bypass order allowing the abortion to proceed. After meeting *ex parte* with the young pregnant girl, a state judge could issue an order that permitted the abortion procedure. It she satisfied the judge that she was "mature and well enough informed to make intelligently the abortion decision on her own, the court must authorize her to act without parental consultation or consent."

Justice Powell wrote the decision for the Court. Unlike Blackmun, he acknowledged the fundamental importance of the traditional nuclear family. "The guiding role of parents in the upbringing of their children justifies limitations on the freedom of minors."[51] However, he continued, the Massachusetts statute imposed an "undue burden upon the exercise by minors of the right to seek an abortion" because of the possibility of parental obstruction. "Every minor must have the opportunity—if she so chooses—to go directly to a court without first consulting or notifying her parents."[52] If the judge believed it was best for the child to consult with the parents before the abortion, there would be appropriate judicial action. However, concluded Powell, "this is the full extent to which parental involvement may be required."[53]

> In *Danforth*, individual privacy rights trumped the rights of parents. After *Belotti*, judges trump parents. . . . At best, *Belotti* partially vindicated parental authority. At worst, it validated the idea that parents can be entirely removed from the abortion process even if their child was judged not to be ready to make that decision on her own.[54]

Clearly, the Court dissenters loudly objected to the Court's weakening of the common law concept of family. Bitterly, Justice Anthony Kennedy, in his *Hodgson* dissent, wrote:

> The primacy of the parents [right] to speak and act on their children's behalf, . . . [and the] family tie is a concept which this Court now seems intent on declaring a constitutional irrelevance.[55]

VI. Back into the Vortex: The "Partial Birth" Abortion Controversy

Events do not await shifts in Court personnel. Eight years after *Casey*, its last watershed abortion rights case, the U.S. Supreme Court, in January 2000, agreed to review the constitutionality of state laws that banned "partial birth" abortions. For the first time since the *Casey* decision, "the Justices will address a woman's right to end a pregnancy, a matter that has split the Court and the country for three decades."[56] It probably granted certiorari because of conflicts in two federal appellate circuits: The CA8 overturned partial birth bans in Nebraska, Arkansas, and Iowa; however, the CA7 upheld similar laws in Wisconsin and Illinois.

Could a state prohibit an abortion procedure referred to as a "partial birth abortion" without clashing with a woman's right to choose? Between 1992 and 1999, thirty-one states[57] banned partial birth abortions.[58] In twenty states, including Nebraska, lower federal courts blocked enforcement by issuing either permanent injunctions or temporary restraining orders until the constitutional questions have been answered.

Republican Congresses passed laws barring the use of federal funds for partial birth abortions in 1996, 1997, and 2000. Democratic President Bill Clinton successfully vetoed them. This type of abortion, hated bitterly by pro-life advocates, is referred to by them as the "brain suction." (The medical term for the abortion procedure is "D and X," "Dilation and Extraction.") It is a three-day procedure, generally performed between the twentieth and twenty-fourth weeks of pregnancy, the midterm of the pregnancy. On the third day, the physician removes the fetus from the woman's uterus.

> However, the head, which is too big to pass through the dilated cervix, remains in the internal cervical opening. At this point, the physician takes a pair of blunt curved scissors and forces the scissors into the base of the skull.

This enables the doctor to remove the skull contents with a suction device. "The head will then compress, enabling the physician to remove the fetus completely from the woman."[59]

Stenberg v Carhart[60] came to the Court from Nebraska. In 1997, the state legislators, under heavy pressure from out-of-state religious pro-life groups, passed a law banning partial birth abortions.

> No partial birth abortion shall be performed in this state, unless such procedure is necessary to save the life of the mother whose life is endangered by a physical disorder, physical distress, or physical injury, including a life-endangering physical condition caused by or arising from the pregnancy itself.

The law defined "partial birth" as

> an abortion procedure in which the person performing the abortion *partially delivers vaginally a living unborn child before killing the unborn child* and completing the delivery. ['Partially delivers . . .' is defined to mean] deliberately and intentionally delivering into the vagina a living unborn child, *or a substantial portion thereof,* for the purpose of performing a procedure that the person performing such procedure knows will kill the unborn child and does kill the unborn child. [My emphasis.]

Violation of the statute, a Class III felony, carried a prison term of up to twenty years, a fine of up to $25,000, and automatic revocation of the doctor's license to practice medicine in Nebraska.

Only one legislator voted against the ban. "It was an ugly time," recalled the lone dissenter, Nebraska Senator Ernie Chambers. State officials were "bullied and intimidated by some of those so-called pro-life people who had come from Washington."[61]

Legislators who defended the legislation said that they wanted to ban the seldom-used "gruesome" D and X procedure, usually performed late in the second trimester and beyond. They maintained that the procedure is "medically unnecessary and looks disturbingly close to infanticide."

Data presented in the federal courts and in the briefs submitted to the Supreme Court indicate (1) more than 90 percent of abortions, nationally, occur during the first trimester, before twelve weeks of gestational age. Using a procedure, "vacuum aspiration," not subject to the Nebraska statute, is the most common protocol. (The procedure involves the insertion of a vacuum tube into the uterus to evacuate the contents. It is performed on an outpatient basis under local anesthesia.) (2) Approximately 10 percent of all abortions occur during the second trimester of pregnancy (twelve to twenty-four weeks). The most commonly used surgical procedure (used 95 percent of the time) is the "intact dilation and extraction," IDE protocol, in which an arm or a leg of a live fetus may be pulled, using a surgical instrument, into the vagina. After that occurs, the surgeon then removes the limb, then the rest of the fetus, and, finally, scrapes the walls of the uterus with a curette to ensure that no fetal tissue remains. Surgeons view the D and E protocol as a partial birth procedure, in many respects similar to the D and X procedure. (3) The D and X protocol is used in a small number of mid- and late-term abortions where the fetus's head is too large to safely use the IDE procedure protocol. There are no reliable data on the number of D and X abortions performed annually; estimates range between 640 and 5,500 per year. According to Dr. Carhart's testimony in the federal district court, D and X is used because it

> reduces the dangers from sharp bone fragments passing through the cervix, reduces the likelihood of leaving infection-causing fetal and placental tissue in the uterus, and could help to prevent potentially fatal absorption of fetal tissue into the maternal circulation.

Case Study: *Stenberg v Carhart,* 1999

Dr. LeRoy Carhart was the only Nebraska doctor who performed partial birth abortions and other medical procedures on woman more than sixteen weeks pregnant. He went into federal district court seeking a declaratory judgment that the Nebraska statute violated the federal Constitution, and asking for an injunction forbidding its enforcement. After a trial on the merits, where both sides presented medical expert testimony, the trial judge held the statute unconstitutional. Don Stenberg, the Attorney General of Nebraska, took his appeal to the CA8.

That federal appellate court affirmed the judgment of the trial court and Stenberg requested, and received, certiorari from the U.S. Supreme Court.

Stenberg's argument before the Justices refuted the CA8's conclusion. The law

> is not an openly worded Rorschach test. The plain terms of the statute regulate the D and X procedure and no other. Unlike the D and E procedure, in which the object is to dismember the unborn child, the thrust of the D and X procedure is to kill the child after almost complete delivery.

He told the Court: "The state's interest here is in drawing a bright line between infanticide and abortion."

Carhart maintained that the method a physician uses "should be determined by the individual woman's situation, the age of the fetus, and the doctor's decision on what is best." Simon Heller, Carhart's attorney, told the Justices that "this law is so broadly written it could prohibit most second trimester abortion" procedures protected by earlier Supreme Court decisions. He maintained that the statute's language, "deliberately and intentionally delivering into the vagina a living unborn child, *or a substantial portion thereof*," effectively meant that D and E as well as D and X were banned abortion protocols. Both procedures "delivered into the vagina" a "substantial portion" of the fetus.

The Court heard oral argument in late April 2000. One reporter noted that the arguments were "strangely subdued" and the "mood remarkably low-key, almost quiet at times."[62] Justice Scalia was the only one who raised "larger moral issues and homed in on a medical procedure that pro-life advocates maintain is cruel and unnecessary." "The state," he said in a very quiet manner (unusual for him), "could have been concerned about rendering society callous to infanticide." In response to Scalia's comments about the horror of the D and X procedure, Heller said, "Abortion methods are, by their nature, unsightly. *They all involve fetal demise.*"

Outside the Court, reported the press, police arrested twenty-three pro-life demonstrators because they refused to take down a freestanding antiabortion sign that was larger than federal regulations permitted.

On June 28, 2000, the last day of the Court's 1999–2000 Term, the decision came down. "A bitterly divided Supreme Court handed abortion rights advocates a double victory yesterday," wrote Ed Walsh and Amy Goldstein.[63] By a 5:4 vote, the Court struck down the Nebraska law. Justice Breyer wrote the opinion for the five-person majority.

However, it was an unbelievably fractured Court: there were eight opinions written in *Stenberg*. There was the majority opinion and three concurring opinions written by Justices Stevens, Ginsburg, and O'Connor. There were four dissents, written by the Chief Justice, and Justices Scalia, Kennedy, and Thomas. (The only justice not writing in *Stenberg* was Justice Souter.)

The "abortion problem," wrote Breyer, contains "virtually irreconcilable points of view." Taking those into account, "this Court, in the course of a generation, has determined and redetermined that the Constitution offers basic protection to the woman's right to choose. See *Roe; Casey.*"

The three principles in *Casey* determine the *Stenberg* outcome.

First, before viability, the woman has a right to choose to terminate her pregnancy. Second, a law designed to further the State's interest in fetal life, which imposes an undue burden on the woman's decision before fetal viability, is unconstitutional. Third, subsequent to viability, the State in promoting its interest in the potentiality of human life may, if it chooses, regulate, and even proscribe, abortion, except where it is necessary, in appropriate medical judgment, for the preservation of the life and health of the mother.

"We hold that this statute violates the Constitution," Breyer wrote for the majority. It does so for two reasons. The law prohibits *any* partial birth procedure except where the protocol is necessary to save the mother's life. "Second, it imposes an undue burden on a woman's ability to choose a D and E abortion, thereby unduly burdening the right to choose abortion itself."

> Even if the statute's basic aim is to ban D and X, its language makes clear that it covers a much broader category of procedures (including D and E). . . . All those who perform abortion procedures using that method must fear prosecution, conviction, and imprisonment. The result is an *undue burden* upon a woman's right to make an abortion decision. We must consequently find the statute unconstitutional.

Justice Scalia's dissent was a typical "Nino"-the-defender-of-morals-and-virtue broadside.

> I am optimistic enough to believe that, one day, *Stenberg v Carhart* will be assigned its rightful place in the history of this Court's jurisprudence beside *Korematsu* and *Dred Scott*. . . . The [majority's] notion that the Constitution of the United States . . . prohibits the States from simply banning this visibly brutal means of eliminating our half-born posterity is quite simply absurd. . . . In the last analysis, [it is] my judgment that *Casey* does not support today's tragic result. . . . *It is a value judgment*, dependent upon how much one respects (or believes society ought to respect) the life of a partially delivered fetus, and how much one respects (or believes society ought to respect) the freedom of the woman who gave it life to kill it. *Evidently, the five Justices in today's majority value the former less, or the latter more, or both, than the four of us in dissent, Case closed.* [my emphasis.]

Stenberg came down during the presidential campaign of 2000. The outgoing President, Democrat Bill Clinton, understood well what Scalia was saying. At a June 28, 2000, press conference, he said:

> I think that in the next four years, there will be somewhere between two and four appointments to the Supreme Court, and depending on who those appointees are, I think the [*Roe/Casey*] rule will either be maintained or overturned. And I think that it's very much in the balance, depending on what appointments are made in the next four years.[64]

There is, however, another "take" on the actions of the Justices of the Supreme Court, one that rebukes Scalia's derisive observation. The trio who wrote the joint opinion in *Casey*, Justices Souter, O'Connor, and Kennedy, stated:

> Some of us as individuals find abortion offensive to our most basic principles of morality, but that cannot control our decision. *Our obligation is to define the liberty of all, not to mandate our own moral code.*

After *Stenberg*, Justices Souter and O'Connor would tack on Scalia's closing comment: "Case closed."

Gary Bauer, in 2000, the chairman of American Values and an unsuccessful candidate for the GOP presidential nomination said of the opinion: "It comes perilously close to legalizing infanticide." Dr. Carhart, who was in the Courtroom when the decision was announced, said afterward: "I don't think it could have gotten any better." Understandably, Republican presidential candidate George W. Bush was "disappointed" with the Court's decision. A spokesperson read a statement attributed to him: "Governor Bush believes it is possible to construct a ban on partial birth abortion that passes constitutional muster and, unlike Vice President Gore, he will work to do so."[65]

VII. Summing Up

This chapter's focus is on *not having* a child. Court majorities have changed since the 1970s; conservative jurists have replaced Justices who aggressively defended the fundamental right of a woman to choose whether or not to terminate a pregnancy. The pendulum has swung from *Roe* to *Webster* to *Casey* and then to *Stenberg*. Its future arc is dependent on who sits and, as Justice Scalia reminds the public, on the values they bring with them when they arrive at the Court.

Since 1973, Court personnel have changed dramatically. For the most part vacancies have been filled by conservative-minded presidential appointees firmly committed to the sanctity of life, especially fetal life. *Roe* remains, but it is a much different container of rights than it was when Blackmun read his opinion in Court in January 1973.

However, something needs to be said, albeit briefly, about the other side of the abortion coin: giving birth. *Having* a child has its own set of constitutional issues. Some of them, for example, the rights of children of illegal aliens,[66] the rights of illegitimate children,[67] and adoption of children born out of wedlock in a foreign country where one of the two parents is an American citizen,[68] have been examined and decided by the U.S. Supreme Court.

Other issues associated with having children, for example, the extremely controversial issue of noncoital reproduction (i.e., cloning, in-vitro fertilization, egg donation, surrogate motherhood, and artificial insemination)[69] and same-sex adoption, are percolating in the lower state and federal courts and will eventually arrive at the U.S. Supreme Court's doors. The next edition of this book may address the at-present barely emergent, highly inflammatory legal and moral and religious question: Should the established right to procreate coitally (dating from *Skinner*) extend to encompass a fundamental right to noncoital procreation? To date, no court has explicitly dealt with this issue.[70] But controversial cases raising this question may be docketed in the next decade.

Chapter 5 will examine what the U.S. Supreme Court has said about intimate family relationships after the children have emerged, whole and healthy, from the mother's womb.

5

Raising the Child
"Father Knows Best"?

The idyllic picture of American family life portrayed by the Supreme
Court clearly does not match the contemporary reality.
—American Psychological Association[1]

During a discussion of a parental authority case in 1978, Justice
Potter Stewart declared:

This is not an easy case. Issues involving the family are among the most difficult that [we] have to face, involving serious problems of policy disguised
as questions of constitutional law.[2]

Hard cases make bad law.[3] This axiom has been exhibited throughout the
book. This chapter is no exception. The reason is simple: cases involving the
intimate, often sexual, relationships between people exhibit, in sharp focus,
the values of the Justices. The men and women who sit on the U.S. Supreme
Court draw on their own value systems to answer the policy problem disguised as a question of constitutional law.

This is especially true when the constitutional issues revolve around the
care and well-being of the child in the home. The home ostensibly provides
respite from external stresses. In our culture, home is associated with comfort, safety, and leisure activities. It is the essence of what is private, from the
privacy of the marital bedroom to the private decisions of parents about
raising and caring for their children.

As "cultural signifier and idealized symbol, 'home' is the place in our unconscious memory to which we want to return. . . . It is deeply idealized and
cherished notwithstanding the reality that the home is also a place that

many choose to leave."[4] As seen in earlier chapters, the ideal of the home has been shattered by the reality of intimate violence directed, for the most part, at women and children living in it. The brutal reality of spousal violence "represents an invasion of this quintessentially private space."[5]

Parental conduct, whether in disciplining the child or in general decision making on behalf of the child,

> is generally protected unless it constitutes abuse or neglect of the child. Courts consistently reiterate the common law presumption that parents act in the best interest of their children. The legal construct of the family is based on the presumption that "parents possess what a child lacks in maturity, experience, and capacity for judgment."[6]

I. "This Is Really a Ridiculous Case to Be Absorbing Our Time"

Stanley v Illinois[7] came to the U.S. Supreme Court during its 1971 Term. The litigation went all the way to the high bench because an unmarried father of three children lost custody of his two minor children when their mother died. Peter Stanley and Joan Stanley lived together, intermittently, without ever marrying, for eighteen years and had three children.

When Joan died, Peter Stanley turned the two minor children over to the care of Mr. and Mrs. Ness. They took the children into their home. According to Chief Justice Burger's reading of the facts in the case, the Nesses became, *de facto*, the actual custodians of the children. Stanley

> took no action to gain recognition of himself as the father, through adoption, or as a legal custodian, through a guardianship proceeding. He seemed, in particular, to be concerned with the loss of welfare payments he would suffer as a result of the designation of others as guardians of the children.[8]

Stanley lost his children because Illinois child custody statutes contained a presumption that unwed fathers were not fit to raise their minor children; however, the statutes did not make the same presumption about unmarried mothers and married fathers (who were divorced, separated, or widowed). Without the benefit of any hearing to examine parental fitness, and without any proof of neglect by the father, the children were declared wards of the state and placed with court-appointed guardians.

The legal issue that intrigued the Court enough to grant certiorari in the case was whether the Illinois statutes[9] violated the Fourteenth Amendment's Equal Protection and Due Process Clauses. The presumption was clear: *husbands and mothers, even unwed mothers, were fit to raise the child; unwed fathers were unfit.*

After reading the briefs and hearing oral argument, the initial response by the seven brethren[10] was to "*Dismiss* the petition as *Improvidently Granted*" (called a "dig") because the constitutional question had not been properly presented in the lower courts. Justice Brennan was assigned the task of writing the short *per curiam* opinion "digging" *Stanley.*

Justice Marshall, after reading Brennan's "dig," wrote his friend a short note: "I shall try my hand at a short dissent to your *per curiam.*"[11] However, Justice Blackmun and the Chief quickly "joined" the Brennan "dig" order.

Justice White always showed a deep concern about what happened to the children in these kinds of cases. He had unsuccessfully argued for granting certiorarti. After Brennan's *per curiam* "dig" was circulated, White distributed a ten-page dissent from the denial. In it, he argued that the brethren must answer the question "that Illinois would have us avoid: Is a presumption that distinguishes and burdens all unwed fathers constitutionally repugnant?"

Justice Marshall's chambers responded somewhat favorably to the White draft, but Marshall's law clerk said to her boss: "I think a stronger opinion can be drafted, and I would like to go ahead with such a draft." A few days later, Marshall's draft dissent circulated. It was one that raised the question "How does it serve the welfare of illegitimate children to deny parental rights to their fathers?" Employing strict scrutiny, Marshall concluded that the Illinois legislators did not meet the heavy burden of justifying their exclusion of unwed fathers. For Marshall, Illinois unconstitutionally relied on an "over-inclusive stereotype" of the unmarried father to rip Stanley's children away from him.

To the Chief's chagrin (for Burger believed that the Court should wash its hands of the "ridiculous" case), White's draft dissent turned the Court around. From a 1:6 vote, *Stanley* came down as a 5:2 vote to reverse the lower courts' judgment upholding the Illinois statute. "By recounting the facts in the case—unwed fathers seeking to retain custody of their children faced hurdles—often insurmountable in fact—that unwed mothers did not,"[12] Justice White persuaded his brethren to change their votes.

Only the Chief and his friend Harry Blackmun voted to affirm the Illinois child custody statute. On November 18, 1971, however, Blackmun wrote White: "I am assuming that you will be converting your dissent circulation of November 8 into a majority opinion. This is just to let you know that I shall probably join you now in a vote for reversal."

A few days before Thanksgiving 1971, Burger told the conference, in a letter to Justice White, that he would file a dissent in this case "as soon as I can put it together."

> I believe that when the whole record is sorted out it can be made clear that Stanley has not only failed but has affirmatively refused to use state remedies pointed out to him by the Illinois judge. *This is a really ridiculous case to be absorbing our time and, paradoxically, I will spend a little more time trying to demonstrate that.*

In early December, Burger circulated his dissent, noting in a cover letter that "I cannot escape a feeling that we are getting into a 'quicksand' area by the proposed opinion." For him, Peter Stanley was a greedy unfit father who wanted to continue receiving welfare payments for his two children. His argument to affirm the Illinois court was a uncomplicated one.

There was "no due process issue raised in the state courts, and no due process issue was decided by any state court." He believed that the only question properly before the Court was the equal protection issue. He

> agreed with the State's argument that [it] is not violated when Illinois gives full recognition only to those father-child relationships that arise in the context of family units bound together by legal obligations arising from marriage or from adoption proceedings.

By invalidating the Illinois law, the majority

> ascribes to that statutory system a presumption that is simply not there and embarks on a novel concept of the natural law for unwed fathers that could well have strange boundaries as yet indiscernible.

In the end, Blackmun switched again and joined Burger's dissent.

The rest of the Court, however, joined the White dissent to turn it into the majority opinion. In early February 1972, Justice Marshall told White that "I have decided to withdraw my concurring opinion and to join your opinion in toto." Justices Douglas, Stewart, and Brennan, a few days later, also joined the White opinion reversing the state supreme court's validation of the Illinois child custody laws. The case came down on April 3, 1972. What was a dissent from the "dig" *per curiam* order in early November 1971 turned into the majority opinion of the U.S. Supreme Court in April 1972.

This "ridiculous" case is but another illustration of the *fluidity of choice* in judicial decision making. While most of these controversial cases exhibit fairly hard-and-fast positions by the Justices, occasionally there is something in the opposing position that has an impact on them. As Justice Scalia observed in his *Casey* dissent, all the Justices make "value judgments" in these cases. Because some of his brethren are more doubtful than Scalia, they are open to a particularly skillful draft opinion from the other side. On many occasions, the papers and Memos of the Justices reflect this characteristic: "While I'm leaning to 'join' you, I await the circulation of the dissent."

These cases involving intimate personal relationships touch the Justices deeply. The tough cases came to the Court as legal questions involving very personal, very intimate interactions between men and women (as well as gay and lesbian relationships). Consequently, there emerged, at the same time, a Scalia moral certitude reaction, as well as the cautious pragmatism of a Justice O'Connor. For Scalia, traditional moral certainty compelled one type of response to the legal issues. On the other hand, Justices such as Brennan, Douglas, Marshall, and Souter, committed to other values, found another legal chord to strike in these cases.

And there were others, such as Justices Blackmun and O'Connor, who were much more pragmatic than their colleagues on the Court. All these blocs sitting at the same time led to flared tempers and fluidity in decision making.

In this case, Justice White's dissent, founded on his concern for the welfare of Stanley's children, ultimately convinced four colleagues, Justices Douglas, Brennan, Marshall, and Stewart, to decide the case on the merits and to reverse on due process and equal protection grounds. The precedents cited to justify the opinion are ones that have already been discussed and will be discussed in this chapter.

When White wrote that "the Court has frequently emphasized the importance of the family," that "the rights to conceive and to raise one's children have been deemed 'essential,'" and a "basic civil right of man," he cited familiar watershed cases:

The integrity of the family unit, has found protection in the Due Process Clause of the Fourteenth Amendment, *Meyer v Nebraska,* the Equal Protection Clause of the Fourteenth Amendment, *Skinner v Oklahoma*, and the Ninth Amendment, *Griswold v Connecticut.*

Two of these cases have already been examined. *Meyer* is a major precedent that will be discussed in the next segment of this chapter.

II. Raising and Educating Children

The U.S. Supreme Court's placement of the family and family autonomy over the autonomy of children is based on its view that "the protection of liberty under the Due Process clause includes parental authority to raise their children as they see fit."[13] In *Meyer v Nebraska*, 1923, the U.S. Supreme Court initially recognized that "family" fell within the constitutional concept of liberty:

> While this Court has not attempted to define with exactness the liberty thus guaranteed, without doubt, it denotes not merely freedom from bodily restraint but also the right to marry, establish a home and bring up children.[14]

The *Meyer* litigation involved a Nebraska law, passed in April 1919, shortly after World War I ended. It was an act relating to the teaching of foreign languages in public and private schools.

> No person, individually or as a teacher, shall teach any subject to any person in any language than the English language. Languages, other than the English language, may be taught as languages only after a pupil shall have attained and successfully passed the eighth grade (age 12)....

Meyer was a teacher in the Zion parochial school where, in May 1920, he was charged with teaching reading in the German language to Raymond Parpart, a ten-year-old who had not passed the eighth grade.[15] The Nebraska Supreme Court upheld the conviction, saying in part: "the salutary purpose of the statute is clear."

> The legislature had seen the baneful effects of permitting foreigners, who have taken residence in this country, to rear and educate their children in the language of their native land . . . so that they must always think in that

language, and, as a consequence, naturally inculcate in them the ideas and sentiments foreign to the best interests of this country.

Meyer appealed the decision to the U.S. Supreme Court. For the Justices, "the problem for our determination is whether the statute as construed and applied unreasonably infringes the [substantive] liberty guaranteed to the plaintiff in error by the [Due Process Clause] of the Fourteenth Amendment."

> Without doubt, [the Due Process Clause] denotes not merely freedom from bodily restraint but also the right of the individual to contract, to engage in any of the common occupations of life, to acquire useful knowledge, to marry, establish a home and bring up children, to worship God according to the dictates of his own conscience, and generally to enjoy those privileges long recognized at common law as essential to the orderly pursuit of happiness.

The Court majority concluded that there was no "reasonable relationship to some purpose within the competency of the state to effect." The statute "as applied is arbitrary." Furthermore, "it is the natural duty of the parent to give his children education suitable to their station in life." Meyer's right to teach "and the right of parents to engage him so to instruct their children, we think, are within the liberty of the [Due Process Clause]."

Justice Holmes, joined by Justice Sutherland, dissented. He argued for greater judicial restraint instead of a new kind of "substantive" due process, believing that while all citizens should speak the same language, the Nebraska "experiment" was a reasonable one; it was not an infringement upon the liberty found in the Fourteenth Amendment.

Two years later, in *Pierce v Society of Sisters*,[16] the Court once again underscored the substantive nature of the liberty interest of parents to direct the "upbringing of children under their control." An Oregon initiative passed in 1922 and supported by nativist organizations like the Ku Klux Klan was a product of post–World War I xenophobia about "Bolshevism," anti-Catholicism, and fears about foreigners coming to the United States. The initiative required

> every parent, guardian, or other person having control or charge or custody of a [normal] child between eight and sixteen years to send him to a public school for the period of time a public school shall be held during the current year; failure to do so is declared a misdemeanor.

The Society of Sisters was an Oregon corporation, established in 1880 to provide instruction for young persons by establishing and maintaining academies or schools. It provided secular and sectarian education according to the tenets of the Roman Catholic Church. The society's lawyers claimed that the Oregon law

conflicts with the right of parents to choose schools where their children will receive appropriate mental and religious training, the right of the child to influence the parents' choice of a school, the right of schools and teachers therein to engage in a useful business or profession, and is accordingly repugnant to the Constitution and void.

A three-judge federal district court concluded that the initiative violated the Due Process Clause of the Fourteenth Amendment. The federal court enjoined the state from enforcing the law, and the state sought a writ of certiorari from the U.S. Supreme Court.

Justice McReynolds, the author of the *Meyer* opinion, wrote the opinion for the Court in *Pierce*. Allowing the act to stand would lead to the "destruction of appellees primary schools."

We think entirely plain that the Act of 1922 unreasonably interferes with the liberty of parents and guardians to direct the upbringing and education of children under their control. . . . The legislation bears no reasonable relation to some purpose within the competency of the State. The child is not the mere creature of the state: those who nurture him and direct his destiny have the right, coupled with the high duty, to recognize and prepare him for additional obligations.

In a 1944 case, the U.S. Supreme Court said:

It is cardinal with us that the custody, care, and nurture of the child reside first in the parents, whose primary function and freedom include preparation for obligations the State can neither supply nor hinder.[17]

Prince was one of more than a dozen Jehovah's Witnesses cases heard by the Court in a ten-year period, all involving clashes between the religious organization and state authority. The Witnesses claimed that the First Amendment's guarantee of freedom of religion allowed them to act on behalf of their religious beliefs—without any state interference.

Prince came from the Massachusetts courts and involved the constitutionality of a state statute that prohibited minors (defined as a boy under twelve or a girl under eighteen) from

> selling, expose or offer for sale any newspapers, magazines, periodicals or any other articles of merchandise of any description, or exercise the trade of bootblack or scavenger, or any other trade, in any street or public place.

Sarah Prince, a Jehovah's Witness, was the aunt and custodian of Betty Simmons, a nine-year-old Witness. Prince was convicted for violating the child labor law because she allowed her own children and Betty to engage in "preaching work" by distributing their religious newspapers, the "Watchtower" and the "Consolation" on the streets of Brockton, Massachusetts. She appealed her conviction on First Amendment freedom of religion grounds. The state courts ruled against her and she took her case to the U.S. Supreme Court.

As the Court noted,

> Two claimed liberties are at stake. One is the parent's, to bring up the child in the way he should go, which, for appellant, means to teach him the tenets and the practices of their faith. The other freedom is the child's, to observe these, and among them is "to preach the gospel by public distribution of 'Watchtower' and 'Consolation,' in conformity with the scripture: 'A little child shall lead them.'"[18]

The Court majority balanced the "right of freedom of conscience and religious practice" against "the interests of society to protect the welfare of children." While the majority, in an opinion written by Justice Wiley Rutledge, acknowledged

> the private realm of family life which the state cannot enter, but the family itself is not beyond regulation in the public interest, as against a claim of religious liberty. And neither rights of religion nor rights of parenthood are beyond limitation.

And the Massachusetts child labor law was state action that was shown "to be necessary for or conducive to the child's protection."

Parents may be free to become martyrs themselves. But it does
not follow they are free, in identical circumstances, to make martyrs of their
children before they have reached the age of full and legal discretion when
they can make that choice for themselves.

Associate Justice Frank Murphy dissented. He argued, vainly, that the law
prohibiting "a child from exercising her constitutional right to practice her
religion on the public streets cannot, in my opinion, be sustained." Religious
training and religious activity, whether performed by an adult or a child, are
categorically

protected by the Fourteenth Amendment against interference by state action, except insofar as they violate reasonable regulations adopted for the
protection of the public health, morals and welfare.[19]

The Court has said many times that the parents' right to raise their children
is not absolute and can be interfered with if the state can show, in a narrowly
tailored law, a compelling reason for such interference. Inevitably, what is
seen is a Court balancing act, weighing the rights of the parents against the
responsibility of the state to legislate for the public health and welfare, especially the welfare of minor children.

The state, said the Court in *Prince,* "has a wide range of powers for limiting parental freedom and authority in things affecting the child's welfare."[20] And in the *Wisconsin v Yoder* case, the Court said:

The power of the parent may be subject to limitation if it appears that
parental decisions will jeopardize the health or safety of the child, or have a
potential for significant social burdens.[21]

Yoder involved the constitutionality of a Wisconsin compulsory education statute that required all youngsters between the ages of seven and sixteen to "attend school regularly." Violators of the statute were subject to fine
and imprisonment. Jonas Yoder and Wallace Miller, respondents in the case,
were members of the Old Order Amish religion, while Adin Yutzy, the third
respondent, was a member of the Conservative Amish Mennonite Church.
They and their families were residents of Green County, Wisconsin.

Moreover, the Court knew the demographic realities. Amish communities were found in nineteen states and in nine of them they "have been

subjected to prosecutions similar to this one while administrative accommodations have been reached in the others," wrote Douglas's law clerk to his boss in a Bench Memo.[22]

The respondents declined to send their children, Vernon Yutzy, age fourteen, Barbara Miller and Frieda Yoder, age fifteen, to public school after the children completed the eighth grade in public school. The three parents were charged, tried, and convicted of violating the compulsory-education law. The three were each fined five dollars. They claimed that the law violated their freedom of religion protected by the First and Fourteenth Amendments. Having their children attend high school was "contrary to the Amish religion and way of life."

At their trial, many religious and education experts testified. All focused on "the impact that compulsory high school attendance could have on the continued survival of Amish communities as they exist in the United States today." Their objection to continued public schooling "is firmly grounded in these central religious concepts." The state's lawyers, using the *Prince* precedent, argued that the state can override religion when the welfare of children was involved.

The trial judge concluded that the law did interfere with the Amish families' right to "act in accordance with their sincere religious belief" but also said that the age requirement was a "reasonable and constitutional exercise of governmental power." The circuit court affirmed the convictions. However, the Wisconsin Supreme Court sustained the parents' First and Fourteenth Amendment claims and reversed the convictions. Wisconsin appealed to the U.S. Supreme Court and the Court granted certiorari on May 24, 1971.

Case Study: *Wisconsin v Yoder,* 1972

The Court's Conference was held on December 10, 1971. Only seven justices participated because Justices Powell and Rehnquist had just joined the Court.

For the Chief Justice, the Amish parents' First Amendment argument was decisive. "The First Amendment pulls against the state's response. This is an ancient religion, not a new cult,"[23] Burger said. "Being raised on an Amish farm is equal or better than vocational school training." He voted to affirm, as he agreed with the Wisconsin Supreme Court judgment.

Douglas also affirmed, maintaining that "*Pierce* governs." Brennan agreed with Douglas. Potter Stewart also affirmed, saying that "it would be difficult to sustain if the group merely did not want its children to be able to read." Then Justice Byron White spoke. He again focused on the children in Amish families: "There has been little talk of the interests of the children. The rights of children have independent standing. They are not competent to make the decision the Amish want." For him, the case was "about sectarian children preparing for multiple societies, as much as or more than about what the majority grandly called the 'demands of the [First Amendment's] religion clauses.'"[24]

Justice Marshall also affirmed, but noted that "Black Muslims go back before Christ" but were not treated as an established religion. Finally, the junior Justice, Harry Blackmun, voted to affirm "on this full and devastating record," although he said the Court should not "paint [the decision] broadly for all cases, however."

Surprisingly, there were four opinions written in *Yoder*. Chief Justice Burger wrote the opinion for the majority. Stewart filed a separate concurring opinion, joined by Justice Brennan. White also filed a separate concurring opinion, joined by Justices Brennan and Stewart. Justice Douglas wrote an opinion, dissenting in part from Burger's views.

Burger's opinion emphasized the nature of the Court's balancing process. Wisconsin's interest in universal education for all children between seven and sixteen must be balanced against the Amish's religious freedom arguments. On balance, in this case, Burger concluded that the Amish

> have amply supported their claim that enforcement of the compulsory formal education requirement after the eighth grade would gravely endanger if not destroy the free exercise of their religious beliefs. . . . As the record so strongly shows, the values and programs of the modern secondary school are in sharp conflict with the fundamental mode of life mandated by the Amish religion; modern laws requiring compulsory secondary education have accordingly engendered great concern and conflict. . . . By exposing Amish children to worldly influences contrary to beliefs, and by substantially interfering with the religious development of the Amish child, [the law] contravenes the basic religious tenets and practice of the Amish faith, both as to the parent and the child.

The case, for the majority, "involves the fundamental interest of parents, as contrasted with that of the State, to guide the religious future and education of their children."

The history and culture of Western civilization reflect a strong tradition of parental concern for the nurture and upbringing of their children. This primary role of the parents in the upbringing of their children is now established beyond debate as an enduring American tradition.[25]

In his concurring opinion in *Yoder,* White wrote of his concern for the Amish kids:

> It is possible that most Amish children will wish to continue living the rural life of their parents. . . . Others, however, may wish to become nuclear physicists, ballet dancers, computer programmers, or historians, and for these occupations, formal training will be necessary.

He noted that the trial record indicated that "many children desert the Amish faith when they come of age." However, he joined the judgment of the majority because

> the sincerity of the Amish religious policy here is uncontested, because the potentially adverse impact of the state requirement is great, and because the state's valid interest in education has already been largely satisfied by the eight years the children have already spent in school.

Justice Douglas dissented in part in the arrests of the two parents whose children did not testify in the state court trial. Only Frieda Yoder spoke in court and she loudly indicated that it was her choice not to attend school after the eighth grade for religious reasons. But Douglas did not know whether Barbara Miller and Vernon Yutzy felt the same way Frieda did.

> It would be an invasion of the mature child's rights to permit such a [parental] imposition [of religious principles] without canvassing his views. . . . Recent cases have clearly held that the children themselves have constitutionally protectible interests.

Because two of the children were not heard at all, and because Douglas believed "that the children should be entitled to be heard," he dissented from the Court's judgment.

The U.S. Supreme Court has repeatedly indicated that parents' authority is dominant in the education of their children as well as in the religious upbringing of their children. *Stanley v Illinois,* the "ridiculous" case involving termination of parental rights, is another area where family conflicts have led to court involvement. Most recently in the 1996 case, *M.L.B. v S.L.J., individually and as next friend of the minor children, S.L.J. and M.L.J., et ux.,*[26] the Justices grappled with another child custody case—with a procedural wrinkle.

After eight years of marriage, M.L.B. and S.J.L. were divorced in June 1992. The children remained in their father's custody, as the parents had agreed at the time of the divorce. In November 1993, the father, who had remarried, filed suit in Chancery Court seeking to end his former wife's parental rights and to have his new wife formally adopt his two children. M.L.B.'s parental rights to her two minor children, a boy and a girl, were "terminated forever" by the Mississippi Chancery Court judge in December 1994.

The two children were formally awarded to the children's natural father and his second wife (whose adoption of the children the judge approved). M.L.B. filed a timely appeal. However, Mississippi law "conditioned her right to appeal on prepayment of record preparation fees estimated at $2,352.66." Lacking funds to pay, she sought leave to file the appeal *in forma pauperis.* The Mississippi Supreme Court denied her application because, under Mississippi precedent and law, there is no right to proceed *in forma pauperis* in civil appeals. She then requested and was granted a writ of certiorari by the U.S. Supreme Court. The question of law: May a State, consistent with the Due Process and Equal Protection Clauses of the Fourteenth Amendment, condition appeals from trial court decrees forever terminating parental rights on the affected parent's ability to pay record-preparation fees?

In a 6:3 opinion, the U.S. Supreme Court reversed and remanded the decision of the Mississippi Supreme Court. Associate Justice Ruth B. Ginsburg delivered the opinion of the Court. Associate Justice Kennedy wrote a concurring opinion. Chief Justice Rehnquist and Justice Thomas each wrote dissenting opinions.

In addition to raising the parent-child relationship, Ginsburg wrote, *M.L.B.* forces the Court to "confront the 'age-old problem' of providing equal justice for poor and rich, weak and powerful alike."[27] The case demands close scrutiny by the Court, because a family association "of basic importance in our society" is at stake. Ginsburg cited precedents where unanimous Courts were of the view that (1) "the interests of parents in their relationship with their children is sufficiently fundamental to come within the finite class of liberty interests protected by the Fourteenth Amendment," and that (2) "few consequences of judicial action are so grave as the severance of natural family ties."

> Choices about marriage, family life, and the upbringing of children are among associational rights this Court has ranked as "of basic importance to our society." M.L.B.'s case, involving the State's authority to sever permanently a parent-child bond, demands the close consideration the Court has long required when a family association so undeniably important is at stake. . . . In accord with the substance and sense of our [earlier decisions] we place decrees forever terminating parental rights in the category of cases in which the state may not "bolt the door to equal justice."

The Court majority ordered Mississippi to provide the court transcript that M.L.B. needed for her appeal.

There were two dissenting opinions. Justice Thomas's dissent was the harsher. He rejected the Court's historic concern for equal justice for poor as well as rich. The Court's *"fetish for indigency,"* he wrote, is categorically misplaced because of one fundamental reason:

> The Equal Protection Clause does not impose on the states an affirmative duty to lift the handicaps flowing from differences in economic circumstances. [That clause] shields only against purposeful discrimination. It is not a panacea for perceived social or economic inequity; it seeks to guarantee equal laws, not equal results.

In the 1999 Term, the Justices dealt with a very sensitive issue associated with the education of children: Must a state provide "supportive services" for a wheelchair-bound and ventilator-dependent youngster so that he could attend public school?[28] When Garret F., the respondent in the case, was four years old, his spinal column was severed in a motorcycle accident. Though paralyzed from the neck down, his mental capacities were unaffected.

Justice Stevens, for a seven-person Court majority, noted that Garrett

> is able to speak, control his motorized wheelchair through use of a puff and suck straw, and to operate a computer with a device that responds to head movements. Garret is currently a student in the Cedar Rapids Community School District, he attends regular classes in a typical school program, and

his academic performance has been a success. Garret is, however, ventilator-dependent, and therefore requires a responsible individual nearby to attend to certain physical needs while he is in school.

During Garrett's early school years, his parents and his extended family provided for his physical care during the school day. However, after many years, Garret's mother (Charlene F.) asked the school district to "accept financial responsibility for the health care services that Garret requires during the school day."[29] The district denied her request, for it believed that it was not legally obligated to provide continuous one-on-one nursing services.

Charlene F., however, relying on the federal Individuals with Disabilities Education Act (IDEA)[30] and on Iowa law, requested and received a hearing before the Iowa Department of Education. (IDEA authorized federal financial assistance to states that agree to provide children like Garret F. with special education and "related services.") An administrative law judge (ALJ) received extensive information concerning Garrett's special needs, as well as the school district's treatment of other special needs students, and reports of assistance provided to ventilator-dependent students in other states.

The ALJ's forty-seven-page report supported the mother's contention that the district had to "bear financial responsibility for all of the services in dispute, including continuous nursing services." The school district challenged the report's findings in federal district court, but the court approved the ALJ's ruling and granted summary judgment against the district. The U.S. Court of Appeals affirmed, noting that because Iowa is a recipient of federal funds under the IDEA, it "had a statutory duty to provide all disabled children a 'free appropriate public education,' which includes 'related services.'" The school district's lawyer immediately filed a writ of certiorari in the Court, which was granted during the Court's 1998 Term "in order to resolve this conflict."

For the Justices, the conflict revolved around the meaning of the term "related services" in the IDEA. Congress defined it as those supportive services that "may be required to assist a child with a disability to benefit from special education." And there is no dispute that in-school services at issue are within the covered category of "supportive services." However, were "medical services, that is, services performed by a physician," a part of the "related services" concept or were they an exclusion? This was a key to resolving the conflict; Congress limited medical services to those that are "for diagnostic and evaluation purposes."

The school district's argument was essentially an economic one. It created a case-by-case multifactor test to determine whether the district would pay for the services. (1) Was the care continuous or intermittent? (2) Could existing school health care personnel provide the service? (3) What would the service cost if district personnel could not perform it? (4) What were the potential consequences if the service was not performed? Using this test, the district refused to pay for Garrett's in-school health care services.

The Court rejected the use of such a non-legally-supported test. Further, the district did not explain why these characteristics "make one service any more 'medical' than another." "Through its multi-factor test, the District seeks to establish a kind of *undue-burden* exemption primarily based on the cost of the requested services. [All four factors are] related to costs." The district's policy was clearly counter to the IDEA. And Stevens said that for the Court to accept the test—and the results in Garrett's case—"would require us to engage in judicial lawmaking."

> Congress intended [with passage of the IDEA] to "open the door of public education" to all qualified children and "required participating States to educate handicapped children with non-handicapped children whenever possible." . . . This case is about whether meaningful access to the public schools will be assured, not the level of education that a school must finance once access is attained. The District must fund such "related services" in order to help guarantee that students like Garrett are integrated into the public schools.

Associate Justice Thomas again dissented, joined by Justice Kennedy. For the Justice from Pin Point, Georgia, the majority's action was "unwarranted" judicial lawmaking. The majority's major error was to focus "on the provider of the services, rather than the services themselves."

> Congress enacted IDEA to increase the *educational* opportunities available to disabled children, not to provide medical care for them. As such, where Congress decided to require a supportive service—including speech pathology, occupational therapy, and audiology—that appears "medical" in nature, it took care to do so explicitly. Congress specified these services precisely because it recognized that they would otherwise fall under the broad "medical services" exclusion.

Congress, contrary to Stevens's view, required the states "to provide an education that is only 'appropriate' rather than requiring them to *maximize* the potential of disabled students." The majority's interpretation of IDEA has "imposed upon the States a burden of unspecified proportions and weight." In Garrett's case, because he

> requires continuous, one-on-one care, throughout the school day, all agree that the district must hire an additional employee to attend solely to respondent. This will cost a minimum of $18,000 per year.

The majority's ruling disregards the principle of judicial restraint and "blindsides unwary States with fiscal obligations they could not have anticipated. I respectfully dissent," concluded Thomas.

Garrett's case leads to another issue, the parents' responsibility for the mental and physical health and welfare of their children.

III. The Mental and Physical Health and Welfare of the Child

Intimate spousal and child abuse is, unfortunately, a fundamental family relationship dilemma. The state has imposed on family privacy and autonomy when necessary "to protect children in matters of physical and emotional well-being."[31] And the U.S. Supreme Court has been asked by parents to determine whether the state action violates the Fourteenth Amendment.

Can a divorced parent bring suit against her former husband and his girlfriend in federal district court under "diversity of citizenship" jurisdiction[32] for alleged torts committed against her two daughters, L.R. and S.R.? Carol Ankenbrandt went into federal district court to seek damages for her two girls. Both were sexually and physically abused by her former husband, Jon Richards, and his girlfriend, Debra Kesler.[33]

The federal trial judge granted Richards's motion to dismiss the lawsuit, adhering to a nineteenth-century U.S. Supreme Court precedent stating that "the subject of 'domestic relations' of husband and wife, parent and child, belongs to the laws of the States, and not the laws of the United States." Because the suit fell under the "domestic relations" exception, the federal court lacked jurisdiction to hear the case. The U.S. Court of Appeals affirmed, without a written opinion.

Ankenbrandt appealed to the U.S. Supreme Court and the Court granted certiorari to address the "following questions": Is there a domestic relations exception to federal jurisdiction? If so, does it permit a district court judge to abstain from exercising diversity jurisdiction over a tort action for damages?[34]

Justice White wrote the opinion for the Court. (Justices Blackmun, Stevens, and Thomas wrote separate concurring opinions.) Justice White continually evidenced great concern about a child's mental and physical development. He wrote an opinion answering the questions in a way that allowed the mother to bring her suit in the federal court.

While there has been a "domestic relations" exception in federal jurisprudence for almost two centuries, it was a narrow one. Because, White reasoned,

> the domestic relations exception encompasses only cases involving the issuance of a divorce, alimony, or child custody decree, we necessarily find that the Court of Appeals erred by affirming the District Court's invocation of this exception.

The federal trial judge, White wrote, should not have abstained from hearing the case. "Absent any pending proceeding in state tribunals, therefore, the application by the lower federal courts of the abstention doctrine was clearly erroneous."

> The exception has no place in a suit such as this one, in which a former spouse sues another on behalf of children alleged to have been abused. . . . Accordingly, we reverse the decision of the Court of Appeals and remand the case for further proceedings consistent with this opinion.

Can a father take color photographs of his partially nude minor daughter? Or is such behavior subject to state constraints and punishment? Clearly, this is a question that barely scratches the surface of a major problem in contemporary American society: child pornography. In the face of this problem, Massachusetts and almost forty other states passed criminal statutes to punish those involved in the business of child pornography. Massachusetts passed General Law 272:29A in 1982. It provided punishment of between ten and twenty years in prison, and a fine of up to $50,000, for any person who [with lascivious intent][35] hired, coerced, solicits, or entices, employs, procures, uses, causes, encourages, or knowingly permits a child under 18 years of age to pose or be exhibited in a state of nudity or to participate or engage in any live performance or in any act that depicts, describes, or represents sexual conduct for purpose of visual representation or reproduction in any book, magazine, pamphlet, motion picture film, photograph or picture.[36]

In 1984, the respondent in the case,[37] Douglas Oakes, took about ten color photos of his well-endowed fourteen-year-old stepdaughter, L.S., who was at the time attending modeling school. The photos depict the daughter sitting, reclining, and lying on top of a bar, clad only in a red and white striped bikini panty and a red scarf. "The scarf," wrote Justice O'Connor in the judgment of the Court, "does not cover L.S.'s breasts, which are fully exposed in all the photographs."

Indicted, tried, and convicted of violating 29A, Oakes was sentenced to ten years imprisonment. A divided Massachusetts Supreme Judicial Court reversed his conviction, however, holding that Oakes's posing of his stepdaughter was "speech for First Amendment purposes because it could not 'fairly be isolated' from the 'expressive process of taking her picture.'" The court struck down the statute because it was "substantially over-broad under the First Amendment." It would make criminal, the court argued, the conduct of "a parent who takes a frontal view picture of his or her naked one-year-old running on a beach or romping in a wading pool." The dissenters argued that "permitting a minor child to pose for [nude] photographs is no more speech than is setting a house on fire in order to photograph a burning house."

The U.S. Supreme Court granted certiorari to review the state supreme court's decision. After certiorari was granted, the Massachusetts law was amended, adding the "lascivious intent" language to the nudity portion of the statute. Although one of the arguments was mooted by the revision of the law, the other one was still live: Was Oakes's conviction under 29A "as applied" constitutional? Under the circumstances, the majority vacated and remanded the case back to the state court.

Justice Brennan, joined by Justices Marshall and Stevens, dissented. For the trio, "nudity, without more, is protected expression." Because the Massachusetts statute's

prohibition extends to posing or exhibiting children "in a state of nudity," rather than merely to their participation in live or simulated sexual conduct, the statute clearly restrains expression within the ambit of the First Amendment.

Brennan distinguished between the production of child porn and a father taking nude photographs of his minor child. The "coercive enlistment, both overt and subtle, of children in the production of pornography is a grave and widespread evil which the States are amply justified in seeking to eradicate." Massachusetts "lacks an overriding interest, however, in prohibiting adults from allowing minors to appear naked in photographs." The trio would affirm the decision of the state supreme court.

There is another less-than-ideal parent-child situation that unfortunately traumatizes the lives of many family members in America: sexual abuse of a young child. In October 1986, a Howard County, Maryland, grand jury charged respondent Sandra Ann Craig with child abuse, first- and second-degree sexual offenses, perverted sexual practice, and assault and battery.[38] At the parents' demand, the prosecutors sought to invoke a Maryland statutory procedure that permits a judge to receive, by one-way closed-circuit television, the testimony of a child witness who is alleged to be a victim of child abuse. The trial judge must first determine whether testimony in the courtroom "will result in the child suffering serious emotional distress such that the child cannot reasonably communicate."[39]

Once the procedure is invoked, the child witness, the prosecutor, and the defense counsel withdraw to a separate room. The judge, jury, and the defendant remain in the courtroom. The child is then examined and cross-examined by counsel. A video monitor records and displays the witness's testimony to those in the courtroom. The defendant remains in electronic communication with defense counsel, and objections may be made and ruled on as if the witness were testifying in the courtroom itself.

Before the *Craig* trial began, the state presented expert testimony that Brooke Etze, the abused six-year-old girl, would suffer "serious emotional distress such that Brooke could not reasonably communicate [when asked to testify at trial]." The defendant's lawyer objected to the use of the procedure on the Sixth Amendment's "Confrontation" Clause grounds.[40] The trial judge overruled, arguing that Craig retained "the essence of the right of confrontation." The jury found Craig guilty on all counts, and the Maryland Court of Special Appeals affirmed the conviction.

The Court of Appeals of Maryland, however, reversed and remanded for a new trial. It concluded that the showing by the prosecutor that Brooke could not testify in the same room as the defendant Craig "was insufficient to reach the high threshold required by [the Confrontation Clause guarantee]." The U.S. Supreme Court granted certiorari "in order to resolve the important Confrontation Clause issues raised by this case."

In a 5:4 decision, the Supreme Court, in an opinion written by Justice O'Connor, overturned the State Supreme Court decision. In a difficult balancing act, called by the dissenters, "interest-balancing analysis where the text of the Constitution simply does not permit it," Justice O'Connor concluded that the Maryland statutory process did not violate the Sixth Amendment's Confrontation Clause protection.

> We have never held that the Confrontation Clause guarantees criminal defendants the absolute right to a face-to-face meeting with witnesses against them at trial. . . . Any exception to this right would surely be allowed only when necessary to further an important public policy.

That amendment's central purposes were realized in the use of the innovative technology. While face-to-face confrontation was important and may not "easily be dispensed with," it was not an indispensable element of criminal procedure, especially given the state's interest in preventing additional emotional harm to the young witness for the prosecution. "[Face-to-face confrontation] is not the *sine qua non* of the confrontation right." The "critical inquiry in this case," wrote O'Connor was "whether use of the procedure was necessary to further an important state interest." O'Connor concluded that the state had a "substantial interest in protecting children who are allegedly victims of child abuse from the trauma of testifying against the alleged perpetrator," and that the procedure was necessary to further that state interest.

> We conclude today that a State's transcendent interest in the physical and psychological well-being of child abuse victims may be sufficiently important to outweigh, at least in some cases, a defendant's right to face his or her accusers in court.

Associate Justice Scalia, and his very odd trio of "joiners," Justices Brennan, Marshall, and Stevens, dissented. For him, the Confrontation Clause was unmistakably clear. "Seldom has this Court failed so conspicuously to sustain a categorical guarantee of the Constitution against the tide of prevailing current opinion."[41] Because, he concluded, "the text of the Sixth Amendment is clear, and because the Constitution is meant to protect against, rather than conform to, current 'widespread belief,' I respectfully dissent."

In 1979, the U.S. Supreme Court tackled yet another tough issue regarding the treatment of a mentally impaired child. It had to wrestle with the question of what "process is due" minor children whose parents "voluntarily" admitted them to a state mental hospital. A class-action suit, *Parham. Commissioner, Department of Human Resources of Georgia v J.R., et al.*,[42] was brought by the appellees, children who were being treated in a Georgia mental institution. They asked for: (1) a declaratory judgment from the federal judge that Georgia's procedures for "voluntary" commitment of children under the age of eighteen violated the Due Process Clause of the Fourteenth Amendment and (2) an injunction against their future enforcement.

The challenged admission process had a number of gates that must be entered by the parents and the hospital administrator before a minor child could be admitted. It began with an application for hospitalization signed by a parent or guardian. The superintendent of the mental facility then admits, temporarily, any child for "observation and diagnosis." If, after observation, medical experts find "evidence of mental illness" and that the child is "suitable for treatment" in the facility, the child may be admitted "for such period and under such conditions as may be authorized by law."

Under Georgia law, any "voluntary patient" who has been hospitalized for more than five days may be discharged at the request of a parent or guardian. Even without such a parental request, the superintendent has an

> affirmative duty to release any child who has recovered from his mental illness or who has sufficiently improved that the superintendent determines that hospitalization of the patient is no longer desirable.

At the time of the lawsuit, there were eight regional mental hospitals in Georgia. The superintendents of seven of these facilities were deposed for the trial. The eighth hospital, in Rome, Georgia, had no children being treated. Each hospital set its own specific procedures for the admission and discharge of children. And there is "substantial variation among the institutions with regard to their admission procedures and their procedures for review of patients after they have been admitted." There were a total of 141 children in the seven regional facilities; the average stay was 193 days (although the average stay at J.L.'s and J.R.'s facility was 456 days).

The two minor children in the suit were J.L., who was "voluntarily" admitted by his parents, and J.R., who, as a neglected child, was admitted by the state, his formal guardian. J.L. (who died when he was about fourteen years old) was first admitted to a regional hospital in 1970 when he was six. The admitting physician interviewed J.L. and his parents, who were divorced. J.L. was diagnosed as having a "hyperkinetic reaction of childhood." J.L., his mother, and his stepfather participated in family therapy while he was hospitalized. In 1972, the child was returned to his mother to live at home but go to school at the hospital. However, the parents could not control their son's behavior and, after a few months, requested readmission. In 1974, the parents relinquished their parental rights to the county. He could not be placed in a foster-home "with a warm, supported, truly involved couple." In October 1975, J.L. (with J.R.) filed the lawsuit, requesting a court order placing him "in a less drastic environment suitable to his needs [i.e., a foster home]."

When he was three months old, J.R. was declared a neglected child by the county and taken from his natural parents. He was placed in seven different foster homes before his admission to the mental health facility at the age of seven. He was disruptive in school. "Because of his abnormal behavior, J.R.'s seventh set of foster parents requested his removal from their home." The Department of Family and Children Services sought his admission to a regional mental health center. He was diagnosed as borderline retarded, and "suffered an unsocialized, aggressive reaction of childhood." Admission to the regional health center was recommended because "he would benefit from the structured environment" of the hospital and would enjoy living and playing with boys of the age."

The Georgia processes were challenged by the appellees. They claimed that the Fourteenth Amendment's Due Process Clause guaranteed them a "post-admission adversary-type hearing by an impartial medical panel."[43]

A federal three-judge district court, after hearing evidence, including "expert and lay testimony and extensive exhibits and after visiting two of the State's regional mental health hospitals," ruled that Georgia's mental health statute was unconstitutional: There were no procedural safeguards for the child. The law

> failed to protect adequately the appellees' due process rights and that the process due the children included at least the right after notice to an adversary-type hearing before an *impartial tribunal*.

In addition, the court ordered the state to "expend funds to provide alternative treatment facilities for forty-six juveniles who, in the opinion of the District Court, did not require hospitalization."[44]

The U.S. Supreme Court noted "probable jurisdiction" to answer the question posed by the incarcerated children and their lawyers:

> Whether a statute authorizing commitment of juveniles to mental health facilities at the request of the parent and the concurrence of the institution deprives the juvenile of liberty without due process.[45]

The U.S. Solicitor General's Office, headed by "General" Wade McCree, submitted an *amicus curiae* brief and participated in oral argument. The federal government's view was that the Georgia statute's principal failure was that there was no flexible, informal, *nonadversarial* process whereby any person "adversely affected by the commitment order may challenge it before an independent tribunal, either before or after commitment."

For a number of reasons, the question was a troublesome one for the brethren, one that led to scheduling a second oral argument in October 1978. It went to the core of the parent-child relationship, and many of the Justices were wary of a scheme that had no process for reviewing the parents' decision to seek hospitalization for their child.

Additionally, it was a question raised the same time the Court was wrestling with the question of parental notification and consent when their minor pregnant child sought an abortion (*Bellotti*). For Justice Powell, the author of the *Bellotti* decision (the Massachusetts parental-notification abortion case), there had to be some parallelism between parental authority in *Parham* and parental authority in *Bellotti*.

Case Study: *Parham v J.R.*, 1979

"This is a complicated case," were the first words Sam Estreicher wrote to his boss, Justice Powell a few days before the first *Parham* oral argument (set for December 7, 1977). He thought the Georgia "scheme does not provide the process that is constitutionally due" a child.[46] There were no provisions "for representation of the distinct interests of the minor child, which on occasion may conflict with the interests of the parents." Also, given the less-than-perfect state of the field of psychiatry, without an independent review, medical errors may deprive the child of liberty without due process. The child does have a liberty interest in ensuring that his admission is the best possible avenue of action his parents and the state could take. "Civil commitment is a deprivation of liberty; it is the harshest action the State can take against the individual through the administrative process," Estreicher argued. He implored his boss to consider the possibility of a flexible, non-adversarial hearing by an independent tribunal, especially for children under fourteen years of age.

In the December 7, 1977, Conference Session after oral argument in *Parham*, Powell relied on Estreicher's urgings. The eight members (Justice Blackmun was absent from the Conference Session) voted to reverse the substantive recommendation of the three-judge district court (regarding the disposition of forty-six children then in Georgia mental hospitals). As Justice Brennan said: "Courts should not start operating state hospitals."

However, there was no consensus on the question of what process is due the children "voluntarily" committed into these facilities. Voting to reverse the district court on the procedural due process issue were Justices Stewart and Rehnquist. Stewart remarked that he could not "reject a [fundamental] presupposition of our society, i.e. that parents make these decisions for children."

Voting to affirm the district court were Justices Brennan, Marshall, and Stevens. Brennan, the senior Associate Justice spoke after Burger. He agreed with the Solicitor General. There was no need for the "full panoply of due process." There should be an informal hearing and the "child's representative need not be a lawyer." Marshall echoed Brennan's views: "[You] don't need a full judicial hearing; there should be an independent decision maker—who could be a social worker."

Voting to affirm in part on the procedural question were the Chief Justice and Justice Powell. Burger said that the district court ignored the fundamental importance of parental authority. Further, there were "no findings that any member of the class was not mentally ill [or that] parents of all class members were unfit to exercise parental authority." However, he did comment that "maybe there should be an outside psychiatrist." Justice Powell said that he would affirm

> to the extent of holding the Georgia procedure inadequate. I would afford more flexibility for the state to formulate informal non-adversary procedures. There should be an established mode of independent review.

However, Powell then said that the parents' decision, "if concurred in by doctor, should be presumptively right."

Justice White was not sure as to the procedural question. As always, he was concerned about the children. He maintained that "the child must have an independent 'champion' but [doesn't] need a lawyer. The state should have some verification procedure and that commitment not be allowed on the sole say of the parents." Blackmun was absent and did not participate in the *Parham* discussions.

Burger assigned the opinion to Justice White. White, however, had changed his mind on the procedural question. On December 12, he asked the Chief to "reassign" the case to a Justice who had "affirmed the procedural holding." Burger immediately sent a Memo to his colleagues:

> In the "sticky" complexities of this week's assignments I have apparently "miscued" on this case and assignment to Byron is withdrawn. My view was that the statute as written could not be sustained but that as applied it could pass muster. I will re-examine, with a cleaner mind than I had late Saturday, and you will hear more. It may be one where Harry's vote on possible re-argument may be crucial in light of my bifurcated posture.

A few days later, Chief Justice Burger wrote his brethren:

> I do not now pass on whether there is a liberty interest in minor children which precludes commitment on the application of a parent. Assuming, *arguendo*, that there is such an interest, I believe the Georgia statute as construed and applied to provide the inquiry by way of informal information gathering, satisfies due process. For "lineup" purposes, this places me in the company of Potter, Byron, and Bill Rehnquist. If other votes remain as recorded, the case is 4-4 and in my view merits re-argument.[47]

Although the clerks and their bosses were puzzled by the Burger comments, on January 13, 1978, the brethren voted to schedule reargument the following Term.

The Justices revisited *Parham* in October 1978. The Conference Session took place on October 13. This time, with Justice Blackmun participating, the majority voted to reverse the district court's opinion in its entirety. Only three Justices, Brennan, Marshall, and Stevens, voted to affirm the district court's procedural due process order. Brennan said bluntly: "The child needs protection against unlawful commitment." Marshall said: "There should be some independent decision-maker, not a judge or lawyer, [it] could be a social worker. It should not be an adversarial hearing." Stevens again called for an "independent decision maker." There must also be a procedure developed to determine whether the parent is fit to speak for the child.

Five others, Chief Justice Burger and Justices Stewart, White, Blackmun, and Rehnquist, voted to reverse both parts of the district court order. For Burger this time around, "Georgia's statutes afford abundant protection." Stewart reiterated his position about the primacy of parental decision making. "The commitment is voluntary and premised on the age-old premise that a parent speaks for a child. [The Court's early precedents] indicate that the Constitution requires the State to leave parents free to act for children without any oversight. Until and unless the parent is found to be unfit, commitment should be left to the parent."

White could not go as far as Stewart, for he believed "that the case was close." He believed there "were some limits on parental authority. The real question is whether Georgia has provided [children] some minimal safeguards." Blackmun, although "not at rest with my vote," nevertheless voted to reverse. "Georgia's procedures are constitutionally valid but the opinion should make it clear that some safeguards are needed." Rehnquist, noted Powell, "agrees generally with Potter Stewart and Byron."

Justice Powell's new clerk, Eric, was more cautious than Sam Estreicher had been, and Powell reflected this attitude in conference. He told the conference that he was "very tentative on the procedural due process issue and I may affirm in part." However, "the way our opinion is written will have a great deal to do with how I finally come down." For him, the "key necessity is to ascertain the fitness of the parents [and the] social worker. If the parents are not fit, there should be a guardian *ad litem* for the child."

Given the voting lineup, 6:3, Burger assigned the opinion to himself. His first draft did not circulate until February 1979. It was, as Powell wrote to his law clerk, "verbose." He would "probably have to write, but I want to give the Chief Justice a chance to rewrite his rambling opinion."

By mid-March both the Brennan and Stewart opinions circulated among the chambers. According to Powell's law clerk, Brennan's opinion called for only a postcommitment "full adversary hearing." Eric warned Powell off joining any part of the opinion, for "it is full of rather inflammatory dicta with which I do not think you should be associated." It was also not a well-written opinion, although not as bad as the Chief's. "There is no attempt to make a careful distinction between what the Constitution requires and what WJB thinks would be good policy."

Justice Stewart's concurring opinion, Eric continued, "is appealing in its straightforward simplicity." His theory is that "so long as the presumption that a parent speaks for a child is intact, no constitutionally protected interest of the child is invaded by the 'voluntary' commitment to a mental hospital." It is, Eric felt, a "rather extreme position. [It] seems to permit an absolute 'hands off' stance by the state, no matter what conditions in the institution might be like or how long the confinement lasts."

Finally, his clerk cautioned Powell about doing too much in *Parham,* lest it became diffuclt for Powell to hold his court in the *Bellotti v Baird* opinion he was writing.

> Perhaps it would not be a good idea to argue in *Parham* for the general analysis we hope will command a court in *Bellotti.* It would be unfortunate to lose majority support for a good idea just because it was raised in the wrong case.

The following day Powell wrote a letter to Burger, with copies to the Conference. He made an effort, ultimately successful, to persuade Burger to modify his opinion so that Powell could "find common ground, if this is possible." Burger's draft "was helpful in discussing generally the range of possible dispositions of the issues in the case. Already Bill Brennan and Potter have views that differ rather substantially in certain respects."

Attached to Powell's letter was a Memo stating Powell's views, in summary terms, about how these "'voluntary child commitment' cases should be analyzed and resolved." The Virginian told his Chief "that we were not too far apart on most of the questions" and he hoped that the Chief could use the "thoughts" in the memo in the next version of the opinion.

Two months later Burger answered Powell's letter. "Rather than respond to it at the time, I have made changes [in my draft opinion] in an effort to accommodate your views." However, Burger rejected Powell's views about postcommitment due process, saying "that my review of the record convinces me that this question is not really before us. I think it is a question that should be dealt with by the District Court on remand."

Powell immediately responded, saying, in part, "[C]ertainly I will go as far as I can in joining you." In a letter marked "Personal," Burger immediately shot back:

> *In an effort to meet your points I am losing other votes.* Unless you join me fully, I will have no choice but to return to my basic position—which I

think is the correct one. I submit that you are underestimating the dangers of "overloading" states with an excess of due process.

Powell, however, continued to press for changes in Burger's opinion. On June 1, 1979, he told Burger that "there still remains some arguable tension in the language—though not the holdings." Powell then offered some suggestions for lessening the "tension." In reality, the tension existed between Burger's intemperate words about the demise of the traditional nuclear family, citing *Danforth* opinion dicta[48] in his *Parham* draft, and Powell's *Bellotti* opinion emphasized the opposite view. "[Your argument] tends to undercut the critical assumption in my *Bellotti* opinion that parents *do* have an important role to play in their daughters' abortion decisions."

Further, in *Bellotti*, "I do not question" the Massachusetts authorization of a judicial by-pass hearing in Superior Court, while Burger does question the state's right to authorize some kind of postcommitment hearing.

My conclusion in *Bellotti* is that providing for recourse to a hearing before a judge is valid. If we can resolve—by what I perceive to be relatively minor language changes—my concerns about *Bellotti*, I will be happy to join [your opinion].[49]

A few days later Burger circulated his third draft, accommodating Powell's suggestions. Powell wrote back: "I am now happy to join your opinion in this case."

There were three opinions written in the case, announced on June 29, 1979, the last day of the Court's Term. Chief Justice Burger wrote the majority opinion for the Court. He was joined by Justices White, Blackmun, Powell, and Rehnquist. Justice Stewart wrote a separate concurring opinion. Justice Brennan, joined by Justices Marshall and Stevens, wrote the third opinion, concurring in part and dissenting in part.

Burger's opinion, the fourth and final version, held that the district court erred in holding unconstitutional Georgia's procedures for admitting a child for treatment to a state mental hospital. On the record presented, the state's fact-finding processes are *minimally* consistent with constitutional guarantees of due process of law. Balancing the rights of the child, the primary role of the parents, and the state's interest, a balancing test devised by Justice Powell a few years earlier,[50] the majority concluded: "Not withstanding a child's protectible liberty interest in not being confined unnecessarily for medical treatment," the parents have the "dominant role, the *plenary authority,* in the decision [to commit], absent a finding of neglect or abuse."

Clearly, in *Parham,* Justice Powell had his cake and ate it. He pushed the Chief to change *Parham* substantively (something done with regularity by the brethren during Burger's tenure as Chief).[51] He also "held his court" in the *Bellotti* case. Powell's work, and the work of his law clerks, brilliantly underscores the ubiquitousness of politics in U.S. Supreme Court decision making.

What about corporal punishment of the child by school authorities? Can parents object on the grounds that such actions violate their child's constitutional rights? *Ingraham v Wright*[52] presented the Justices with questions concerning the use of corporal punishment in public schools. The petitioners, James Ingraham and Roosevelt Andrews, were junior-high-school students enrolled in the Charles R. Drew Junior High School in Dade County, Florida. (In October 1970, the school board approved Policy 5244; it provided for corporal punishment in the school system.)

The two students brought suit in federal district court against the school officials, Willie J. Wright, the school principal, and other high school and county education officials, alleging a deprivation of constitutional rights. "The evidence showed that the paddling of petitioners—using a wooden paddle to a recalcitrant student's buttocks—was exceptionally harsh."[53] Initially, Ingraham's punishment

> was to be five "licks," meaning five whacks on the buttocks with a flat wooden paddle about two feet long and two inches wide. [He] refused to "stoop over and get [his] licks." Two [administrators] hoisted Ingraham, struggling, onto a table and held him there so that Wright could administer the punishment. Ingraham counted more than twenty whacks in all. He left school and went home and found his backside "black and purple" and "tight and hot." His mother took him to a local health clinic [where] the examining doctor diagnosed the injury as a "hematoma." [This punishment] resulted in serious bruising and absence from school for 11 days.[54]

The constitutional rights violated were, the students argued, (1) the Eighth Amendment's prohibition of cruel and unusual punishment and (2) the Due Process Clause of the Fourteenth Amendment because they were entitled to a hearing before the punishment was inflicted.

The district court judge dismissed the complaint against the officials, finding "no constitutional basis for relief" in federal court because there was no "violation of a federal constitutional right."[55] A three-judge panel of the CA5 reversed,

> concluding that the punishment was so severe and oppressive as to violate the Eighth and Fourteenth Amendments, and that the procedures failed to satisfy the requirements of the Due Process clause.

Upon a rehearing, the CA5, sitting *en banc,* rejected the panel's conclusions and affirmed the judgment of the district court judge. The federal court of appeals

> went beyond the DC in holding that corporal punishment is not "punishment" within the Eighth Amendment and that it deprives a schoolchild of no "liberty" interest under the Fourteenth Amendment. The court refused to look at each individual instance of punishment to determine if it had been administered arbitrarily [in violation of the Fourteenth Amendment].

The U.S. Supreme Court granted certiorari, limited to two questions:

> First, whether the paddling of students as a means of maintaining school discipline constitutes cruel and unusual punishment in violation of the Eighth Amendment; and, second, to the extent that paddling is constitutionally permissible, whether the Due Process Clause of the Fourteenth Amendment requires prior notice and an opportunity to be heard.

This was not a new constitutional issue for the justices.[56] However, the question that quickly divided them, in the conferences and in the written dialogues that followed, was "whether to extend due process safeguards to new areas [of parent-child-state conflict]."[57]

Case Study: *Ingraham v Wright,* 1977

The Justices were of at least three minds when James Ingraham's petition for certiorari came to them for a vote in late May 1976. In the secret Conference Session, three Justices voted to grant certiorari (Justices Stevens, White, and Stewart), four voted to deny (the Chief and Justices Powell,[58]

Rehnquist, and Blackmun). However, two brethren, Justices Brennan and Marshall, voted to "join 3," which meant that certiorari was granted limited to the Eighth Amendment and Fourteenth Amendment (procedural due process) questions.[59]

The case was argued in Court in early November 1976. For Powell, there was no need for the Court to interpose in the case. As he wrote to his clerks, he quickly dismissed the two constitutional grounds for bringing suit: "The eighth amendment applies to punishment for crimes—not to school discipline, and no prior due process hearing is required." He thought that, as a matter of tort law, "just as a policeman is liable at common law—and under USC Section 1983—if he employs excessive force in making an otherwise valid arrest," excessive force may not be used by school administrators. The remedy, he believed, was the same: a civil suit for damages against the school administrators *after* the alleged injury occurred. "This makes a good deal of sense," he concluded.

The Chief Justice opened the discussion and, as he did on occasion, passed on the procedural due process issue. He would, however, affirm the CA5 on the cruel and unusual punishment issue. "The eighth amendment was never intended to cover school discipline." Justice Brennan spoke next. He voted to reverse the CA5 on both questions. "When school punishment is excessively severe, as here, it is cruel and unusual punishment!"

Justice Stewart spoke and voted next. He affirmed the CA5 on the cruel and unusual punishment issue but voted to reverse its procedural due process judgment. "Corporal punishment in schools is not 'punishment' within the meaning of the eighth amendment," he said. Further, "there is no life, liberty, or property taken away" in this case. But then he said he was "not at rest," that he was "quite uncertain whether there should be some limited prior hearing."

Justice White was next. As in the past, he was concerned about the treatment kids received from their parents and others. He was

not completely at rest but [I'm] inclined to agree with Brennan. Kids are compelled to go to school. This view, however, *does* involve a major expansion of the Eighth Amendment but this may be desirable.

However, he voted to reverse the CA5 on the procedural due process question, saying: "[O]ur prior cases do not require a hearing for deprivation of minor privileges." (He was to change his mind on this question a few months later.)

The next to speak, Justice Marshall, said that "teachers [and administrators] have a common law defense to corporal punishment. However, this case is so outrageous, [I] may have to reverse on [substantive] due process."

Justice Blackmun would affirm the CA5 on the Eighth Amendment issue. He said that

Professor Rogow [counsel for Ingraham] must have been on the lookout for an outrageous case. The basic issue is whether there is enough of a constitutional right to sue in federal court rather than in state courts.

He voted to reverse the CA5 on the procedural due process question.

Powell voted to affirm the CA5 on the cruel and unusual punishment matter. "The eighth amendment does not apply to schools." Punishment in schools is very different from "punishment pursuant to the criminal justice system. I would not expand the eighth amendment of the Constitution to class-room discipline." And there is, he said, "nothing to the procedural due process claim. Remedies are available under state law and are adequate," he concluded. Justice Rehnquist agreed with Powell. "The eighth is confined to criminal process and [Ingraham] does not have a right to a due process hearing." The "freshman" Justice, John P. Stevens, spoke last. He agreed with Justice Brennan and would have reversed the CA5 on both questions. "There is an invasion of 'liberty' for whatever time a child (even seconds) is detained. If the punishment is severe, there should be a prior hearing," he concluded.

After the brethren spoke and voted, Powell's tally sheet showed a 6:3 vote to affirm the CA5 on their Eighth Amendment judgment (the three in dissent were Justices Brennan, White, and Stevens). It showed a 5:3:1 vote to reverse the CA5 judgment that a student did not have a right to a hearing before punishment (the three who voted to affirm the CA5 were Justices Blackmun, Powell, and Rehnquist). Burger passed on the latter vote in the conference; however, a few weeks later he "advised me [Powell] he prefers my view that there is no due process right."

The following week, Burger assigned the writing of the majority opinion to White. An embarrassed White promptly responded to Burger: "My notes show that I was in the minority on the Eighth Amendment point. Someone else should perhaps take this on." The same day, November 15, 1976, Burger reassigned the opinion to Justice Powell.

The Virginian had a problem, however. It was expressed on the first page of a Memo from his law clerk: "The Eighth Amendment issue is easy; the due process [question] is more difficult but it can be worked out."

Six brethren agreed "on the proposition that corporal punishment . . . is not 'punishment' within the reach of the Eighth Amendment." However, the question of whether the absence of a hearing before the punishment denied Ingraham a procedural process due him was another matter entirely. As Powell's law clerk wrote:

> My understanding is that there are tentatively four votes to affirm (CJ, HAB, LFP, and WHR), three votes to reverse (WJB, BRW, and JPS), and two undecided but leaning toward reversal (PS, TM). *A reversal seems at this point more likely to win a Court.*

Given this problem, Powell and his law clerk, Charlie Ames, had to find a way to cobble together at least a five-man court to reverse on the "what process is due" issue. They had two options: (1) there "was no 'liberty' interest implicated, and no process is due," and (2) there "is a 'liberty' interest present in the right to be free from unjustified physical assaults." But that interest is protected by tort actions in state court against the unacceptable actions of school officials.

Powell's response to Charlie Ames's ideas and initial draft of the opinion was very positive: "Your draft opinion is an exceptionally fine piece of work. It has all the indicia of careful scholarship." However, wrote Powell, although "I know how 'fed up' you must be working on *Ingraham*, I would appreciate your doing a rather critical 'rewrite' of [some] portions."

> We have to consider this case with special care. It would be a major case in any term of court, it will be scrutinized critically by scholars, and its implications may well surprise even us. *To be sure, we may never get it by four of my Brothers!*

Less than a month later, and two internal drafts later, Powell still felt uncomfortable with it. "It will not be easy to obtain a Court in this case—however the opinion is written." The new draft still reflected the majority vote at Conference ("no Eighth Amendment right and no procedural due process right") and Powell hoped the others would agree.

If we cause tremors of anxiety among my "conservative" Brothers by declaring a constitutional right in personal security, the conclusion that claims of deprivation are satisfied by common law remedies will be viewed as a judicial "earthquake" by my "liberal" Brothers. The only hope of winning a Court in these circumstances, at least as I view it, is to write this case as narrowly as we possibly can, and still remain faithful to the analysis we have evolved.

The following day, February 12, 1977, Powell sent another Memo to Ames. Powell was concerned about getting the votes of his "conservative" brethren.

I am inclined to think that our best chance to win a "Court" is to return to an idea we discussed some weeks ago; that the analogy between being in "custody" of police and in "custody" of school authorities is sufficiently close for us to rely on it in a primary sense. [In both situations] there are two elements involved: "custody" and "punishment." And both are present where a child is in school under a compulsory attendance law. . . . I believe relatively little revision would be required to narrow the focus to the infliction of penal sanctions in a custodial situation. *I am inclined to think this is the way to win a Court.* It also leaves for another day some of the more difficult questions.

The first draft circulated to the brethren, on March 17, was the third one prepared by Powell. In it, he wrote that the Fourteenth Amendment did not require notice and a hearing before punishment because that practice is authorized and limited by the common law. However, there is a "liberty" interest, within the meaning of the Fourteenth Amendment, implicated where school authorities deliberately punish a child for misconduct by restraint and infliction of "appreciable physical pain."

Freedom from bodily restraint and punishment is "within the liberty interest in personal security that has historically been protected from state deprivation without due process of law." Florida provides "significant protection" against unjustified punishment of school children. "If the punishment is later found to be excessive, the school officials may be held liable in damages or be subject to criminal penalties. Imposing "additional administrative safeguards "as a constitutional requirement" would, reasoned Powell, "significantly intrude into the area of educational responsibility that lies primarily with the public school authorities."[60]

Justice Stewart was the fifth vote needed by Powell. Stewart "joined" the Powell draft immediately: "I shall have no problem whatever in joining your excellent opinion." It took the circulation by Powell of two additional drafts before he received "join" letters from the other three (Justice Rehnquist, on April 8, 1977; Justice Blackmun, on April 11; and the CJ, on April 13).

As Powell had predicted, his "conservative" brothers were indeed uncomfortable with his views about the liberty interest of schoolchildren. For example, Justice Rehnquist, on March 25, 1977, wrote Powell:

> I indicated [in Conference] that I felt there was no protected liberty or property interest that could be invoked by the school child. I still remain of that opinion, but am not intractable. My only hesitancy with your opinion relates to the holding that there is a protected liberty interest; I think your treatment of the Eighth Amendment issue and the due process issue is admirable. Since you and Potter both agree that there is a protected liberty interest in the school child, I am confident that my view to the contrary would not pick up a majority of the Court.

Rehnquist suggested a few changes in the "liberty" interest segment of the draft opinion, which were later incorporated into the majority opinion by Powell. However, the bottom line for Rehnquist was clear: "*you can count on mine* as a vote to affirm the Fifth Circuit."

As soon as Powell's draft was first circulated in mid- March, Justice White wrote the Conference a Memo: "In due course, I shall file a dissent in this case." In his dissent, White maintained that egregious corporal punishment can be the subject of the protections afforded by the Eighth Amendment and that schoolchildren are constitutionally entitled to a hearing before punishment.

> Although there were no ears cut off in this case, the record reveals beating[s] so severe that if they were inflicted on a hardened criminal for the commission of a serious crime, they might not pass constitutional muster. . . . [It is] plainly wrong to believe that there is a recognized difference between criminal and non-criminal punishment for purposes of the Eighth Amendment. [Regarding the second question raised in the litigation, White wrote:] There is no basis in logic or authority for the majority's suggestion that an action to recover damages for excessive corporal punishment affords substantially greater protection to the child than the informal conference mandated by *Goss,* i.e., a mandated procedural safeguard.

He quickly circulated the dissent and immediately received a "join" from Justice Brennan. A few weeks later, Justice Marshall "joined" White's dissent. And, on April 14, Justice Stevens "joined" White's dissent. He wrote Powell on the same day: "Although I have high regard for your analysis, I have decided to join Byron's entire dissent."

The final vote was 5:4. The decision was announced in Court on April 19, 1977.

In cases such as *Parham* and *Ingraham*, the Court majority adopted a very flexible, very pragmatic view of the procedures that may be "due" by carefully examining the context in which the due process was raised. Counter to the dissenters' arguments, the conservative majority, from the 1970s on, steadfastly refused to expand the meaning of due process guarantees to new and novel areas of parent-child-state relationships. They have succeeded in avoiding what they believe is an uncritical "dilution" of the liberty interest in the Fourteenth Amendment.

Since the mid-1980s, in the courts and in public policymaking, another parent-child issue has become visible—and contentious: the quality of life of a terminally ill child (or competent adult—see next chapter) has taken precedence over the sanctity of life.[61]

This dilemma is seen when babies are born prematurely, or have major medical problems, or are born terminally ill. It has become a very realistic problem because of the advances in medical technology, advances that have allowed physicians to use cutting-edge technology to keep these infants alive. In 1992, for example, almost six billion dollars was spent caring for such infants.[62]

This parental trauma raises the critical legal, medical, and ethical question: What is "the best interest of the child"? And, until very recently, this was a question answered by the parents with the advice of their doctor. As the Court noted in *Prince*:

It is cardinal with us that the custody, care and nurture of the child reside first in the parents, whose primary function and freedom include preparation for obligations the state can neither supply nor hinder.

The parents' ability to make such choices for their child has been based, since *Prince*, on the Fourteenth Amendment's "liberty" concept.

There is, however, a fundamental tension between parental rights and adolescent autonomy. The law defers to family autonomy over the autonomy of the minor child. Children's rights are not coextensive with those of adults. They are limited in reality. Since the middle of the twentieth century, the U.S. Supreme Court has said that, generally, the Fourteenth Amendment and the Bill of Rights protect minors as well as adults from unconstitutional state action.

However, when the Justices look at specific cases,

> it is apparent that there are countervailing, limiting principles. The Court has made it clear that there are some activities of children that may be subject to state regulation to a greater degree than those of adults.[63]

IV. Children's Rights: Visiting the Grandparents

Does a child have a right to visit his or her grandparents? Or can the parents limit such bonding between grandparents and grandchildren? Is it in the child's "best interest," based on the parents' perspective, not to have the grandparents visit the child? Can a court order grandparent visitation without infringing upon the right of family privacy?

"Certainly, there are those extreme situations where denial of contact with a grandparent is appropriate."[64]

> However, there are also many times when the grandparent, who has played a critical role in a child's life, is suddenly left without the right to visit that child because "Mom and Dad said so." Maybe it is because Grandma and Grandpa said the wrong thing; or because Grandpa can no longer give Mom and Dad the extra money they need; or because Mom and Dad are afraid Grandma will discover they are abusing their child.[65]

Given the reality of such child-parent-grandparent tensions, and given the commitment to the ideal of the family, including the grandparents, all fifty states have laws granting grandparents—and, in some states, other nonparental third parties—visitation rights under certain circumstances. The Washington State grandparent visitation statute, however, was the broadest of all the state laws. *Any* person at *any* time may request visitation rights from a state judge.

The grandparents used the Washington law because they were denied the opportunity to visit with their two granddaughters more than once a month. The mother challenged the constitutionality of the state law. And, in that case,[66] just recently, the U.S. Supreme Court said that that was a matter for the parents to decide, not the children, not the grandparents, and certainly not for the state to decide.

Jennifer and Gary Troxel "doted on their young granddaughters," began the *Washington Post* story.[67] It ran one week before oral arguments between the Troxels' lawyers and the lawyers for the mother of the two girls, Tommie Granville, took place in the Court's ornate marble palace. The Troxels' son, Brad Troxel, had lived with Tommie from 1989 to 1991. Although the two had not been married during that time, she gave birth to his daughters Natalie and Isabelle.

Brad committed suicide in May 1993. His parents sought the right to visit their granddaughters, but Tommie, who by then was married to Kelly Wynn, a local businessman, wanted to keep the grandparent-granddaughter contact to only one weekend a month.

In 1993, Tommie was literally the head of a "Brady Bunch" family of ten: eight children and two adults. Prior to her intimate relationship with Brad, Tommie had been married and had three children. When she married Kelly, his two children by a previous marriage became part of the Wynn family, along with Brad's two daughters. A short time after her marriage to Wynn, Tommie gave birth to a child. As someone wrote, "Tommie Wynn's situation presents a snapshot of modern America—a 'blended' family."[68]

Like the *Inez Moore* case discussed earlier, this litigation forced the Court to respond to questions involving parental rights, in this case, how the law should respond to changing notions of "family." Courts across the country, especially state courts,

> have been asked to rule on visitation battles involving not only grandparents, but also other blood relatives, former boyfriends of a child's mother, former foster parents, the biological mother of a child after adoption, and gay partners of a child's biological parent.[69]

The dispute involved a Washington State law allowing grandparents or *any* third party to seek visiting rights "at *any* time" with a child if a court determined that such a visitation would be in the "child's best interest." Because of their unsuccessful battle with the mother of their grandchildren, in December 1993 the Troxels entered state court to seek better visitation rights. They wanted an entire weekend every other week with their grandchildren.

The judge gave them a once-a-month visitation from Saturday at 4:30 P.M. to Sunday at 6 P.M.

Tommie appealed to the Washington Supreme Court. In 1998, that court struck down the statute[70] because it impinged on the parents' constitutional privacy interests. The court ruled that "parents have a right to rear their children without state interference and said visitation could be imposed only if necessary to prevent harm to the child."[71] A state can interpose in a family matter "only to prevent harm or potential harm to the child." In *Troxel*, the state supreme court found that the challenged statute

> does not require a threshold showing of harm and sweeps too broadly by permitting any person to petition at any time with the only requirement being that the visitation serve the best interest of the child.

And as in so many cases involving the family and family and personal autonomy that reach the U.S. Supreme Court, in *Troxel* the Court disintegrated into splinter groups. As Justice O'Connor, the author of the judgment of the Court said, in an aside while announcing the opinion in *Troxel* in June 2000: "Unfortunately, the members of this Court were as divided as the parties in the case before the Court."[72]

There were six opinions written by the Justices, including three dissenting opinions. And there were strange bedfellows: Justice O'Connor was joined by Chief Justice Rehnquist and by Justices Ruth Ginsburg and Stephen Breyer. Justices Souter and Thomas wrote separate concurring opinions. Justice Scalia dissented, as did Justices Stevens and Kennedy; each wrote a dissenting opinion.

Case Study: *Troxel v Granville*, 2000

On Wednesday, January 12, 2000, the case was argued in Court. All the Justices, "six of them grandparents themselves,"[73] with the usual exception of Justice Clarence Thomas (who was raised by his grandparents and who was, at the time, raising a great-nephew) asked questions that underscored their efforts to understand the complexity of family relations in the twenty-first century.

The lawyer for Tommie Wynn argued that courts should enter the family environment only when a child is at risk. "Unless there is some threat of harm, parents should be in charge of deciding who spends time with their children and how much." The grandparents' lawyer told the brethren that court-ordered visitations "for relatives intrude only slightly on a parents' rights. He beseeched the Court to consider a grandparent's deep bonds with a grandchild."

Chief Justice Rehnquist, one of the Court's six grandparents, worried that the Washington State law would allow a distant relative to suddenly appear and seek visitation time "to take her to the movie every Friday." Justice O'Connor, another grandparent, called the statute "breathtakingly broad." Justice Souter, the only Justice without children, was worried lest "anyone walking in off the street" get visiting rights to a child regardless of the parents' wishes. Scalia, during the give-and-take, asserted that a child "does not belong to the courts" but to the parents.

That Friday in Conference the Justices discussed *Troxel* and other cases heard earlier in the week. Six of the Justices concluded that the Washington State law was "breathtakingly broad" and as such "exceeded the bounds of the Due Process Clause." The state had, in effect, deprived Tommie Granville Wynn of her "liberty" to raise her children without due process of law. Chief Justice Rehnquist asked Justice O'Connor to write the opinion for the Court.

The Washington State law violates Tommie Granville Wynn's due process right to make decisions concerning the care, custody, and control of her daughters. The Fourteenth Amendment's Due Process clause "provides heightened protection against governmental interference with certain fundamental rights and liberty interests of fit parents," O'Connor wrote in her plurality opinion.

The Washington law is put to use solely on a judge's determination of a child's best interest; "a parent's estimation of the child's best interest is accorded no deference." First of all, the Troxels never alleged that Tommie was an unfit parent and there is, wrote O'Connor, "a presumption that fit parents act in their children's best interests." Also, the trial judge "gave no weight to Granville's having assented to visitation even before the filing of the petition or subsequent court intervention."

> The combination of these factors demonstrates that the visitation order in this case was an unconstitutional infringement on [Tommie] Granville's fundamental right to make decisions concerning the care, custody, and control of her two daughters.

Pragmatically, O'Connor concluded:

> There [is] no need to consider the question whether the Due Process Clause requires all non-parental visitation statutes to include a showing of harm or potential harm to the child as a condition precedent to granting visitation or to decide the precise scope of the parental due process right in the visitation context.

She carefully sidestepped commenting on the Washington Supreme Court's observation that the U.S. Constitution allows the state to interfere only to prevent harm to the child.

Justice Souter's short concurring opinion stated: "The case ends with the state supreme court's assertion that the state legislation sweeps too broadly in authorizing any person at any time to request (and for a judge to award) visitation rights." There is no need to decide whether harm is required or to consider the exact scope of parental rights in this area. "I would say no more."

Justice Thomas's very brief concurrence said that in these cases, the "strict scrutiny" standard must be applied "to infringements of fundamental rights." Applying the standard in *Troxel,* he concluded that the

> state lacks even a legitimate governmental interest—to say nothing of a "compelling interest" in second-guessing a fit parent's decision regarding visitation with third parties. On this basis I would affirm the judgment below.

Justice Stevens's dissent addressed the character of parental authority. For him, the Court has never said that a parent's right to make decisions about her child was an absolute right; there are limits to these rights.

> The constitutional protection against arbitrary state interference with parental rights should not be extended to prevent the states from protecting children against arbitrary exercise of parental authority that is not in fact motivated by an interest in the welfare of the child.

Justice Scalia's dissent was a typical "Nino" broadside. In it, he came close to seconding Justice Goldberg's views about the Ninth Amendment presented in the 1965 *Griswold* litigation.

> In my view, a right of parents to direct the upbringing of their children is among the "inalienable rights" which the Declaration of Independence

proclaims. And in my view that right is also among the "other rights retained by the people" which the Ninth Amendment says the Constitution's enumeration of rights "shall not be construed to deny or disparage." However, if we embrace this unenumerated right, I think it obvious that we will be ushering in a new regime of judicially prescribed, and federally prescribed, family law. I have no reason to believe that federal judges will be better at this than state legislatures; and state legislatures have the great advantages of doing harm in a more circumscribed area, of being able to correct their mistakes in a flash, and of being removable by the people.

Justice Kennedy wrote the third dissent. Because of errors in the state supreme court's decision invalidating the statute, Kennedy would reverse and remand to the state supreme court.

Given the error I see in the State Supreme Court's central conclusion that the best interest of the child standard is never appropriate in third-party visitation cases, that court should have the first opportunity to reconsider this case. I would remand the case to the state court for further proceedings.

The *Troxel* judgment was a very pragmatic one, limited to the peculiar facts in the case. Like all the others, the judgment drew upon the values of the Justices. It was written by the Court's leading pragmatist, Justice Sandra Day O'Connor.

There is yet another very disturbing but still largely invisible issue involving children and parents: parental abuse by their offspring.[74]

Elder mistreatment[75] occurs in all segments of our population, irrespective of race, sex, ethnic, or socioeconomic background. Victims often feel powerless. Much mistreatment occurs within the family and the elderly person is often simultaneously embarrassed by the abuse, fearful of future mistreatment, and paradoxically, protective of the abuser. Because it most often occurs in private residences against persons who have limited contact with outsiders, its is among the most hidden of contemporary America's problems.[76]

In the 1970s the American community became aware of the "battered child and/or spouse" syndrome. However, the "battered parent" problem is still largely an invisible tragedy. In the twenty-first century there are only two ways the legal and political systems try to protect the elderly. They are (1)

laws that criminalize mistreatment of the elderly, and (2) regulations requiring health professionals (doctors, nurses, and others) to report in-
stances of suspected elder abuse by offspring, thereby "triggering state protective services. These forms of protection are ineffective," conclude many
legal and health care scholars.[77]

Compounding the dilemma is a demographic reality: America's population is a "graying" one. Persons older than sixty-five years of age are the
fastest-growing segment of the population. In 1900, this segment constituted abut 4 percent of the population; in 1950, 8 percent; in 1980, 11 percent. It is projected that by 2030 persons older than sixty-five will be almost
22 percent of the population.[78] Given the probability of the problem of
elder abuse likewise growing in the future, there will be increased efforts to
pass legislation to provide for greater protection of the elderly. And with the
passage of such legislation, there will be the inevitable litigation that will,
sooner or later, involve the Justices of the U.S. Supreme Court.

V. Summing Up

Raising a child, as any parent knows, is an ongoing challenge. Dozens of decisions are made daily by parents regarding the care, custody, education,
and nurturing of their children. For centuries, courts have deferred to the
idea of parental authority; judges often wrote opinions extolling the virtues
of the traditional nuclear family. The U.S. Supreme Court, in early-twenti-
eth-century cases such as *Meyers* and *Pierce*, even spoke of the "fundamental" liberty of Mom and Pop to bring up their children without governmental interference.

However, parental authority, these judges and courts have said, is not absolute because Mom and Pop are not angels and frequently act to harm their
children, intentionally or not. There are occasions where the state is empowered to intervene and to counter such negative parental behavior.
Clearly, in this area of intimate family relations, a balancing process takes
place in judicial decision making. The elements in the balancing equation
are (1) parental authority, (2) the child's health and nurturing, and (3) the
state's interest in ensuring the health, welfare, and well-being of its residents.

Each of these factors is given a weight in a court's effort to determine
what is in the "best interest" of the child. Very subjective assessments take
place because of the emotional complexity of the legal dilemma. Should the

child be able to challenge her "voluntary" admission into a medical facility? Should a mother lose custody of her children because she does not have the fees necessary to continue her legal battle to retain them? Can the state protect the emotional well-being of a child who has been sexually abused and then must testify against the alleged abuser in court?

As seen, even the Justices of the U.S. Supreme Court cannot agree on what is in the best interest of the child. Inevitably, there is a "muddling through" by them in the effort to resolve the legal-political-ethical dilemmas surrounding the society's commitment to the right of parental authority in the raising of children.

This chapter has presented an array of cases that emphasize the question Justice White always raised: "What's happening to the kids?" Whether litigation involved child custody, or the raising and education of children, or the mental and physical health and welfare of the child, the Court's primary focus and concern has been whether the autonomous development of the child has been impeded or enhanced—by the parents or by the state.

The answers were often presented in multiple-opinion decisions, without four Justices "joining" a "majority" opinion. Some, such as Justices Scalia and Thomas, have held very traditional views of the family, parental decision making, and the role of legislators and judges. Others, particularly Justices Brennan, White, and O'Connor, have placed the health and well-being of the child above conventional standards of parental and state authority. In this chapter as in the preceding ones, there is deep division evidenced in the Court's efforts to resolve these intimate questions.

An equally troublesome question, alluded to in this chapter, is the focus of the next chapter. Chapter 6 examines how the U.S. Supreme Court has responded to arguments that had their beginning with the reasoning found in *Griswold* and *Roe*: Does a competent person, with a fatal illness, have the right to terminate life support systems? Does another competent but terminally ill person, in chronic unbearable pain, have the right to commit suicide with the assistance of a physician? And what is the "best interest" of the child who is in a permanent vegetative state (PVS)? And who should answer these questions?

6

"Let Me Go!"
Death in the Family

Water me no more
With glucose and saline,
I am pod not seed,
I will not bloom.
And puff me no more
with oxygen.
The monitor's beam
May dance on the screen
Forever fed by
your green tanks and bottles,
your plastic tubes and pumps
mimicking order, but
I am chaos.
Your respirator reaches out,
seizes my throat,
chokes all speech.
Mute, my thoughts show
On no screen.
How do I sign
'Let me go'?
   —Conrad Rosenberg[1]

The right to have an abortion was the premier privacy issue of the 1970's," wrote a reporter in 1985. "This decade, it's the "right-to-die.""[2] That the "right-to-die" was seen as a "premier" issue is paradoxical because Americans have had a "discomfort with death. Medicine and contemporary culture have combined to erase death from our imaginations."[3] However, as a doctor wrote, the reality is that "most of us will face some form of high-tech dying, and we need to be ready for it."[4]

Very slowly, in great part because of the recent, sensational advances in medical technology, what Sherwin Nuland called the "medicalization of death,"[5] that keep people alive longer, we are confronting the paradox that ensues from those scientific breakthroughs: the machines keep the body breathing and feeding while the person's cerebral cortex, which controls thought and consciousness, ceases to function. An observer noted, in 1991, that

> over the past twenty years, medical technology has advanced so much that it is now possible to resuscitate people after they have stopped breathing or their hearts have stopped beating. Thus, it is possible to extend "life" in some form. Medical technology has effectively created a twilight zone of suspended animation where death commences while life, in some form, continues.[6]

There are other poignant and tragic "right-to-die" cases that raise moral issues of the highest order. For example, can a *permanently disabled* competent person elect to end all life-sustaining medical technology? Elizabeth Bouvia's case made international news in the 1980s. She was a quadriplegic cerebral palsy victim who, beginning in 1983, checked into California hospitals in order to die by not being fed. Her request was denied a number of times, always upheld by state judges. However, in April 1986, the California Court of Appeal, Second District, in *Bouvia v Superior Court*, 225 Cal Report, 297, 1986, ruled that she had the right to refuse force-feeding even if that refusal sped her death: "We do not believe that all and every life must be preserved against the will of the sufferer."[7]

Another dreadful "right-to-die" issue is seen in the many "Baby Doe" cases, where the parents of a horribly deformed infant request doctors not to perform any heroic measures to save the life of the infant. The initial "Baby Doe" case came from New York. The baby was born with an open spine, water on the brain, and an abnormally small head.

> Even with surgery, her doctors said, she might live to age 20 but would always be severely retarded, paralyzed from the waist down, epileptic, in pain and faced with repeated expensive operations. Her parents decided to forgo surgery, meaning she would probably die by age 2.[8]

Because of medical breakthroughs, a major ethical-medical-political-legal drama moved to the U.S. Supreme Court stage in the past decade. Can a *competent* terminally ill person, at that person's request, be removed from life support systems? Can an *incompetent* person, in a permanent vegetative state (PVS),[9] have a surrogate order the hospital to remove all life-support systems? Finally, can a *competent*, terminally ill person commit suicide with the aid of a physician? These are the essential questions that the end-of-life drama raised in state and federal courts. By 1990,[10] the play reached the marble palace on First Street in Washington, DC.

Is euthanasia, i.e., a human-induced, gentle, painless, merciful, or "good" death, legally wrong (setting aside the moral/ethical dimensions) because it violates the essential dignity and worth of human life? Or does a person have a protected liberty interest in the Due Process Clause of the Fourteenth Amendment that enables her to make a very personal choice about living or dying? For the state legislators and for the judges, the essential civil liberties question is this: "What role may the individual play in his or her own death?"

The Justices of the U.S. Supreme Court, along with many state and federal jurists, reluctantly agreed to examine this intensely private manifestation of the idea of personal autonomy. In so deciding, the judges have begun "to make choices for human beings lying in the twilight between life and death," wrote U.S. Court of Appeals Judge Calabresi in 1996.

In responding, the Justices of the U.S. Supreme Court have defined what personal conduct is permitted and what is not permitted and have essentially allowed the fifty states to determine, for their citizens, the legal parameters in which these profound choices are made. In so deciding, the Justices have had to draw upon the latest medical/scientific data. They, like so many others in modern society, have come to understand that medicine and medical technology have made it easier for a person to terminate life as well as to postpone death.[11]

I. *"This Case Should Never Have Been Started"*

In a 1990 "right-to-die" case, the Justices accepted the "long recognized" common law premise that a *competent* person has a right to control his own body.[12] There is also a Fourteenth Amendment constitutional "liberty" interest, though not absolute, in this area for *competent* persons: "The principle that a competent person has a constitutionally protected liberty interest in refusing unwanted medical treatment may be inferred from our prior decisions."

There was, in *Cruzan's* dicta, the triumph of self-determination, of *competent* patient autonomy.[13] John Stuart Mill's principle was primary and generally outweighed the interest of the state in maintaining, at all costs, the sanctity of life for a *competent* person. In effect, the Court implied that each *competent* human being had a right to control his or her own body, so long as the person's actions do not interfere with or injure another person.

A person can elect *not* to receive life-sustaining medical technology. As Chief Justice Rehnquist said:

> The [common law] doctrine of *informed consent* is viewed as generally encompassing the right of a competent individual to refuse medical treatment. . . . For purposes of this case, we assume that the U.S. Constitution would grant a competent person a constitutionally protected right to refuse lifesaving hydration and nutrition.[14]

But what about an *incompetent* person's constitutional right to terminate medical measures? Does she have the same due process 'liberty' interest a *competent* person possesses? The first "right-to-die" case involving an *incompetent* person captured headlines across America. Karen Ann Quinlan was the "central figure in this tragic case."[15]

In April 1985, Karen, "an attractive and vivacious young [twenty-one-year-old] woman,"[16] went to a birthday party with a number of friends. At the affair, she had some hard drinks and took phenobarbital and Librium. Because she was acting "kind of strange," her friends, thinking she was drunk, took Karen home and put her to bed. They returned a short time later and found she was not breathing. A policeman called to the scene started her breathing, although she never regained consciousness. Karen had "inexplicably ceased breathing for two fifteen-minute intervals."[17] She was comatose when brought to Newton Memorial Hospital and remained so until her death.

During the time her breathing stopped, Karen suffered anoxia, a deprivation of oxygen to the brain that leads to brain damage and, if deprivation lasts more than five minutes, brain death. She had "slipped into a chronic persistent vegetative state [PVS]."[18] She no longer "had any cognitive function," the doctors concluded. At the hospital, she was "kept alive" by being placed on a respirator. She was nourished through a nasal-gastric tube. She never woke up from her coma.

The record bespeaks the high degree of familial love which pervaded the home of Joseph Quinlan and reached out to fully embrace Karen, although she was living elsewhere at the time of her collapse. The [record] showed him to be deeply religious [Roman Catholic], imbued with a morality so sensitive that months of tortured indecision preceded his belated conclusion to seek the termination of life-supportive measures sustaining Karen.[19]

"I'm convinced," said the father, "it is our Lord's will that Karen be allowed to die." His bishop supported Quinlan's decision:

Competent medical testimony has established that Karen Ann Quinlan has no reasonable hope of recovery from her comatose state by the use of any available medical procedures. The continuance of mechanical (cardio-respiratory) supportive measures to sustain continuation of her body functions and her life constitute extraordinary means of treatment. *Therefore, the decision of Joseph Quinlan to request the discontinuance of this treatment is, according to the teachings of the Catholic Church, a morally correct decision.* [Emphasis in original.][20]

The doctors, however, refused to remove the medical devices because of the (very slim) possibility of being charged with murder, the possibility of a medical malpractice suit, and because of their interpretation of medical standards, practice, and ethics that called for continuation of extraordinary life-supportive medical efforts.

Joseph Quinlan needed a lawyer. He worked at Warner-Lambert in New Jersey and asked someone in the legal department for the name of a lawyer in the area of medical law. That man commuted to New York with a thirty-year-old attorney, Paul W. Armstrong, who had recently, in 1973, received his law degree from Notre Dame Law School. Armstrong was a Legal Aid lawyer attending New York University Law School nights to study constitutional law and medicine for his L.L.M. degree. "This fellow recommended me. He said I had been studying in the area," Armstrong recalled decades later.[21]

With Armstrong as his *pro bono* attorney, Joe Quinlan went to state court to receive the authority to act as his daughter's guardian, in order to disconnect the medical machines. "What had been a private nightmare for the Quinlan family became the opening round in an ongoing national debate."[22] *New York* magazine's cover on October 6, 1975, featured the Quinlan story; the headline read "The Girl in the Coma." *Newsweek's* cover, on

November 3, 1975, read "A 'right-to-die.'" National television shows featured stories on the question the Quinlans raised in their lawsuit. And when the New Jersey Supreme Court issued its opinion in 1976, it was quickly translated into thirty-two languages.[23]

Although there was overwhelming witness testimony recommending termination, the Chancery Court judge, Robert Muir, refused to allow Karen to be taken off the machines. "There is a duty to continue life-assisting apparatus. There is no constitutional 'right-to-die' that can be asserted by a parent for his incompetent adult child."

Quinlan appealed to the New Jersey Supreme Court. When the judges heard the case, at the end of January 1976, Karen was

> emaciated, having suffered a weight loss of at least 40 pounds, and undergoing a continuing deteriorative process. Her posture is described as fetal-like and grotesque; there is extreme flexion-rigidity of the arms, legs, and related muscles and her joints are severely rigid and deformed.[24]

After the oral argument, in conference the justices agreed that Quinlan should be appointed guardian and that he had the right to disconnect the medical machines. However, "it remained unclear on what grounds they would base the decision." As one of the justices said,

> *This case should never have been started,* but it was started and it's here. Usually we try to contribute something towards a solution. I guess that's our primary and ultimate function here.[25]

The court overturned Muir's ruling. The six Justices unanimously held, in an opinion written by former Democratic Governor and at the time Chief Justice Richard J. Hughes, that one could find a "'right-to-die'" in the common law and in U.S. Supreme Court decisions such as *Griswold v Connecticut* and *Roe v Wade.* "It is the issue of the constitutional right of privacy that has given us most concern," Hughes wrote.

> Though the Constitution does not explicitly mention a right of privacy, U.S. Supreme Court decisions have recognized that a right of personal privacy exists and that certain areas of privacy are guaranteed under the Constitution. . . . In *Griswold,* the Court found the unwritten right of privacy. . . . [We believe that it is] broad enough to encompass a patient's decision to decline medical treatments under certain circumstances, in much the

same way as it is broad enough to encompass a woman's decision to terminate pregnancy under certain conditions. *Roe v Wade.*

Following the U.S. Supreme Court's use of the balancing test in all the cases involving clashes between the family and the state, the New Jersey Supreme Court said:

> We think that the State's interest [to preserve life] weakens and the individual's right to privacy grows as the degree of bodily invasion increases and the prognosis dims. Ultimately, there comes a point at which the individual's rights overcome the State interest.

Since Karen was comatose, the Court concluded that "Karen's right of privacy may be asserted on her behalf by her guardian under the peculiar circumstances here present." The New Jersey Supreme Court remanded the case back to Judge Muir with instructions to appoint Mr. Quinlan as Karen's guardian "with full power to make decisions." Specifically, it included the decision to withdraw the life-support system "without any civil or criminal liability therefor, on the part of any participant, whether guardian, physician, hospital, or others."

The U.S. Supreme Court denied certiorari in *Quinlan* and the decision of the New Jersey Supreme Court was implemented.[26] (The Court denied certiorari in one other "right-to-die" case until it granted certiorari in *Cruzan* in 1989.) Almost two dozen other state courts took note of the New Jersey response to the question—and the denial of certiorari by the high bench—and issued "right-to-die" rulings when they confronted other personal tragedies in search of a humane solution.[27] The case, wrote one observer, was

> truly historic.... The New Jersey Supreme Court was proclaiming the principle of equal rights in the arena of health. Medical paternalism was converted into a democratic process whereby family members could speak for incompetent persons.[28]

In May 1976, Karen was taken off the respirator, but she remained on the nutrition (nasal-gastro) tube. At the time the idea of removing her feeding tube was viewed as "utterly repugnant."[29] Ironically, she breathed on her own for nine more years. She died on June 11, 1985, unable to overcome a whole-body infection.

II. Terminating Life Support for an Incompetent Family Member: Passive Euthanasia

The *Quinlan* decision sharply focused America's attention on some very discomforting matters involving death and dying. It was estimated that there were between 10,000 and 15,000 persons in a PVS across America at that time.[30] Further, at the time, "the annual national health care bill for patients in PVS has been estimated as ranging from $120 million to $1.2 billion."[31] Fourteen years later, after having twice passed up the opportunity to have their say in the matter, the U.S. Supreme Court Justices finally granted certiorari in an appeal from Missouri. The question was the one the New Jersey justices had grappled with in 1976: Does the *right of privacy* and the concept of *personal autonomy* encompass an incompetent person's *"right-to-die"* by shutting off the life-support system that maintains that person's life?

The case, *Cruzan by Cruzan v Director, Missouri Department of Health,*[32] came to the Court from Missouri. It had the same general fact-situation that was seen in *Quinlan:* A young female adult in a PVS kept alive by medical equipment and the latest medical technology, even though her parents wanted to take her off all life-supportive systems. Nancy did not have any cognitive functions; she was considered brain dead.[33]

Twenty-five-year-old Nancy Cruzan had been in a terrible auto accident in which her brain had been deprived of oxygen for between twelve and fourteen minutes. It was January 1983; she was returning home from her job on the night shift of a cheese factory when she lost control of her Nash Rambler on icy Elm Road in Jasper County, Missouri.[34] Trooper Dale Penn of the Missouri Highway Patrol discovered Nancy face-down in a ditch thirty-five feet from her car. She did not have any detectable respiratory or cardiac functions. The paramedics arrived and successfully revived these two functions.

She never regained consciousness. She suffered significant anoxia. Her doctors informed the parents that Nancy was soon to become brain dead because her cerebral cortex was failing. She seemed awake but was totally unaware of her surroundings. She was not on a respirator but she needed food; without sustenance, she would die of hunger. Nancy would, however, remain unconscious in a vegetative state for decades unless the hydration and feeding tube was removed and she was allowed to die.

The accident occurred in 1983. In early 1987, after seeing absolutely no change in their unconscious daughter in that period of time, Nancy's parents, Joyce and Joe Cruzan, requested that the tube be removed and that their daughter be allowed to die a natural death. "You try your damnedest as long as there's hope," said Joe Cruzan in 1990, "and then when there is none anymore, you must let her go."[35]

Nancy's heartbroken parents described their daughter as "an unconscious shell in a room full of strangers."[36] At the time of their request, Nancy was

> completely and permanently disabled. She remained unconscious and was completely oblivious to her environment except for primitive [vegetative] reflexes. While she would never recover, she was not terminally ill.[37]

Rehabilitative efforts were fruitless. She was a spastic quadriplegic. The parents based their request on the constitutional right to privacy, which, in their situation, involved the very personal and intimate decision to allow their child to die.

In 1988, a state court granted permission for the parents to have the feeding and hydration tube removed. Relying on the testimony of several friends of Nancy, her mother, and her sister, the judge concluded that she had clearly expressed herself on the question of the death: "A person in Nancy's condition had a fundamental right under the State and Federal Constitutions to refuse or direct the withdrawal of 'death prolonging' procedures."

However, on appeal by the state's Attorney General, William Webster, the Missouri Supreme Court, in a divided vote, reversed the judge's order. It ruled that the state was committed to the "sanctity of human life" as expressed in the state's "Living Will" law. In cases such as the Cruzans', "clear and convincing evidence" had to be presented showing that an incompetent patient, when competent, clearly and convincingly indicated that life-support systems should not be used on her in the event she became medically incompetent as a result of an accident.

The Cruzans then appealed to the U.S. Supreme Court, which granted certiorari and heard the case during its 1989 Term. The question for consideration by the Court was whether Nancy Cruzan had any rights under the U.S. Constitution that would require a hospital to withdraw life-sustaining treatment from her under these circumstances.[38]

The case brought instant national media attention. After all, the Court's grappling with the question of who was empowered to make life-and-death decisions in such a situation—the family, the doctor, or the state—was one that family members across America understood and experienced themselves. The federal government was invited by the Court to participate in the oral arguments and U.S. Solicitor General Kenneth Starr, a Reagan appointee, spoke in support of the Missouri statute.

The Court received *amicus curiae* briefs from more than forty groups and persons representing the views of hundreds of thousands of Americans. The groups urging reversal of the state supreme court ruling included the AIDS Civil Rights Project, the American Academy of Neurology, the American Hospital Association (Paul Armstrong, the Quinlans' attorney was the counsel of record in the brief), the National Hospice Organization, and the Society for the Right to Die. An equal number of pressure groups called upon the Court to affirm the Missouri Supreme Court's decision. These included Agudath Israel of America, the American Academy of Medical Ethics, the Catholic Lawyers Guild of the Archdiocese of Boston, the Association for Retarded Citizens of the United States, Doctors for Life, Knights of Columbus, and Focus on the Family.

Since *Roe*, the watershed abortion rights decision, was announced in 1973, there were four new justices on the Court, all appointed by two conservative Republican Presidents (Ford and Reagan): Justices Stevens, O'-Connor, Scalia, and Kennedy. The other five had all participated in *Roe*, with Brennan and Marshall joining Blackmun's majority opinion, and White and Rehnquist writing in dissent.

Politically, the case was a dynamite one for Republican President George Bush. He had campaigned in 1988 on behalf of the sanctity of life. For the president, as it had been for his predecessor, Ronald Reagan, there was no "right-to-die." And his Solicitor General, Kenneth Starr, had prepared a powerful brief that underscored the President's commitment to the "sanctity of life."

Case Study: *Cruzan v Director, Missouri Department of Health*, 1990

In a narrow 5:4 vote, the Court, with Chief Justice William Rehnquist writing the majority opinion, upheld the judgment of the Missouri Supreme Court. As with so many other controversial right of privacy cases, *Cruzan* had five separate opinions; three were the majority and two concurring opinions (written by Justices Scalia and O'Connor); the other two were dissents written by Justices William J. Brennan and John P. Stevens. Justice Marshall, along with Justice Blackmun, joined both dissents.

Rehnquist assigned the opinion to himself because of the stress within the five-person majority (himself, and Justices O'Connor, Scalia, White, and

Kennedy). Two of the five, Justices O'Connor and Scalia, were tenuous "joins" who could bolt if the Rehnquist draft opinion did not give them enough substantive argumentation for them to "join." This was because their views on the question of the right to die were at opposite ends of the spectrum.

Scalia believed that federal courts should not get into this very dramatic, tragic, and very personal issue. It was a matter for state legislatures and state courts, not the U.S. Supreme Court. For him, and for only Scalia among the brethren, a person does *not* have a constitutionally protected liberty interest in the Due Process Clause to refuse unwanted medical treatment.

Justice O'Connor's argument was very different. She argued, aggressively, that there *was* a protected "liberty" interest found in the Due Process Clause, for a competent person to refuse unwanted medical treatment, including the machine delivery of food and water. For her, the state's invasion into the body is "repugnant to the Due Process Clause." She did not rule out a Court decision that the Constitution requires the state to implement the decisions of an incompetent patient's duly appointed surrogate if the state provides very clear procedures for surrogates and judges to follow.

Somehow, Rehnquist had to balance these two irreconcilable views in his majority opinion or else he would have only a "judgment" of the Court. He "faced an unenviable task of reconciling these seemingly irreconcilable views. He attempted to do so by writing both cautiously and cryptically." His opinion implied,

> without quite holding, that a competent person would have the constitutional right to refuse lifesaving hydration and nutrition. It did not follow, however, that such treatment should be terminated for an incompetent person

if the state acted to preserve the lives of all those who could not speak for themselves.[39]

At the very end of the Term, June 25, 1990, the Court announced its decision upholding the state court decision. Justice Brennan's dissent in *Cruzan* was one of his last opinions from the high bench; he announced his retirement less than one month later.

In *Cruzan,* Rehnquist's majority wrestled with the possibility of expanding the right of privacy to difficult decisions involving the death and dying of persons who are incapable of making their own choice. Naturally, his opinion rejected such an expansion of the right to privacy.

What about a patient such as Nancy Cruzan, comatose when brought into the hospital and very near brain death? She was incompetent and the question for the Justices was whether a state could establish guidelines by which doctors could "pull the plug" or not, on such unconscious, brain-dead incompetent patients—without facing criminal charges for murder. For the Rehnquist majority, "the question is simply and starkly whether the U.S. Constitution prohibits Missouri from choosing the *rule of decision* [the clear and convincing evidence rule] which it did."

The majority concluded that the state's rule of decision as to whether a doctor could cut off life support was not in violation of the Constitution's prohibitions. It refused to extend the right of privacy to an unfettered "right-to-die." On balance, the state, and not the family, is better able to serve as the surrogate for an incompetent patient such as Nancy Cruzan.

Missouri accomplished this by establishing the procedural rule that "requires evidence of the incompetent's wishes as to the withdrawal of treatment be proved by clear and convincing evidence." For the majority, such a "procedural requirement" by Missouri is plainly constitutional. (Even though Nancy's family and friends presented evidence that she did not wish to vegetate on a machine, the state supreme court adjudged that the information did not rise to the level of "clear and convincing evidence.")

> Read most charitably, Rehnquist's opinion represents an uneasy compromise between the positions of Justices Scalia and O'Connor. [He] can hardly be blamed for being caught between two firmly held and fervently asserted views.[40]

Justice Scalia began by noting that

> the various opinions in this case portray quite clearly the difficult, indeed agonizing, questions that are presented by the constantly increasing power of science to keep the human body alive for longer than any reasonable person would want to inhabit it.

He then directly addressed the question of whether the issue is a matter for the federal courts to resolve. His categorical response was never! Instead, the Court should have clearly announced that "Federal courts have no business in this field. The Constitution has nothing to say about the 'right-to-die.'" In his acerbic style, he then said:

The point at which life becomes "worthless," and the point at which the means necessary to preserve it become "extraordinary" or "inappropriate," are neither set forth in the Constitution nor known to the nine Justices of this *Court any better than they are known to nine people picked at random from the Kansas City telephone.*

Justice O'Connor's concurring opinion reflected her view that a competent person had a liberty interest in choosing to withdraw life-supportive medical devices "and that the refusal of artificially delivered food and water is encompassed within that liberty interest." Her opinion sought to explain "why I believe this to be so." For Justice O'Connor, the idea of liberty is "inextricably entwined with our idea of physical freedom and self-determination." Regarding the right to die of an incompetent patient in a PVS, while she joined Rehnquist's opinion, she said that "today's decision does not preclude a future determination that the Constitution requires the States to implement the decisions of a patient's duly appointed surrogate."

Justice Brennan dissented, joined by his friends Justices Marshall and Blackmun. (Justice Stevens also dissented.) He and the other dissenters rejected the "balancing" formula repeatedly used by Rehnquist and the other conservatives. The dissenters believed that Nancy Cruzan

has a fundamental right to be free of unwanted artificial nutrition and hydration, which right is not *outweighed by any interests of the State. . . .* I respectfully dissent. Nancy Cruzan is entitled to choose to die with dignity. . . . Dying is personal. And it is profound. For many, the thought of an ignoble end, steeped in decay, is abhorrent. A quiet, proud death, bodily integrity intact, is a matter of extreme consequence. . . .

For Justice Brennan, family members were more competent to make these life-and-death decisions than was the state. For the three jurists, "the state is a stranger to the patient." They concluded that the Missouri statute violated the Fourteenth Amendment's Due Process Clause and that Nancy Cruzan had the "right-to-die."

Justice Stevens, in his dissent, joined by Justices Marshall and Blackmun, wrote that for him,

the critical question is not how to prove the controlling facts [regarding the views about death of the patient in a PVS] but rather what proven facts should be controlling. . . . The failure of Missouri's policy to heed the interests of a dying individual with respect to matters so private is ample evidence of the policy's illegitimacy.

The Court's narrow 5:4 holding in *Cruzan* was a setback for the dissenting Justices. They envisioned a broad right of privacy but that was not to occur in this area of intimate family relationships. As Rehnquist argued successfully in other constitutional cases before his Court, the balance between family rights and the interest of the states in these cases had to tip in favor of the state.

Nancy Cruzan, despite the majority's ruling in her case, did not "remain a passive prisoner of medical technology." In a follow-up hearing before the state probate judge, Cruzan's parents presented additional witnesses in the effort to implement Rehnquist's ruling that "clear and convincing evidence" be presented to show Nancy's views on death. The probate judge granted, again, the family's petition and the state supreme court affirmed that decision.

The response in the state was dramatic. Nineteen demonstrators were arrested for attempting to enter the hospital with the intent to reattach Nancy Cruzan's feeding and hydration tube.[41] Sharon Orr, one of Nancy's nurses, was frustrated and angry when the second Missouri Supreme Court decision came down: "The Humane Society won't let you starve your dog," she exclaimed to a news reporter.[42]

On December 14, 1990, the hospital removed Nancy Cruzan's feeding tube. Twelve days later, December 26, 1990, Nancy Cruzan died. The official cause of death was listed as dehydration.[43]

III. Physician-Assisted Suicide: Active Euthanasia

"It's the dying that's the problem," said a terminally ill cancer patient to his psychiatrist.

I can't bear the sickness. I hate the hospital, the chemotherapy, the nausea, the waiting in hallways for procedures, the endless pills. I'm becoming someone else. But I don't want to endlessly talk about it, particularly with my wife. She's got enough to deal with.[44]

Most people dread becoming someone, or something, else. Further, "most of us have parents or other loved ones, and we've lived through a dying experience that forces us to think about these things," Justice Ruth Bader Ginsburg said at one point during the January 1997 oral arguments in the two physician-assisted suicide cases. This end-of-life dilemma is one that millions of spouses and offspring deal with continually.

Much earlier that winter day, two protesters spoke to each other in front of the Supreme Court building about the pros and cons of the right of a terminally ill person to choose to die:

> "Disease is mutilation," [said] Carol Poenisch, 42. Her mother was stricken with Lou Gehrig's disease. "Have you ever seen a woman with cancer, where the bone gets eaten away, and her back collapses? Is that a life?" "Whether it's a life or not, I don't think the Constitution supports suicide," says Marc Spindelman. An American flag snaps in the wind above his head. He asks Poenisch why she flew here all the way from Michigan. "My mother was Number 19," says Poenisch. She was Merian Frederick, Jack Kevorkian's[45] 19th assisted suicide, killed in October 1993 by sucking on a plastic tube that fed her carbon monoxide. Before Frederick died, she had lost the ability to speak. She wrote in a note to her three children:
> "I have 2 criteria for meaningful existence.
> 1) a posture that allows me to write without undue fatigue.
> 2) finger and forearm strength that allow typing and writing."
> Then the 72-year-old mother outlined what she could not endure: "When I can't go to the john without help; play my tape books; watch tv."[46]

Justice Ginsburg's observation and the brief dialogue are a part of the context in which the Justices examined the last of the questions associated with the right to die: Could a *competent* person, with a terminal illness, commit suicide with the assistance of a physician? During its 1996 Term, in *Washington State v Glucksberg*[47] and *Vacco v Quill*,[48] the Court attempted to answer that final inquiry about personal autonomy, the "right-to-die," and physician-assisted suicide.

It is a matter that is politically explosive. All states but one[49] have laws that make criminal active participation in the suicide of another person. Prosecutions, however, have been very rare. Within the medical community, doctors and medical ethicists are "deeply divided" on the issue of physician-assisted suicide.[50] Those opposed point to the Hippocratic Oath, taken by all physicians for millennia. It stipulates that a physician "will give no deadly medications to anyone if asked, nor suggest any such counsel."

The American Medical Association's Code of Ethics is equally clear: "Doctors Must Not Kill." The AMA and forty-five other medical associations filed *amicus curiae* briefs with the Supreme Court opposing the legitimizing of physician-assisted suicide.[51] Other medical groups, such as the thirty-thousand-member American Medical Student Association, filed briefs in favor of legalization. "Students are simply being more progressive, I think, in reflecting the general societal understanding that there needs to be better training for physicians and more rights for patients," said AMSA President Andrew Nowalk.[52]

And physicians on both sides of the issue were shocked that the Supreme Court was going to hear the controversy and possibly validate the right to physician-assisted suicide. "That the Supreme Court is even considering it is breathtaking to many of us," [a doctor] said. "If the court upholds the lower courts' decisions, he added, "the next day, every person in this country could walk into a doctor's office or health care facility and demand suicide. What would we do?"[53]

A geriatric social worker described the social context of the constitutional problem of physician-assisted suicide: "Old people want an easy exit. They don't want to be kept alive and suffer great pain. They just want to die in peace."[54] Interest in active euthanasia by aging parents

> sometimes reflects anxiety about overly aggressive medical treatment, sometimes dread about abandonment, and sometimes fear that dying people may suffer simultaneously or sequentially from both misfortunes. . . . A good death is one that is: free from avoidable distress and suffering for patients, families, and caregivers; in general accord with patients' and families' wishes; and reasonably consistent with clinical, cultural, and ethical standards. A bad death, in turn, is characterized by needless suffering, dishonoring of patient or family wishes or values, and a sense among participants or observers that norms of decency have been offended.[55]

State statutes, it was claimed by the student-doctors and the major pressure group in both cases, Compassion in Dying, violated two clauses found in the Fourteenth Amendment. The fundamental right of *competent* but terminally ill patients, found in the Fourteenth Amendment's Due Process Clause, who wished to swiftly bring about their own death through physician-assisted suicide. Such a "liberty" interest, they argued, was also found in the *Cruzan* precedent, which said, in effect, that a *competent* person had the "fundamental" right to choose death over life. The second part of the

Fourteenth Amendment, the Equal Protection Clause, was also violated by the states because that clause directed that "all persons similarly situated should be treated alike."[56] While a terminally ill or PVS patient could have all life-supportive medical treatment withdrawn in order to die, a "similarly situated" terminally ill patient could not choose to die by committing suicide with the assistance of a doctor.

The due process argument was the "logical extension" of a competent person's constitutional right to refuse or to discontinue life-support medical treatment. The equal protection claim was also based on the "logical extension" argument. It was unconstitutional for a state to make the distinction between a physician's complying with a person's decision to withdraw from life-saving medical treatment and that same doctor's affirmatively assisting another terminally ill patient to commit suicide.

The Justices invited the executive branch to participate in the debate. The Clinton administration's brief *amicus curiae* filed with the Justices argued that there was a difference between withdrawing life-support systems from a patient and allowing a patient to actively hasten his death, with the assistance of doctors, by committing suicide.[57] (Duke Law School professor Walter Dellinger, acting U.S. Solicitor General, argued the cause for the United States, as *amicus curiae*, by special leave of the Court.)

Clearly, in the privacy litigation, the Court found itself dealing with controversial questions that literally involved life and death. Contraception and abortion precedents of the 1960s and early 1970s, were thrown into the legal equation as the brethren heard cases that raised the possibility of extending the right of privacy, first found to be a fundamental right in 1965, to a person's right to die.

It has always been a crime to assist a suicide in the State of Washington. The state's present law, passed in 1975, makes "[p]romoting a suicide attempt" a Class C felony, punishable by imprisonment for five years and a fine of up to $10,000, and provides: "A person is guilty of [that crime] when he knowingly causes or aids another person to attempt suicide." Respondents in *Washington v Glucksberg* were four Washington physicians who occasionally treated terminally ill, suffering patients, who declared that they would assist these patients in ending their lives if not for the state's assisted-suicide ban.

They, along with three gravely ill plaintiffs (who died before the Court's decision came down) and Compassion in Dying, a nonprofit organization that counsels people considering physician-assisted suicide, filed the suit against the petitioners, the state and its Attorney General, seeking a declaration that the ban is, on its face, unconstitutional. They asserted a "liberty" interest protected by the Fourteenth Amendment's Due Process Clause that extends to a personal choice by a mentally competent, terminally ill adult to commit physician-assisted suicide. Relying primarily on *Planned Parenthood of Southeastern Pa. v Casey*[58] and *Cruzan v Director, Missouri Department of Health,*[59] the U.S. District Court agreed, concluding that Washington's assisted suicide ban is unconstitutional because it placed an "undue burden" on the exercise of that constitutionally protected liberty interest. The *en banc* CA9 affirmed Chief Judge Barbara Rothstein's decision.

In *Dennis Vacco, Attorney General, New York State v Timothy Quill, M.D.*, New York, like most states, made it a crime to aid another person to commit or attempt suicide. However, as in all states, patients may refuse life-saving medical treatment. Respondents were three New York physicians. They asserted that, although it would be consistent with the standards of their medical practices to prescribe lethal medication for mentally competent, terminally ill patients who are suffering great pain and desire a doctor's help in taking their own lives, they are deterred from doing so by New York's assisted-suicide ban.

The doctors, and three gravely ill patients (who died before the final decision was handed down by the Court), sued the state's attorney general, claiming that the ban violates the Fourteenth Amendment's Equal Protection Clause. In SD, New York, U.S. District Court, Chief Judge Thomas P. Griesa heard the case and disagreed with the doctors. He ruled that the patients did not have a "fundamental right" to physician-assisted suicide and that the New York State statutes criminalizing such conduct did not violate the Equal Protection Clause.

But the CA2 reversed, holding (1) that New York accords different treatment to those competent, terminally ill persons who wish to hasten their deaths by self-administering prescribed drugs than it does to those who wish to do so by directing the removal of life-support systems, and (2) that this supposed unequal treatment is not rationally related to any legitimate state interests.

The two states, losers in the lower federal appellate courts, brought petitions for certiorari to the U.S. Supreme Court. The petitions were granted at the beginning of the Court's 1996 Term. Oral arguments were scheduled for both cases on January 8, 1997.

Very early, about 5:00 A.M., on the cold wintry dark morning of January 8, hundreds of protesters from both sides began picketing and lining up for tickets to hear the oral argument. Near them, an unidentified chorus was singing to no one in particular: "We are strong and gentle people, and we are singing for our lives."

Members of the anti-physician-assisted-suicide group Not Dead Yet picketed, in wheelchairs, in front of the Court. Their signs shouted in the darkness: "Not Dead Yet," "Hitler Would Be Proud," and "Your Mercy Is Killing Us." Across the street, a group from the Hemlock Society picketed in support of the right to choose death by suicide. "There's no point when I'm half dead making me stay alive," says Roy R. Torcaso, a white-bearded, withered man from the organization. "The government has no right to tell me I have to live and suffer."

> "Will nature take its course, or will we turn doctors into angels of death?" said Bob Castagna, executive director of the Oregon Catholic Conference, grasping the ticket a court officer just handed him, marked "Admission Card #2."

"For the people on the steps of the Supreme Court," observed a news reporter,

> the issue is all about the gray zones: the physical, religious, moral and legal uncertainties that surround a hastened death. Justice Antonin Scalia said recently that he felt like someone being asked to deliver cosmic wisdom. "*Why would you leave that to nine lawyers, for heaven's sake?*" he said.[60]

Case Study: *Washington State v Glucksberg,* 1997; *Vacco v Quill,* 1997

Harold Glucksberg and Timothy Quill were two of the protagonists in this medical-ethical-political-legal conundrum. They were medical doctors practicing, respectively, in Washington and New York State. Their arguments on behalf of their terminally ill patients led the Justices into another complex problem facing families across the world.

As in the other difficult family relationship crises, the Justices of the Court had many different views. Ultimately, while the two opinions of the Court were 9:0 votes, there were six opinions filed in each case. Chief Justice Rehnquist wrote the majority opinion for the Court in both cases, joined by four other justices. Along with his opinions, five others wrote separately to offer their views on the question. This quintet included Justices O'Connor, Stevens, Souter, Ginsburg, and Breyer.

These differences were heard in the oral argument on that cold January morning in the nation's capital. Wrote one veteran Court reporter:

> Taking on one of the most important constitutional questions of the decade, the Supreme Court yesterday expressed grave concerns over the implications of declaring that dying patients have a right to a doctor's help in committing suicide. During the solemn two-hour hearing, the justices pursued not just legal questions, but evolving societal attitudes, the role of modern medicine, their own personal experiences and moral considerations that thread through the emotional issue. In the end, it appeared a majority would not vote to establish a right to physician-assisted suicide.[61]

The oral arguments plainly revealed the conundrum the Justices found themselves in: trying to balance the alleged liberty interest of the individual family member against the interests of the state to preserve life by prohibiting physician-assisted suicide. Eight Justices participated in the two hours of oral argument, for the two state cases were heard back to back. (As is so most of the time, Justice Clarence Thomas was the sole nonparticipant in the oral arguments.)

Oral argument in the Supreme Court can be an exciting, invigorating experience for the Justices and for onlookers. Each Justice has a different approach to questioning the lawyers facing him or her. Some are polite, others scold. Observed one scholar: "Justices ask questions to clarify issues for themselves, but they also use questions to shape their colleagues' perceptions of a case."[62]

It can be a dreaded experience for the lawyer trying to make his or her case before the nine Justices. It is the first time since the Court granted certiorari many months before that the nine jurists focus on the specifics of a case among themselves.

Generally, each side receives thirty minutes, including rebuttal time. On the lectern is a white light and a red light. With five minutes left, the white light is illuminated. When the thirty minutes have expired, the red light goes on and the counsel is finished. "In one case, the red light went on and the attorney asked, 'May I finish my sentence?' 'Yes,' Chief Justice Rehnquist responded, 'assuming it's a short one.'"[63]

With the exception of Thomas, the Rehnquist Court justices are a lively bunch of jurists who insist on interrupting the lawyers facing them.

Justice Ginsburg reports that "there are many more questions than there were in the days when I was arguing before the Court" in the 1970s. "Then, you could get at least five or six sentences out consecutively. Now we tend to interrupt not only counsel, but each other."[64]

The first to speak in the physician-assisted suicide oral arguments[65] was William Williams, a senior Assistant Attorney General of the State of Washington. His task was to refute the arguments of the doctors.

Respondents offer a line that is unstable and inconsistent with the concept of ordered liberty. It is inconsistent with liberty in three respects. First, it is limited to a very few of our citizens. Secondly, those few must justify their exercise of this so-called constitutional right. Thirdly, this right, if it is to be exercised at all, if it is to be recognized at all, must be closely regulated. And their equal protection argument demonstrates just how unstable the line is, because they suggest that flowing from this court's assumed recognition of a right to refuse treatment in the *Cruzan* case, there is a seamless stream of constitutional rights that flows from that decision.

The meaning of "liberty" interest consumed all the parties in the oral argument. Williams started that discussion and was immediately interrupted by Justice Ginsburg, who is recognized as a notorious interrupter of counsel and colleagues alike. She asked:

In the *Cruzan* case, the court recognized a liberty interest and yet it upheld restrictive legislation. . . . So couldn't one take the same approach here, there is a liberty interest, but because of the risks and dangers involved, considerable state regulation is permissible?

"Even if you find a liberty interest," Williams answered, "the same important state interests that were present in *Cruzan* are present in this case."

Justice O'Connor then asked: "What are the state interests you would argue support the law here in the event that a liberty interest is recognized?" Williams indicated three important state interests: "Life, i.e., preventing suicide," "preventing abuse and undue influence [on the terminally ill person by the family or the doctor]," and "regulating the medical profession."

Rehnquist then chimed in:

It would be very difficult to assume a liberty interest and rule in your favor in this case, would it not? Because if we assume a liberty interest but nonetheless say that, even assuming a liberty interest, a state can prohibit it entirely, that would be rather a conundrum.

Williams disagreed with the Chief Justice and said so: "I believe the state, the same important state interests that were implicated in the *Cruzan* case are implicated here but more strongly. . . ." But Rehnquist interrupted:

But in *Cruzan* what we were dealing with was a state rule that said you had to prove a certain thing by clear and convincing evidence. Here we're not dealing with any sort of an evidentiary rule; we're dealing with an outright prohibition.

Continuing, in his inimitable ironic fashion, Scalia said: "*We can say there's a liberty interest in murdering people, however, it's outweighed by the state's interest in preserving the rights of its citizens. I guess we could do that, couldn't we?*" To which Williams could say only, "That's correct."

Justice Scalia then made the following observation: "I suppose that proclaiming a liberty interest is cost-free so long as you can proclaim them and then say, however they can be outweighed by various social policies adopted by the states." Williams said, quietly, "That's true."

U.S. Solicitor General Walter Dellinger shared some of Washington State's thirty minutes and spoke next. Justice O'Connor asked him: "It's your brief that takes the position that there is a liberty interest, but nonetheless, the law should be upheld." He agreed but qualified the view of the government: "There is *no* general liberty interest in dying." And he threw the "slippery slope" argument out:

While the individual stories are heartrending . . . it's important for this court to recognize that, if you were to affirm the judgments below, lethal medication could be proposed as a treatment, not just to those in severe pain, but to every competent terminally ill person in the country.

Justice Souter, however, asked Dellinger: "I don't know how to weight this probability and this risk. Help me out on that." Scalia jumped in at this point:

You say there is a liberty interest which tosses the whole matter into this Court so that it's up to us to decide whether indeed the states are right or wrong that this is a dangerous practice. And, if we think they're wrong, then the liberty interest must prevail.

Before he could answer comfortably, the red light went on and Dellinger sat down.

The next speaker was Kathryn Tucker, representing the respondent doctors. She began:

This case presents the question whether dying citizens in full possession of their mental faculties at the threshold of death due to terminal illness have the liberty to choose to cross that threshold in a humane and dignified manner. . .

The Chief stopped her: "[That] is not an issue here. . . . It's that they want assistance from a physician to do it, that's what we're arguing about." Admonished, she corrected herself and attempted to bridge the patient's right with the need for physician assistance:

These dying patients want a peaceful death, they want a humane death and they want a dignified death. And, in order to access that kind of death they need the assistance of their physician. . . .

Scalia intervened: "Why is it limited to those on the threshold of death? I mean suppose . . . the doctor says you're going to be in terrible pain for 10 years. . . . Why shouldn't I have the right to suicide." She answered:

A patient who is confronting death . . . has a very different choice than the one you posit. This individual does not have a choice between living and dying. This dying patient whose dying process has begun and is underway, this individual has only the choice of how to die. Will that death be brutal, will that death be peaceful.

She was able to continue for another minute:

We are asking simply that this court recognize the vital liberty interest at stake and that it is a protected choice but [we are] not asking this court to engage in legislation, we are not asking this court to promulgate a code for regulation of the practice. We do think it should be left to the states.

Rehnquist, however, was not that sanguine about the future:

You're not asking that now. But surely that's what the next couple of generations are going to have to deal with, what regulations are permissible and what not if we uphold your position here.

Neither was Justice O'Connor sanguine about the future; she observed: "There is no doubt that . . . if we upheld your position, *it would result in a flow of cases through the court system for heaven knows how long.*"

For Justice Kennedy, who had been quiet, there was a need to raise another major facet of the litigation: "This is a question of ethics and of morals and of allocation of resources and of our commitment to treat the elderly and infirm." And legislators were much better at defining a problem and creating policy than judges.

The next to speak was New York Attorney General Dennis Vacco. Should the state remain neutral when one of its citizens decides to take his life with the assistance of a physician? No. "It is New York's view, however, that the Constitution does not require this to be the case."

Ginsburg started: "*Tell us why the* [CA2] *was wrong* [when it overturned the state law because it denied equal protection of the law to similarly situated patients]?" Vacco did, stating there was a fundamental difference between refusing treatment and dying and affirmatively committing suicide with the aid of a doctor.

In the first context the individual who is at the . . . end stages of their life as the 2nd Circuit defined it, are exercising their right . . . to refuse treatment. That right which has been recognized for centuries as springing from the common law, the right of being free from bodily interference, the right to be free from battery; [the] right to be let alone.

In contrast, are those individuals who are not asserting a right, that [is,] their rights to bodily integrity, but instead attempting to assert, as the plaintiff respondents in this case are claiming, that there is some right to have a third party, in this instance physicians help kill themselves. And we believe that these two acts are clearly distinguishable.

Justice Ginsburg asked Walter Dellinger the same question. His answer:

There is an important common sense distinction between withdrawing artificial support so that a disease will progress to its inevitable end and providing chemicals to be used to kill someone. The historic distinction between *killing someone and letting them die* is so powerful that we believe that it fully suffices here.

Harvard Law School professor Laurence H. Tribe was the advocate for Dr. Timothy Quill and his colleagues. Tribe is an internationally respected legal scholar. He is also a very experienced practitioner before the U.S. Supreme Court. Justice Breyer, however, had a question for him at the very beginning of his oral argument:

> However you define the liberty interest, there are tremendously difficult procedural questions of what would be the safeguards of voluntariness, a much more difficult question . . . than what you might think. And how do you decide terminal condition? What's your response to the proposition that different [interest] groups, interacting with the legislature, are far more suited . . . to come up with an answer than a court writing a constitutional provision.

Tribe did not directly answer the sharp query from Justice Breyer. Instead, he tried to discuss the "liberty" interest of the dying patient who was not on any life-support system. "The person has a right to say, 'leave me alone.'"

But Justice Stevens wanted more specificity from Tribe: "Tell us what you think the liberty interest is."

Tribe answered:

> The liberty interest in this case is the liberty, when facing imminent and inevitable death, not to be forced by the government to endure a degree of pain and suffering that one can relieve only by being completely unconscious. Not to be forced into that choice, that the liberty is the freedom, at this threshold at the end of life, not to be a creature of the state *but to have some voice* in the question of how much pain one is really going through.

Souter quietly responded: "Why does the voice just arrive when death is imminent?"

Tribe's final observation paraphrased Shakespeare:

The court's jurisprudence has identified, I think for good reason, that life, though it feels continuous to many of us, has certain critical thresholds: *Birth, marriage, child-bearing. I think death is one of those thresholds.* That is, it is the last chapter of one's life after all.

At the end of the two-hour oral argument, which clearly took its toll on all the participants, jurists and counsel alike, the Chief Justice thanked the lawyers, closing with the traditional remark: "The case is submitted."

Almost six months later, the Supreme Court handed down the judgments in the two physician-assisted suicide cases. There were six opinions written by the Justices in *Washington v Glucksberg*. Chief Justice Rehnquist wrote the majority opinion, joined by Justices O'Connor, Scalia, Kennedy, and Thomas.

The question presented in this case is whether Washington's prohibition against "causing" or "aiding" a suicide offends the Fourteenth Amendment to the U.S. Constitution. We hold that it does not.

Rehnquist's opinion held that the Washington statute did not violate the Due Process Clause, either on its face or as applied to competent, terminally ill adults who wished to hasten their deaths by obtaining medication prescribed by their doctors. The Chief Justice concluded that the liberty interest attached to the Due Process Clause did not include a right to commit suicide with the included right to assistance in doing so.

An examination of the nation's "history, legal traditions, and practices" revealed that the asserted "right-to-die" with the assistance of physicians as "not a fundamental liberty interest" protected by the Due Process Clause. "For over 700 years, the Anglo-American common law tradition has punished or otherwise disapproved of both suicide and assisting suicide."

Nor was the asserted right consistent with the line of "deeply rooted" substantive due process precedents. While that clause

provides heightened protection against governmental interference with certain fundamental rights and liberty interests,[66] the right to commit suicide with the aid of another has no place in our Nation's traditions.

And, wrote Rehnquist;

we have always been reluctant to expand the concept of substantive due process because guideposts for responsible decision-making in this uncharted area are scarce and open-ended.

Finally, the state's ban on physician-assisted suicide was at least "reasonably related" to the promotion and protection of a number of Washington's "important and legitimate" interests, including "the unqualified interest in the preservation of human life."

The opinion closed with the observation that

throughout the Nation, Americans are engaged in an earnest and profound debate about the morality, legality, and practicality of physician-assisted suicide. Our holding permits this debate to continue, as it should in a democratic society. The decision of the CA9 is reversed, and the case is remanded for further proceedings consistent with this opinion.

Justice O'Connor wrote the same separate concurring opinion for both state cases. "Death," she began, "will be different for each of us."[67] She joined Rehnquist's opinions because she, too, believed that there was no generalized right to "commit suicide." She wrote separately to present her position, one markedly different from Rehnquist's.

All parties in both cases agreed that a competent patient who was suffering from a terminal illness and who was in constant pain had no legal barriers to obtaining "palliative" medication from qualified doctors to alleviate such suffering—"even to the point of causing unconsciousness and hastening death." There was, in her judgment, "no need to address" the "narrower question" raised in this case: "Whether a mentally competent person who is experiencing great suffering has a constitutionally cognizable interest in controlling the circumstances of his or her imminent death." Clearly, she left open the answer to that question, suggesting instead that her answer would differ from the Chief's response.

Justice Stevens also wrote a concurring opinion for both cases. He believed that there was no categorical "liberty" to kill oneself with the assistance of a physician. However, he insisted, "in a more particularized challenge to a general rule [prohibiting physician-assisted suicide]" a terminally ill and competent patient who sought to hasten death with the assistance of a doctor "might prevail." He maintained, there is room for further debate about the limits the Constitution places on the power of the state to punish the practice [of physician-assisted suicide]. . . . It does not mean that every possible application of the statute would be valid.

Justice Souter concurred in the judgment of the Court. Given the substantial dispute that emerged, internationally, over the effectiveness of assisted suicide guidelines, Washington's asserted interest in protecting terminally ill patients was a valid counterbalance against the due process argument of the doctors in the case. He wrote separately, and at great length, to explain why he believed the right to "commit suicide" with some assistance was not a fundamental right protected by the Constitution. It can never be considered an indispensable facet of a society based on the concept of "ordered liberty" enunciated in *Palko*.

Justice Ginsburg concurred as well, in both cases. "I concur in the Court's judgments in these cases substantially for the reasons stated by Justice O'-Connor in her concurring opinion."

Justice Breyer's was the fifth separate concurring opinion that covered the two cases. He joined most of the O'Connor opinion because her "views, which I share, have greater legal significance than the Court's opinion suggests."

For Breyer, the core of a person's liberty interest was "the right to die with dignity." The Rehnquist description of the liberty interest, the "right to commit suicide with another's assistance," was just too crude.

But irrespective of the exact words used, at its core would lie personal control over the manner of death, professional medical assistance, and the avoidance of unnecessary and severe physical suffering.

"Were the legal circumstances different," had the state not allowed palliative care, i.e., extensive medication for the alleviation of pain, the state statute "would be more directly at issue." Because terminally ill competent patients in both states could be given massive doses of medication to relieve the pain "at the end of life"—although simultaneously hastening death (known as the "double effect")—the state statute did not violate due process of law.

Vacco was a much shorter ruling. Rehnquist's opinion for the same majority held that New York State's prohibition on "assisting" suicide did not violate the Fourteenth Amendment's Equal Protection Clause. The Court refused to accept the argument that the competent, terminally ill patient who refuses life-saving medical treatment is "similarly situated" to another competent, terminally ill patient who wishes to commit suicide with the assistance of a physician.

There is, as U.S. Solicitor General Dellinger had maintained during oral argument in January, an "important distinction between *letting* a patient die and *making* that patient die."

> The distinction comports with fundamental legal principles of causation and intent. When a patient refuses life sustaining medical treatment, he dies from an underlying fatal disease or pathology; but if a patient ingests lethal medication prescribed by a physician, he is killed by that medication.

The respondent doctors' argument, accepted by the CA2, that the distinction is "arbitrary" and "capricious" and therefor violative of the Fourteenth Amendment was incorrect. "The line between the two acts may not always be clear, but certainty is not required, even were it possible." Logic and contemporary practice support New York's judgment that the two acts are different, and New York may therefore, consistent with the Constitution, treat them differently.

The headlines the following day told the world that the U.S. Supreme Court's "Unanimous Decision Points to the Tradition of Valuing Life."[68] However, as the oral arguments and debates in the six opinions indicated, there were a number of major disagreements within the Court. They were, however, set aside for another set of cases and for petitioners who were still alive when the litigation reached the Court.

The Court essentially punted on the major question, giving the states time to reexamine their public policies and to change them if that was the sense of the state's citizens. Without doubt, however, the two cases put into the national spotlight the end-of-life drama. It has become a premier issue for reluctant legislators, judges, doctors, and the public.

The Justices "very deliberately left it to state governments to decide upon a broad and growing assortment of questions that arise when people under medical treatment must come to terms with death."[69] In 1997, forty-four states had laws criminalizing assisted suicide. However, as Rehnquist noted in his opinion, in thirty states bills had been introduced to weaken those bans. And Oregon's voters approved, by a statewide referendum, the Death With Dignity Act, which finally was implemented in late 1998.

The impact of these decisions on doctors was unclear. During the oral arguments and in the briefs, it was acknowledged that many doctors helped terminally ill competent patients deal with their pain by administering huge doses of morphine or valium on top of a morphine drip to alleviate the pain. This is known as the "double effect"; patients, who have agreed to the final treatment, die painlessly because of this overmedicalization. Ironically, an example of the "double effect" scenario surfaced the day the two right-to-die decisions came down. A Florida jury acquitted Dr. Ernesto Pinzon, accused of murdering a terminally ill patient with massive doses of morphine. He argued, successfully, that "he was only trying to relieve his patient's pain."[70]

Life spans have lengthened since 1900; death comes differently in 2000 than it did in 1900. More people are living longer as America entered the twenty-first century than was the case one hundred years earlier. In 1900, the average American died at age forty-six, and the major causes of death were communicable diseases, with pneumonia seen as the "good" death. In 2000, the average life span of Americans is seventy-seven years, and the major causes of death are chronic ailments such as cancer, AIDS, diabetes, and heart failure "developed months or years before their deaths."[71]

In 2000, the majority of chronically ill patients—more than 80 percent—are in hospitals rather than at home at the end of life. (In 1900, most Americans died at home.) A majority are in great pain and very frightened of dying. There is the need for them to talk about death with their families. They must discuss "living wills," "advance directives," "Do Not Resuscitate" (DNR) instructions to nurses and doctors, and the possible need for surrogates.

Public opinion, too, reflects the growing awareness among families of end-of-life issues. When asked "What are you afraid of?" a majority of men and women answered, "Being in pain at the end of life." Other concerns expressed by seniors were depleting the family's finances, prolonging death by artificial means, and dying itself. In a recent study, "women reported being more fearful than men not only of being in pain, but of dying and having their death prolonged by artificial means."[72] Further, 77 percent of family members believe that physicians should be able to use controlled substances to effectively manage the pain of their child or parent. This suggests that families as well as patients are aware of the "double effect," but are more concerned with alleviating the constant pain and suffering of a loved one.[73]

IV. Summing Up

The two women on the Court, Justices Ruth B. Ginsburg and Sandra D. O'-Connor, placed the end-of-life drama in very personal, human terms. *"Most of us have parents or other loved ones, and we've lived through a dying experience that forces us to think about these things,"* Justice Ginsburg said during the January 1997 oral arguments. In her June 1997 written opinion, Justice O'Connor wrote: *"Every one of us at some point* may be affected by our own or a family member's terminal illness."

The other jurists surely saw the end-of-life cases in the same way. For some, especially Justice Scalia, legislators, not federal judges, were the ones to deal with the matter by establishing public policies regarding death and dying. "For God's sake," he uttered at one time, "we judges do not have the secrets of the Cosmos nor the Wisdom of Solomon."

However, the Court did grant certiorari—in *Cruzan, Glucksberg,* and *Vacco*—because the right-to-die question had percolated enough in the state and lower federal courts. There was a need to provide the nation with some answers, however tentative, to the questions that had become very visible in the last two decades of the twentieth century.

In this set of right-to-die cases, as in all the other intimate personal and family relationships previously examined, the Justices could not agree on the correct answers. But they have given Americans some ideas with which to continue the discussions about the end of life.

Justice O'Connor wrote: "[D]eath will be different for each of us." However, given the changed manner in which death will visit "each of us" in this century, most of us will die in hospitals or nursing homes, surrounded by many strangers and a room full of medical equipment. Many patients will be incompetent, in a PVS at the end, and most of us will realize our greatest fear: chronic pain.

There is a great need to educate all of us, including physicians, nurses, other medical professionals, and clergy, about the rights autonomous individuals have when they face death, as well as the proper care for those facing death. Whether or not one agrees with the Supreme Court's opinions in this area of personal privacy and autonomy, they have given Americans food for thought. What was, until recently, the unthinkable issue is now a prime target of discussion in magazines, newsweeklies, made-for-television movies, talk shows. Most important, however, these discussions are occurring in the quiet places in the family home.

7

Family and Personal Privacy in the Twenty-First Century

Hard cases involving intimate personal and family relations continue to arrive in courtrooms around the nation. In July 2001, for example, a frustrated Wisconsin Supreme Court upheld a probation order that barred a man convicted of failure to pay child support *from having more children* unless he shows that he can support all his children.

According to the story in the *New York Times,* thirty-four-year-old David Oakley, "who has nine children by four women and owes $25,000 in child support, faces eight years in prison if he violates the condition." The Wisconsin high court divided 4:3 along gender lines. All four male justices joined in the ruling, finding "the condition a *reasonable mechanism* to deal with a father who has consistently and intentionally failed to pay the child support he owes." It was, wrote Justice Jon P. Wilcox, a restriction "*narrowly tailored to serve the state's compelling interest* in having parents support their children." Nonpayment of child support was a national problem, he wrote. One family in three with a child support order did not receive any money at all; nationally, "parents who did not pay deprived children of about $11 billion a year."

All three female justices dissented, calling the condition placed on Oakley "an unconstitutional intrusion on a basic right to procreate." Justice Diane S. Sykes wrote that the "condition" amounted to "a compulsory, state-sponsored, court-enforced financial test for future parenthood." Another dissenter, Justice Ann W. Bradley, was concerned about the implications for abortion. The order "creates a strong incentive for a man in Oakley's position to demand from the woman the termination of her pregnancy." Furthermore, the condition placed on Oakley is "unworkable since [he] realistically cannot be stopped from having intercourse, protected or otherwise."

Oakley's lawyer, Timothy T. Kay, planned an appeal to the U.S. Supreme Court.[1] If the appeal moves upward, will the Court during its 2001 Term grant certiorari in *Oakley v State*? Will there be four votes to review the case? And, If certiorari is granted, how will a Court majority balance the values in the dispute: the right to have nonprocreative sexual intercourse versus the state's interest in protecting the welfare of its residents?

Will Kay try to use the *Zablocki* precedent? In that 1978 decision, the Court held unconstitutional a state statute that prohibited a parent who failed to comply with child support orders from marrying without court permission. Can that precedent be "stretched" to cover some very different facts in Oakley's case? Will the Justices simply throw their hands up, perhaps laugh at the absurdity of the "ridiculous" case, and deny certiorari?

The U.S. Supreme Court Justices do not know what the fact-situation will be in future privacy and personal autonomy cases until the briefs are filed requesting a grant of certiorari. They do know, however, that petitioners will continually ask them to stretch the parameters of the privacy right to rule in their favor. This has been the reality since the Court, in 1965, "found" a fundamental marital privacy right in the "penumbras and emanations" of the Bill of Rights.

I. "She Kept Screaming"

Anamarie Regino, in 2000, was a four-year-old "morbidly obese" child standing four and one-half feet tall, and weighing more than 130 pounds—"meaning she was three times heavier and 50% taller than an average child her age." Standing up left her breathless. "A short walk across the room is a hike," wrote a reporter. When she was three, Anamarie was taken screaming from her parents and placed in foster care. The state officials said that the child's "life-threatening obesity was her mother and father's fault."[2]

The case became a national sensation when the press and television told the story. The youngster became "a *cause celebre* for the National Association to Advance Fat Acceptance, which sees her case as a 'threat to all the parents of fat children.'"[3] The state relinquished its legal custody of Anamarie in January 2001, and her parents have brought civil suits against the doctors, social workers, and the state itself for allegedly violating the family's liberty interests protected by the Fourteenth Amendment's Due Process Clause.

The parents' claim that they have struggled to

cope with a child whose condition medicine is not able to cure and whose best interests the law cannot easily determine. "They don't know what's wrong, so they blame us," says Adela Martinez-Regino.

"They treated her for four years, doctor after doctor. Not one of them could help. They've played around with her life like she was some kind of experiment, and even now no one can tell me what is wrong."

When Anamarie was born, she was long and skinny. She weighed a normal 6 pounds, 13 ounces. As an infant, the mother knew something was wrong. The baby "was drinking 10, 12 bottles a day and still wanting more," said her mother. At eight months, Ana was 38 pounds and an endocrinologist told her mother, "[W]ater down her formula, she's just going to be a big girl." A bone scan when Ana was one year old showed her to have the bones of a four- to five-year-old. She had all her teeth when she was a year old. When Ana was two years old, her father, Miguel Regina, quit his carpenter's job to stay home full-time because she could not walk. "Her bones and muscles were not strong enough to support her weight of more than 70 pounds." Her diet was varied constantly by the doctors, going from twelve hundred to five hundred calories daily. But she still gained weight. After three years of endless hospitalizations, the medical staff suspected a suspicious cycle of parental abuse. Ana would lose weight during the hospital stay and, after discharge, she gained her weight back and more. The medical staff, including social workers, thought that Ana's parents were trying to hurt their child.

In June 2000, Ana was at her heaviest, 130 pounds—at an age when most children weigh 30 pounds. She entered the hospital again, was put on a liquid diet and by early July her weight was down to 123 pounds. She was released, put on a strict five hundred-calorie-a-day liquid diet, and enrolled in a day-care program at Children's Psychiatric Hospital. Secretly, hospital staff closely watched the little girl to see (by examining her stool) if her parents were giving her solid foods. In late July, they found traces of solid food.

In August, the state officials initiated a plan to take Ana away from her parents. A report was issued indicating that every physician who examined Ana agreed that "continued weight gain could cause fatal heart damage." She would die soon if steps were not taken to remove her from her family. Toward the end of the month, a social worker recommended that Ana be placed in a foster home because her parents "have not been able or willing" to properly control her weight.

The social worker speculated that Ana was a victim of Munchausen Syndrome by Proxy, "a psychological disorder in which parents purposely harm their children in order to draw attention to themselves." The family, the report concluded, "does not fully understand the threat to their daughter's safety and welfare due to language or cultural barriers." On August 25, 2000, Ana was taken from her parents and placed in a foster home. They were charged with child abuse and a fall hearing was set to determine their fate and that of their child.

Ana's parents' lawyer found a new doctor, Javier Aceves, an Albuquerque pediatrician who worked with chronically ill children, to work with their child while in the foster home. He changed her diet and she began losing weight. In late October 2000, an agreement was reached between the lawyer and the New Mexico Children, Youth, and Families Department. The state maintained legal custody of Ana, but physical custody was returned, with Ana, to the parents. She came home on November 10, 2000. However, state social workers visited the home daily, "watching everything the family did."

In January 2001, the family court judge, satisfied that Ana was losing weight and that the parents were not suffering from Munchausen Syndrome by Proxy, dismissed the charges of child abuse and returned legal custody to the parents. Ana's doctor still does not know what is wrong with the child. He is treating her with diet and exercise. "We need to find a diet she can live with and an amount of exercise she can do to control her weight."

In July 2001, the parents filed civil suits against the state, the Children, Youth, and Families Department, a number of Ana's doctors and social workers. Doctors, by law, are required to report suspected child-abuse. But, asked the lawyer, "can obesity really be called a form of abuse?"

The major question courts will examine is whether the state's intrusion into the private affairs of the Regino family, without any proof of improper parental behavior, violated their fundamental privacy right protected by the Due Process Clause of the Fourteenth Amendment.

This vignette's focus is on the countervailing forces that exist in every one of the Court's cases involving the right of privacy and personal autonomy versus state actions that curtail these rights. U.S. Supreme Court decisions have indicated that raising a child is the fundamental responsibility of the parents. However, there no longer exists an impenetrable iron curtain around private family relationships. The state's interest in protecting a family member from abuse is a compelling one. It can take steps, if "narrowly tailored," to ensure that the state interest is manifested. When the state action is challenged in court by individuals such as Miguel and Amelia Regina, the judges have to balance the rights of the parents against the interests of the state. This balancing proceeds all the way to the U.S. Supreme Court.

The Justices of the U.S. Supreme Court, in case after case involving intimate family and personal relationships, draw on the established precedents, the common law, and general rules of equity in their balancing of the arguments. But, "inescapably," in all these hard cases they are "influenced strongly by principles of public policy as well as their moral values," i.e., their own understanding of "individualism and individual worth."[4] Their principles must extend to the most unusual fact-situations presented to them by plaintiffs. For them, there is a consistent application of their moral values in the balancing process that they engage in when deciding family privacy and personal autonomy cases.

In the 2000–2001 Term of the Court, there were two cases the Justices wrestled with involving the personal rights of individuals. The cases exhibited new and novel fact-situations. At their core, however, the litigation forced the nine jurists once again to examine their core values and to apply them in their legal responses.

II. Is the Home Still a Castle?

In chapter 6, the problematic issue discussed was how individuals—patient, family, doctors, and nurses—responded to dramatic advances in medical technology. Clearly, as the case law suggests, law, politics, and medical ethics are trying to keep pace with the rapid advances made by science that keep people alive far longer than many want to live. Scientific advances, however, are not limited to medical breakthroughs.

In the continuing societal effort to reduce crime and arrest criminals, law enforcement agencies, federal, state, and local, have been the beneficiaries of the latest in surveillance technology. These new devices have caused civil liberties groups such as the American Civil Liberties Union (ACLU) a great deal of concern. The ACLU position was classic J. S. Mills: "Privacy makes possible individuality, and thus, freedom."[5] These modern electronic devices, such as thermal imaging machines, the ACLU claims, invade a person's privacy in ways that overwhelm one's freedom and liberty protected by the Due Process Clause.

The thermal imaging device, for example (there are now about ten thousand in use by law enforcement agencies) uses infrared technology—invisible to the naked eye—to detect the escape of heat from within the house being scanned by the device. Law enforcement officials view the images produced on a monitor and take appropriate action, including arrest of a suspect.[6] Using the new technology, a search warrant is not requested by the police because, they maintain, there is no actual physical penetration into the suspect's home.

What was once considered an illegal physical intrusion, a trespass, of a person's property is no longer a literal physical trespass. A helicopter five hundred feet above the suspect's house, or a law enforcement officer in a car across the street from the house, can electronically "enter" the home without having to actually pierce the walls.[7] The thermal imager "operates somewhat like a video camera showing heat images."[8]

Case Study: *Kyello v U.S.*, 2000

Danny Kyello lived in Florence, Oregon. In 1991, Agent William Elliot of the U.S. Department of the Interior came to suspect that Danny was growing marijuana at home. Growing the plant indoors requires high-intensity halogen lamps. In order to determine whether there was that level of heat present in the house, Agent Elliot, joined by Agent Dan Haas, used an Agema Thermovision 210 thermal imager to scan Kyello's house from their parked car. It took only a few minutes. The monitor showed hot spots over the garage and on a sidewall.

With that information, along with an informant's tip and presentation of Kyello's utility bills, the agents were issued a search warrant by a federal magistrate. A search of Kyello's apartment found an "indoor growing operation involving more than 100 plants." Kyello was arrested and indicted on one count of manufacturing marijuana, in violation of 21 U.S.C. Section 841(a) (1).

On appeal the CA9 remanded the case to the federal district court for an evidentiary hearing regarding the "intrusiveness of thermal imaging." The district court concluded that thermal imaging was a "non-intrusive" device that did not penetrate walls or windows. The judge upheld the validity of the warrant and reaffirmed the court's denial of the motion to suppress. A divided CA9 panel initially reversed the district court judge, "but that opinion was withdrawn and the panel (after a change in composition) affirmed, 2:1." The majority held that Kyello "had shown no subjective "expectation of privacy"[9] because he made no attempt to conceal the heat escaping from his home."

The Court granted certiorari and heard oral argument on February 20, 2001. Kenneth Lerner, Kyello's lawyer, argued that, if anything, the expectation of privacy was greater in one's home than it is for someone making a call from a public telephone. He called the use of the thermal imaging device "spying" by the government.[10]

A skeptical Justice Stevens asked Lerner if the police would need a search warrant before "dangling a thermometer from a long pole to measure the temperature of a roof-top." "Obviously," the lawyer answered, "I don't think that we would prohibit things like thermometers or watches or things that we typically use in our daily lives."

According to a legal reporter covering the oral argument,

Lerner seemed to score a point when he suggested that the justices should keep the inevitable progress of technology in mind when they rule on a case involving relatively murky images generated by current devices.[11]

Assistant Solicitor General Michael R. Dreeben, for the United States, argued that there was no physical penetration of the walls of Kyello's house by the thermal imager. Justice Souter immediately countered:

I think there is a reasonable expectation of privacy that what you're doing in your bathroom is not going to be picked up when you take a bath by somebody with one of these thermal imaging devices!

At the Conference Session after oral argument, five jurists came down on Kyello's side, including Justice Scalia. Since he was the senior jurist on the majority side, Scalia assigned himself the opinion. Joining him was a very odd combination of jurists: fellow conservative Justice Clarence Thomas and moderate Justices Souter, Ginsburg, and Breyer.

Scalia concluded that the actions of the law enforcement agents violated the Fourth Amendment's prohibition of unreasonable searches and seizures. In the opinion, he incorporated Lerner's arguments and the bathroom vignette briefly mentioned by Souter a few days earlier.

It would be foolish to contend that the degree of privacy secured to citizens by the Fourth Amendment has been entirely unaffected by the advance of technology. . . . The question we confront today is what limits there are upon this power of technology to shrink the realm of guaranteed privacy. . . . In the search of the interior of homes—the prototypical and hence most litigated area of protected privacy—there is a ready criterion, with roots deep in the common law, of the minimal expectation of privacy that *exists,* and that is acknowledged to be *reasonable.* To withdraw protection of this minimum expectation would be to permit police technology to erode the privacy guaranteed by the Fourth Amendment.

Using thermal imaging, a device "not in general public use," constitutes a search, and "the information obtained by the thermal imager in this case was the product of a search." For it to be used in any criminal prosecution it must be a legal search, i.e., one conducted *after* a search warrant was issued by an impartial magistrate. "It is presumptively unreasonable without a warrant," Scalia noted.

Then Scalia wrote: Not to take this position

> *would leave the homeowner at the mercy of advancing technology*—including imaging technology that could discern all human activity in the home.[12] While the technology used in the present case was relatively crude, the rule we adopt must take account of *more sophisticated systems* that are already in use or in development.

The majority reversed the CA9 and remanded the case for further proceedings. Ironically, liberal Justice John P. Stevens wrote the dissent, joined by three conservative jurists, Chief Justice Rehnquist, and Justices O'Connor and Kennedy.

Justice Stevens argued that there was literally no "through-the-wall" invasion of privacy. The federal agents were doing "off-the-wall" surveillance with the thermal imager and made "indirect deductions" about the manufacture of marijuana behind the walls. There was no Fourth Amendment invasion of Kyello's privacy by the federal agents. Furthermore, to make a constitutional rule to cover *future* technological improvements was "unnecessary, unwise, and inconsistent with the Fourth Amendment."

The *Kyello* case was yet another ironic 5:4 opinion in the area of privacy rights, with O'Connor on the losing side, reflecting the division of views about policy and values. "But it was not the usual 5:4 conservative-liberal split," wrote a Court reporter after the decision came down.

Justice Antonin Scalia wrote the majority opinion in a case that conformed neatly to his view that the Constitution should be interpreted according to the intent of its framers; modern technology that enables the police to gain knowledge that once would have necessitated a physical entry into a private home, he said, requires a warrant. Not to make that leap across time, Justice Scalia said, *"would leave the homeowner at the mercy of advancing technology."*[13]

James Tomkovicz, a professor at the University of Iowa School of Law, who wrote an *amicus* brief supporting Danny Kyello—for the National Association of Criminal Defense Lawyers—said: "The decision sends a message that there are strict limits on how much technology can decrease personal privacy in the home."[14]

Not surprisingly, but very unusual, the Scalia opinion in *Kyello* was hailed by the ACLU. Its national legal director, Steven R. Shapiro, said: "It means that the Fourth Amendment is going to apply to all the high-tech technology that is rapidly being developed. Big Brother must now pay attention to constitutional principles."[15]

Bill Stutz, a professor at Harvard Law School, said:

This is an important case because it is an important issue. It says the Constitution protects some level of privacy that is not defined by current technology. That's very important in a society where technology is advancing as rapidly as in ours. It's not a radical advance, but it's a big deal.

However, Stutz added:

Twenty years from now you may be able to buy thermal imaging technology at a Wal-Mart. Then either we get less privacy or the Court has to draw another line. *Kyello* is not the last word on this.[16]

Kyello is the most recent example of the U.S. Supreme Court majority's reaching out to invalidate an implicit public policy that conflicted with what it believed was a fundamental right, a person's *reasonable* expectation of privacy in his home. A "rule" was fashioned—by an extremely conservative jurist—to protect personal privacy in the home against the use of sophisticated technological devices that could conceivably allow the uninvited observer to determine when the woman of the house was in the sauna.

III. The "Medical Necessity" Exception and Federal Anti-Marijuana-Use Law

In the second case involving personal privacy and autonomy, *U.S. v Oakland Cannabis Buyers' Cooperative, et al.*,[17] the conservatives trumped the moderates. Although it was an 8:0 judgment, there was sharp disagreement between the five conservatives and the three moderates.

Two opinions were written to reflect these differences. (Justice Stephen Breyer took no part in the consideration or decision of the case. As is the Court's custom, he did not explain his recusal. There was, however, an obvious reason: His brother, Charles Breyer, was the U.S. district court judge involved in the legal actions preceding the appeal to the U.S. Supreme Court.)

The case focused on the legality of using marijuana for medical reasons. By the year 2000, almost one-fifth of the states had passed "compassionate use" legislation enabling seriously ill persons to possess and use marijuana for medical reasons.[18] Supporters of such laws argue that marijuana is

> often the only source of relief for cancer patients experiencing excruciating pain or AIDS patients feeling crippling nausea. Some anorexics have used marijuana to maintain their appetites.[19]

In November 1996,[20] voters in California enacted an initiative measure, the Compassionate Use Act of 1996, "to ensure that seriously ill Californians have the right to obtain and use marijuana for medical purposes." However, a federal law, the Controlled Substances Act, 21 U.S.C. Section 841 (a), prohibited the distribution, manufacturing, or possession of marijuana, labeled by the government as a Schedule I controlled substance. The sole exception for marijuana use in the act: "Government-approved research projects." The Clinton administration, fearful that these state "compassionate use" laws would "create a massive loophole" in federal drug laws, had to respond but had only a few options.[21]

Other than sending out letters to doctors "encouraging" them to discuss the "risks, benefits, and legality" of the medical marijuana treatment, the only action the federal government could take was to have federal district courts in the nine states issue injunctions prohibiting the manufacture, distribution, and possession of marijuana for medical use. The U.S. Department of Justice (DOJ) categorically rejected the specter of "dispatching swarms of federal agents to California, and Arizona, for fear of appearing heavy-handed and generating an anti-Washington backlash, senior [Clinton administration] officials said." Besides, the U.S. Justice Department acknowledged that "it lacked the resources and the legal authority for a more aggressive crackdown."[22]

In January 1998, the U.S. government asked the federal district court judge to enjoin the not-for-profit Oakland organization, Oakland Cannabis Buyers' Cooperative, created to help distribute marijuana to qualified persons, from distributing marijuana for medical purposes. The argument the Clinton administration made was the "federalism" claim: Although the cooperative's actions are legal under state law, they violate federal law.

The mayors of four California cities that had well-developed cannabis distribution centers, San Francisco, Oakland, Santa Cruz, and West Hollywood, in March 1998, wrote a letter to Clinton requesting the withdrawal of the lawsuits against the Oakland and other cannabis clubs.

What is now a reasonably well-controlled, safe distribution system—one that has been characterized by cooperation with city officials and one that is inspected by the Health Department—will instead devolve into a completely unregulated, and unregulable, public nuisance,

they argued.[23]

Clinton, however, did not take their advice. The U.S. district court judge, Charles Breyer, concluded that the federal government had established a probability of success on the merits and granted a preliminary injunction.

The cooperative openly violated the federal injunction by distributing marijuana to many persons. The government then instituted contempt proceedings against the cooperative. In its defense, the cooperative argued that the distribution was medically necessary. There was, in the common law, the "medical necessity" exemption that allowed it to provide marijuana to patients who were desperately ill and in great pain. Judge Breyer rejected the defense because there was "insufficient evidence that each patient who received marijuana was in actual danger of imminent harm without the drug." He found the cooperative in contempt and empowered U.S. Marshals to seize the property.

The cooperative appealed the judgment of the district court judge to the CA9. On the merits, the CA9 reversed and remanded, arguing that the medical necessity defense was a "legally cognizable defense" that would likely apply in the instant case. It ordered Judge Breyer to consider "the criteria for a medical necessity exemption, and, should he modify the injunction, to set forth these criteria in the modification order." Breyer eventually modified the injunction to incorporate the medical necessity defense.

The Clinton administration successfully petitioned the U.S. Supreme Court for certiorari to review the CA9's decision that "medical necessity" is a "legally cognizable defense to violations of the Controlled Substances Act." That became the constitutional question of law the Justices had to answer.[24]

Justice Clarence Thomas was the author of the majority opinion, joined by the Chief Justice and Justices O'Connor, Kennedy, and Scalia. He disagreed with the cooperative's contention that "because necessity was a defense at common law, medical necessity should be read into the Controlled Substances Act." Exemptions are a policy matter for legislatures, not judges, he wrote. "Under any conception of legal necessity, one principle is clear: The defense cannot succeed when the legislature itself has made a 'determination of values.'"

> We hold that medical necessity is not a defense to manufacturing and distributing marijuana. The Court of Appeals erred when it held that medical necessity is a "legally cognizable defense." It further erred when it instructed the District Court on remand to consider "the criteria for a medical necessity exemption." . . . Because federal courts interpret, rather than author, the federal Criminal code, we are not at liberty to rewrite it.

Justice Stevens wrote separately, joined by Justices Souter and Ginsburg, to express his critical views of the Thomas opinion:

> Because necessity was raised in this case as a defense to *distribution,* the Court need not venture an opinion on whether the defense is available to anyone other than distributors. Most notably, whether the *defense might be available to a seriously ill patient for whom there is no alternative means of avoiding starvation or extraordinary suffering is a difficult issue that is not presented here.* [My emphasis.]

Reflecting some very basic disagreements on another matter, Justice Stevens wrote:

> The Court *gratuitously* casts doubt on "whether necessity can *ever* be a defense" to *any* federal statute that does not explicitly provide for it, calling such a defense into question by a *misleading* reference to its existence as an "open question." By contrast, our precedent has expressed no doubt about

the viability of the common-law defense, even in the context of federal criminal statutes that do not provide for it in so many words.

Thomas's "over broad language is especially unfortunate," Stevens concluded, "given the importance of showing respect for the sovereign states that [compose] our Federal Union." He concluded:

> I join the Court's judgment of reversal because I agree that a distributor of marijuana does not have a medical necessity defense under the Controlled Substances Act. I do not, however, join the *dicta* in the Court's opinion.

California Attorney General Bill Lockyer called the decision "unfortunate [because] the responsibility for determining what is necessary to provide for public health and safety has traditionally been left to the states."[25]

The decision of the Court did not invalidate the medical marijuana laws in the nine states. Those states are free not to prosecute people who use marijuana for medical reasons "and the federal government rarely prosecutes individuals for marijuana use."[26] However, the message from the conservative Court may have the "chilling effect" of dampening efforts in other states to pass similar medical marijuana legislation.

IV. Summing Up

Family privacy and personal autonomy cases still flood state and federal courts—and will continue to do so. These issues are never wholly resolved because new actions by individuals lead to new responses by state authorities. In all U.S. Supreme Court decision making and doctrinal declaration, the issue before the Court, over the decades, goes through an unfolding from the general to the specific, from a simple issue to a very complex one.

Intimate spousal violence is an example of the evolution of Court doctrine and precedent. Early cases *ignored* the reality of spousal and child abuse. In the past thirty years legislatures have begun to address the problem by passing legislation, VAWA, for example, to protect women from family abuse, especially battering by husbands or boyfriends. Although VAWA's criminal provisions have been legitimized by federal courts (but not by the U.S. Supreme Court, which has denied certiorari in these cases), the U.S. Supreme Court *has* invalidated the civil remedies available to women in

VAWA. Congress may respond to *Morrison* by passing amendatory legislation.

Litigation will continue. Once federal courts examined the dilemma of intimate spousal violence, new variants of the problem emerge. A contemporary example: Can a wife who has been repeatedly brutalized by her husband seek political asylum in the United States? Ms. Aruna Vallabhaneni's "beatings were relentless, severe enough, she claims, to force her to have a hysterectomy, enough to cost her her sense of smell, enough to leave her husband—and two children behind."[27]

Aruna did go to the police in Hyderabad, India, and had her husband arrested. Her father, however, who had arranged the marriage, went to the police and got the charges dropped. Her father and mother then told Aruna that they would commit suicide if she ever did that again. She left India for the United States on a temporary tourist visa. Once in America, she sought political asylum.

She and many hundreds of other battered women have sought sanctuary in the United States by claiming persecution by their husbands and/or families. Under federal law and Immigration and Naturalization Service (INS) regulations, one is eligible for political asylum if it is shown that one cannot return home because of a fear of persecution arising from one of five categories: one's race, religion, nationality, political opinion, or membership "in a particular social group."

Lawyers for these women claimed that their clients were being persecuted because of membership "in a particular social group"—*the woman's immediate family.* (In 1999, 1,085 of 55,000 claims for asylum were from women seeking refuge because of their membership "in a particular social group.")

A CA9 panel has already accepted that novel interpretation of the phrase in a case involving a nineteen-year-old Mexican woman who fled her father's persecution and sought asylum in America. The federal appeals court panel "wholeheartedly supported the idea of domestic-violence-based asylum complaints."[28] The three-judge panel condemned the Mexican government's "inability or unwillingness to control the abusive behavior of domestic violence perpetrators [like the father] and, indeed, [gave] its tacit approval of a certain measure of abuse." The INS has asked the full CA9 to hear the case.

There are pressure groups that are absolutely against such a broadening of the asylum rules. "It's [the CA9 decision] totally ridiculous," said Barbara

Coe, chair of the California Coalition for Immigration Reform. "You get a punch in the mouth, and you're home free."[29]

Sooner or later, petitioners will ask the Justices to grant certiorari to resolve a controversy that has developed involving this more complex issue of intimate spousal violence. It may come as a challenge to the revisions of the INS regulations covering asylum. In December 2000, just before leaving office, Democratic U.S. Attorney General Janet Reno, against the wishes of the INS bureaucracy, issued proposed new asylum guidelines specifically allowing claims involving domestic violence. The Justices may hear a case involving these new guidelines because there were different responses by federal appeals courts about the validity of the amendments. Or the certiorari request may come from battered women denied asylum because the George W. Bush administration rescinded the regulatory change introduced by Reno. In any event, in the future there will be persons and groups who will ask the U.S. Supreme Court to resolve this new question regarding intimate spousal violence.

In 2001, however, the family and personal autonomy cases touched upon the ugly business of child abuse as well as the plight of desperately ill cancer patients who need marijuana to relieve their pain. We see frustrated state judges trying to deal with child-support shirkers and the U.S. Supreme Court jurists struggling to respond to a privacy challenge regarding the use by police—without a search warrant—of the latest in surveillance technology.

These cases illustrate, again, the basic protagonists in this area of family privacy and personal autonomy: An aggrieved individual contesting a state action, or state inaction (recall the *DeShaney* tragedy), allegedly depriving that person of a fundamental right protected by the Due Process Clauses in the U.S. Constitution.

Whether the case touched on the dilemmas of child rearing, or intimate spousal violence, or a death in the family, the major actors were the same. Though the facts differed, the normative legal issue was always privacy and personal freedom versus the interest of the state to intrude on the most intimate relationships between men and women, men and men, and women and women.

This book has discussed a large number of

intense human dramas [that] have recently played on the judicial stage. In the guise of court decisions, they have presented very poignant themes, involving the most sensitive kinds of personal concerns—procreation, birth, health, survival, and dying.[30]

The discussion surrounding each of the cases has, it is hoped, illuminated something else: the very personal—and political, strategic,[31] and ideological—nature of U.S. Supreme Court decision making.

The men and women who decide to decide[32] to hear these human dramas etched in legalese categorically draw upon a host of values they brought with them to the Court. As Justice Powell confessed to his law clerk during the *Bowers* deliberations, he voted on the issue based on *"my age, general background, and convictions."* Every Justice, in moments of candor, would agree with him.

These normative principles—as well as the Justices' strong beliefs about the role of unelected federal judges in the American polity—were embedded in them by the time they walked up the Supreme Court's marble steps to take their seat on the high bench. They were planted in their minds and hearts by their parents, by the books they read, by their ministers and rabbis, their friends and their mentors—in university, in law school, and in politics—and by the myriad of personal experiences they had prior to their elevation to the Court.

The Justices issue value judgments in the guise of judicial opinions. There are more or less even scoopfuls of law, politics, and morality mixed in each opinion they write. There is seen, from time to time, skillful strategy employed by a Justice to find and hold a majority.[33] Examples include Justice Black's countering Fortas's vitriolic opinion in *Time v Hill* (an example of the lack of strategic skill) and Justice Powell's maneuverings in the *Parham* deliberations in order to have his *Belotti* draft opinion make sense—and hold *his* majority.

Although dressed up in the rhetoric of the law, the opinions handed down are reflections of the value judgments—regarding birth and death and every intimate relationship in between—of the nine men and women who serve as Justices of the U.S. Supreme Court. Some, only a minority, were supportive of the fundamental rights of homosexuals. Others, for example, Chief Justice Burger, had nothing but mordant demeaning comments about gays and lesbians. Still others, Justice Powell, for example, expressed disdainful thoughts about homosexuals—and the end of civilization—but also confessed to being ignorant of "those people."

Justice Scalia's sharp dissent in *Casey* is also very appropriate. His blunt observation may be too grating for some but is nonetheless accurate. Court opinions, he said, are "'*value judgments*.' In *Casey* our opponents had five votes and we had four. '*Case closed!*'"

On the other side of the Court's value divide stood Justice Thurgood Marshall. In his final dissent in 1991, a death penalty case,[34] he bitterly blasted Rehnquist's conservative gang: "*Power, not reason, is the new currency of this Court's decision-making*." The only change that occurred, that led to the overturn of an earlier precedent in *Payne*, was "the personnel of this court."

Power, however, has always been the currency of the Court. The most important vote, Justice Brennan said regularly, was the vote of five justices in a case. With four joining your draft you have an opinion of the Court. One talks about the most powerful Justice as the one who possesses that fifth vote in a splintered Court. During the 1967 Term of the U.S. Supreme Court, Justice William J. Brennan, the master "cobbler" of Court majorities of five, did not dissent once.

For most of his tenure on the Court, Justice Lewis Powell was considered the most powerful Justice because of his position on the Court. His votes in the controversial area of affirmative action tell the story. In more than a dozen major affirmative action cases, Powell was *never* on the losing side. His unique 1978 opinion in the higher education affirmative action case, *Regents v Bakke*,[35] is still the standard for affirmative action programs on college campuses across the nation.[36]

Sandra Day O'Connor has taken over Powell's title as the most powerful Justice sitting on the Court in 2003. In the 1999 Term, she dissented only once. Whatever position she took—and takes—was and is the majority's position. Look, for example, at the four North Carolina racial redistricting cases, involving the 12th congressional district. They came to the Court beginning in 1992. In the first three cases, the state legislature's creation of the majority-minority 12th Congressional District (CD) was invalidated. The redistricting was seen by the majority as a racial gerrymander. O'Connor was the fifth vote in these and she wrote the opinions of the Court.[37] The fourth time the reapportioned CD came up, Justice Stephen Breyer wrote the opinion for a five-person majority *validating* the reapportionment. Justice O'Connor was the fifth vote in that case.[38]

It is hoped that power is accompanied by reason in the Justices' judgments—but that is never guaranteed. All 108 men and women who sat and are sitting on the Court claim to have reason on their side. All sincerely believed that the "theory" that "animated" them to reach judgment in the instant case was logical, naturally flowing from a mountain of precedent, and based on the experiences of one's lifetime. Judging, clearly, is a very human enterprise. Triggered by their understanding of how to "read" the words of the Constitution, the Justices bring all their skills and knowledge to the task of resolving the legal controversy.

The Justices, however, are human beings and most of them respond humanely to the poignant issues that have come to them involving birth and death, love and marriage, personal and family privacy. They also make mistakes because even the Justices of the U.S. Supreme Court are fallible creatures.[39] Justice Brennan wished he had been more cautious when he instantly agreed, on the advice of his law clerk, to join Justice White's dissent from a denial of certiorari in the critically important *Bowers* case. And Justice Blackmun confessed error for passing along the "unimportant" abortion cases to a seven-person Court in the fall of 1971.

As seen in the cases discussed in this book, Justices make every effort to consistently draw upon their values and their experiences when balancing personal rights versus state action that intrudes on these rights. However, their beliefs generally reflect an earlier era. Because most of the men and women are nominated for the Court when they are past fifty, they bring with them a host of "traditional values" that they must draw upon when involved in the balancing-of-values judicial decision-making process.

In *Bowers*, a majority of the brethren held extremely traditional views of homosexuality. As activity in the chambers of Justice Powell illustrates, these somewhat elderly jurists were in the dark, were ignorant, about homosexuality. The beliefs and values they have and drew upon were first generated decades earlier. As all know, it is hard to transcend long-held beliefs, attitudes, and prejudices.

Furthermore, the Justices are sensitive sentient human beings, easily hurt by criticism of their work, especially when their Court colleagues critique them in written opinions. And this very human scenario is an understated yet important nonverbal aspect of Supreme Court decision making.[40]

Justice William O. Douglas was probably the most irascible of contemporary Justices. One of Douglas's colleagues, Justice Byron White, said that Douglas "was not tolerant of dumb people." A very remote person, he was quick to criticize his brethren. He had no tolerance for his law clerks. "He didn't horse around with his law clerks," White recalled, "they just slowed him down."[41] Two other Justices, William J. Brennan and Harry A. Blackmun, spoke of the many times Douglas's clerks would come into their offices crying because of something Douglas said to them.[42]

All legal observers, supporters and critics alike, believe that Justice Antonin "Nino" Scalia is a brilliant, ebullient jurist who, like Douglas, continually showed disdain for almost *all* his colleagues at one time or another. However, all agree that he has had little impact on his colleagues' jurisprudence (with the sole exception of Justice Clarence Thomas). Justice Sandra Day O'Connor infuriated Scalia when she did not join the Rehnquist opinion in *Webster*. Her decision denied the conservatives the golden opportunity to strike down *Roe*. Scalia's separate concurring opinion attacked her directly and with typical Scalia venom. At one point, he wrote that O'Connor's analysis "cannot be taken seriously."

A Justice confided to a reporter that O'Connor was "'deeply wounded' by the insults Scalia has sent her way, starting in 1989."

> A former Scalia clerk acknowledges that Scalia "compeltely alienated" O'Connor and "lost her forever," and a former Rehnquist clerk notes how O'Connor's "personality is in many ways just the opposite of Justice Scalia's. She's very willing to build consensus on opinions." But Scalia, says another ex-clerk, is not only "in love with his own language," he also believes that "what he is doing is a matter of principle. He knows how right he is."[43]

If a Justice cannot work cooperatively with colleagues, if there is openly displayed contempt of colleagues, then that jurist will not have much impact on their thinking about constitutional issues. There have been only 108 men and women who have sat as Justices of the U.S. Supreme Court since 1789. Scalia is not the first, nor will he be the last, jurist to ruffle the feathers of colleagues.[44] By acting in such a dyspeptic manner, however, a Justice dramatically reduces his or her influence. Such, too, is the nature of U.S. Supreme Court decision making.

The "vote of five," said Justice Brennan again and again, was the most important vote. Marshaling a Court majority, cobbling together the five men and women who agree on the resolution of the dilemma and who agree on the reasoning presented for their decision, is the highest art of the successful jurist.

And it is the most difficult goal to achieve if there is an ideologically divided 5:4 Court. As one Justice said who wrote the dissent in a tough 5:4 loss to the conservative majority: "*Oh, for a fifth vote.* Maybe Bill Brennan could have gotten it."[45] Probably not, for that case[46] was lost because most of the men and women appointed by conservative Presidents Ronald Reagan and George Bush behaved as expected by the men who appointed them.

Souter's frustration underscores a point made at the very beginning of the book. Presidents appoint "their kind" of person to sit on the nation's highest court. Who sits on the U.S. Supreme Court determines what kind of case docket the Court will have. Who sits also determines, in advance, the outcome of the kinds of controversial cases discussed in this book.

Occasionally, there has been evidence of the "fluidity" of judicial choice. A jurist who voted one way in the Conference Session after oral argument changes his mind after reading other draft opinions (recall Justice Powell's vote change in the *Bowers* case—and his recantation four years later). However, as one Justice said, "[T]he longer justices have been on the bench, the less they give."[47]

And there are the infrequent surprises, Justice Blackmun's *Roe* opinion; Justice Douglas's opinion in *Belle Terre;* and Justice Scalia's opinion in *Kyello.* For the most part, however, one gets what one expects from the brethren who have sat on the Court since 1789.

What is the final word? When reviewing the decisions of the U.S. Supreme Court, the line between law and politics is impossible to draw. Using their own value hierarchy, the Justices continually balance state authority and personal liberty. Unless a President, in the bowels of the White House, clones eight Scalias or eight Brennans, there will be battles on—and off—the bench.

And the final answer? Every opinion that comes down from the marble-column building on First Street will please some and horrify others. A powerful mayor of Chicago in the 1960s said, "[I]f you don't like something, vote early and often and things will change." Better yet, as Senator Joe Biden (D-Del) said: "[Get] two new justices."

Notes

Notes to the Introduction

1. Richard Cumming, editor, Max Lerner, *Nine Scorpions in a Bottle: Great Judges and Cases of the U.S. Supreme Court*, New York: Arcade Publishers, 1937, 1994.

2. Robert A. Sedler, "Abortion, Physician-Assisted Suicide and the Constitution," 12 *Notre Dame Journal of Law, Ethics, and Public Policy* 529, 1998, at 538.

3. See, generally, H. W. Perry, *Deciding to Decide: Agenda-Setting in the U.S. Supreme Court*, Cambridge: Harvard University Press, 1992.

4. The Fourteenth Amendment, ratified in 1868, states in part, in its first section: "No State shall make or enforce any law which shall abridge the privileges or immunities of citizens of the United States; nor shall any State deprive any person of life, liberty, or property without due process of law; nor deny to any person within its jurisdiction the equal protection of the laws." The Fifth Amendment, ratified in 1791, says in part that no person shall "be deprived of life, liberty, or property, without due process of law."

5. See Bernard Schwartz, *The Super Chief: Earl Warren and His Supreme Court*, New York: Oxford University Press, 1986.

6. 347 U.S. 483. See, generally, Richard Kluger, *Simple Justice*, New York: Vintage Press, 1975.

7. 163 U.S. 537. See C. Van Woodward, *The Strange Career of Jim Crow*, New York: Oxford University Press, 1955, 1974.

8. See Howard Ball and Philip Cooper, *Of Power and Right: Justices Hugo L. Black, William O. Douglas, and America's Constitutional Revolution*, New York: Oxford University Press, 1995.

9. "Homosexuality is the sexual and emotional attraction to persons of the same sex." Vetri, "Almost Everything You Always Wanted to Know," at 4.

10. The Warren era came to an end the same year a watershed event took place that triggered the start of the gay liberation movement. In late June 1969, New York City police harassment of gay men and lesbians at the Stonewall Tavern in Greenwich Village led to a major riot. Demonstrations by the gay community in the city lasted for days and led to initial discussions between the gay community and city of-

ficials regarding police treatment of gay men and women, especially persons of color who were gay. From the 1960s onward, particularly in the aftermath of the Vietnam protest movement, and after the development of the African American civil rights movement, and the women's equal rights movement, many individuals attracted to same-sex partners began to understand that they were not the problem. Societal attitudes, the criminal law, and psychological biases were the problem. Vetri, "Almost Everything You Always Wanted to Know," at 12–13.

11. Steven R. Shapiro, national legal director, ACLU, quoted in Edward Walsh, "An Activist Court Mixes Its High-Profile Messages," *The Washington Post,* July 2, 2000, p. A6.

12. Eric Schmitt, "For First Time, Nuclear Families Drop Below 25% of Households," *The New York Times,* May 15, 2001, at A1.

13. Dominick Vetri, "Almost Everything You Always Wanted to Know about Lesbians and Gay Men Their Families, and The Law," 26 *Southern University Law Review* 1, Fall 1998, at 4.

14. Sedler, "Abortion, Physician-Assisted Suicide and the Constitution," at 530–531.

NOTES TO CHAPTER 1

1. From the papers of Justice William J. Brennan, Jr., (WJBP) located in the Library of Congress (LOC), Washington, DC.

2. Black dissent, *Griswold v Connecticut,* 381 U.S. 479, 1965, at 510.

3. The Fourth Amendment, in its entirety, states: "The right of the people to be secure in their persons, houses, papers, and effects, against unreasonable searches and seizures, shall not be violated, and no Warrants shall issue, but upon probable cause, supported by oath or affirmation, and particularly describing the place to be searched, and the persons or things to be seized."

4. The quotes from this section of the chapter all come from the files of Justice Lewis F. Powell (LFPP) located in the Washington and Lee Law School Library Archives (WL), Lexington, Virginia.

5. *Certiorari* is a Latin term that means "produce the record." A writ of certiorari is a centuries-old equitable power of the judges incorporated into the common law and the statutes of the American colonies. Today, petitioners ask the U.S. Supreme Court to grant them a writ of certiorari. If the Court grants it, the Justices will review the case. However, the Court has total discretion in the use of the grant and very few petitions reflect important cases that the Justices wish to hear. In Conference, there must be a "vote of four" to grant the request. In the first decade of the twenty-first century, the Court, annually, will receive more than nine thousand petitions for certiorari. It will grant about eighty or so requests. See, generally, Cooper and Ball, *The U.S. Supreme Court: From the Inside Out.*

6. "Homosexual individuals include both men and women. The term 'homosexual' applies equally to persons of both sexes. The term 'lesbian' refers specifically to homosexual women. There is no similar nonpejorative term exclusively for the male homosexual. The term 'gay' is synonymous with the term 'homosexual.'" Rhonda R. Rivera, "Our Straight-Laced Judges: The Legal Position of Homosexual Persons in the United States," 50 *Hastings Law Journal* 1015, April 1999, at 1019–1020.

7. Days prior to hearing oral arguments, law clerks in the nine chambers prepare "Bench Memos" for their bosses. These substantive Memos, ranging from ten to fifty or so pages, provide the Justices with a review of the salient legal and constitutional questions in the case, the precedents that are relevant, and the possible roads the jurist can take in the effort to answer the question before the Court.

8. "It is clear," answered Powell, "that the issue here is whether there is a substantive due process right—within the meaning of liberty and privacy—to engage in private, consensual sodomy."

9. Powell wrote Mike: "I must say that when Professor Tribe refers to the 'sanctity of the home,' in the context of sodomy, I find his argument repellant. Also, it is insensitive advocacy. 'Home' is one of the most beautiful words in the English language. It usually connotes family, husband and wife, and children—although of course, single persons, widows and widowers, and others also have genuine homes."

10. His law clerk added the following to Powell's short list: "recreational drug use, at least with marijuana; suicide; bestiality; and prostitution."

11. See John C. Jeffries. *Justice Lewis F. Powell, Jr.*, New York: Scribner's, 1994.

12. See Joyce Murdock and Deb Price, *Courting Justice: Gay Men and Lesbians v the Supreme Court*, New York: Basic Books, 2001.

13. Edward Lazarus, *Closed Chambers: The Rise, Fall, and Future of the Modern Supreme Court*, New York: Penguin Books, 1998, 1999, at 336. The conversation between Powell and his gay law clerk, in part, went as follows, according to Lazarus:

Powell: Are gay men not attracted to women at all?
Clerk: They are attracted to women, but there is no sexual excitement.
Powell: None at all?
Clerk: Justice Powell, a gay man could not get an erection to have sex with a woman.

14. See, generally, Sherene D. Hannon, "License to Oppress: The Aftermath of *Bowers v Hardwick*," 19 *Pace Law Review* 507, Spring 1999.

15. *Brown v Allen*, 344 U.S. 443, 1953, at 540.

16. See Howard Ball, *A Defiant Life: Thurgood Marshall and the Persistence of Racism in America*, New York: Crown Publisher, 1999.

17. Lincoln Caplan, "The President's Lawyer, and the Court's," *The New York Times*, May 18, 2001, A27.

18. Memo to the Conference, from Antonin Scalia, January 6, 1987, In Re: *McKleskey v Kemp*, No 84-6811, in the files of Justice Lewis F. Powell, Washington and Lee Law Library.

19. See Cooper and Ball, *The U.S. Supreme Court: From the Inside Out.*

20. See, generally, Henry J. Abraham, *Justices, Presidents, and Senators: A History of the U.S. Supreme Court Appointments from Washington to Clinton*, New York: Rowman and Littlefield Publishers, 1999.

21. President William J. Clinton, 1993–2001, was the first Democratic President since President Lyndon Baines Johnson's appointment of Thurgood Marshall to the Supreme Court in 1967 to have an opportunity to nominate persons to fill vacancies on the Court. In 1993, he nominated Ruth Bader Ginsburg to replace Justice Byron R. White; in 1994, he nominated Stephen Breyer to replace retiring Justice Harry A. Blackmun. Both nominees were easily confirmed by the Senate.

22. The Due Process Clause is found in two places: the Fifth Amendment (constraining the national government) and, after 1868, in the Fourteenth Amendment, which prohibits certain kinds of "state action."

23. In 1830, the U.S. Supreme Court, in the case of *Barron v Baltimore*, 32 U.S. 243, Chief Justice Marshall writing, concluded that the Bill of Rights constrained only the federal government's actions, not the states'. Citizens of the states had to look to state constitutions and statutes for protection of their civil and political rights.

24. 302 U.S. 319, 1937.

25. Richard Polenberg, "Cardozo and the Criminal Law: *Palko v Connecticut* Remembered," 1996 *Journal of Supreme Court History*, pp. 92ff.

26. See, for example, Richard A. Posner, *Cardozo: A Study in Reputation*, Chicago: University of Chicago Press. 1990. The *Palko* case was the last opinion Justice Cardozo announced in Court. He suffered a stroke a few weeks later and retired from the high bench shortly therafter.

27. 395 U.S. 784 (1969).

28. See Lynne M. Kohm, "Liberty and Marriage," 12 *Brigham Young University Journal of Public Law* 253, 1998.

29. 300 U.S. 379, 1937.

30. Robert A. Sedler, "Abortion, Physician-Assisted Suicide and the Constitution: The View from Without and Within," 12 *Notre Dame Journal of Law, Ethics, and Public Policy* 529, 1998.

31. William N. Eskridge, Jr., "*Hardwick* and Historiography," 1999 *University of Illinois Law Review* 631, 1999, at 637.

32. For the Court majorities, sexual privacy is protected as far as allowing a person, in the privacy of the home, to watch a pornographic movie and, by implication, to masturbate. See *Stanley v Georgia*, 394 U.S. 557 (1969).

33. Sedler "Abortion, Physician-Assisted Suicide and the Constitution," at 536.

34. 342 U.S. 165, 1952.

35. See, generally, Eileen L. McDonaugh, "My Body, My Consent," 62 *Albany Law Review* 1057, 1999.

36. 304 U.S. 144, 1938

37. Quoted in Peter Irons, *A People's History of the Supreme Court*, New York: Penguin Books, 1999, at 333.

38. Ibid. at 334.

39. Harlan Fiske Stone Papers (HFSP), LOC, Washington, DC.

40. Robert A. Destro, "*Loving v Virginia* After 30 Years," 47 *Catholic University Law Review* 1207, Summer 1998, at 1214.

41. See Howard Ball, *Hugo Black: Cold Steel Warrior*, New York: Oxford University Press. 1996.

42. Melissa A. Provost, "Disregarding the Constitution in the Name of Defending Marriage: The Unconstitutionality of the Defense of Marriage Act," 8 *Seton Hall Constitutional Law Journal* 157, Fall 1997, at 166.

43. Dennis J. Hutchinson, *The Man Who Once Was Whizzer White: A Portrait of Justice Byron R. White*, New York: The Free Press, 1998, at 452.

44. Thurgood Marshall Papers (TMP), LOC, Washington, DC. Also WJBP, LOC, Washington, DC.

45. TMP, LOC, Washington, DC.

46. WJBP, LOC, Washington, DC.

47. Hutchinson, *The Man Who Once Was Whizzer White*, at 451–452.

48. WJBP, LOC, Washington, DC.

49. Hutchinson, *The Man Who Once Was Whizzer White*, at 452.

50. See Peter Irons, *The Courage of Their Convictions*, New York: Penguin Books, 1988.

51. See J. Woodford Howard, "On the Fluidity of Judicial Choice," 62 *American Political Science Review*, March 1968, 43–56.

52. 510 S.E.2nd 18, 1998.

53. Vetri, "Almost Everything You Always Wanted to Know," at 5–6.

54. 517 U.S. 620, 1996

55. These ordinances contained "an extensive catalog of traits which cannot be the basis for discrimination, including age, military status, marital status, pregnancy, parenthood, custody of a minor child, political affiliation, physical or mental disability of an individual or of his or her associates—and, in recent times, sexual orientation."

56. In its entirety, Amendment 2 stated: "Neither the State of Colorado, through any of its branches or departments, nor any of its agencies, political subdivisions, municipalities or school districts, shall enact, adopt or enforce any statute, regulation, ordinance or policy whereby homosexual, lesbian, or bisexual orientation, conduct, practices, or relationships shall constitute or otherwise be the basis of or entitle any person or class of persons to have or claim any minority status, quota

preferences, protected status or claim of discrimination. This Section of the Constitution shall be in all respects self-executing."

57. *Romer v Evans*, 517 U.S. 620, at 624. Unless otherwise noted, the quotes in this case study are from the majority opinion in *Romer*, written by Justice Anthony Kennedy.

58. Quoted in Kevin G. Walsh,"Throwing Stones: Rational Basis Review Triumphs over Homophobia," 27 *Seton Hall Law Review* 1064, 1997, at 1069–1070.

59. Kevin H. Lewis, "Equal Protection After *Romer v Evans*: Implications for the Defense of Marriage Act and Other Laws," 49 *Hastings Law Journal* 175, November 1997, at 214.

60. Eskridge, "*Hardwick* and Historiography," at 640–641.

61. Implicit in *Skinner v Oklahoma*, 316 U.S. 535, 1942.

62. *Griswold v Connecticut*, 381 U.S. 479, 1965. See also *Carey v Population Services International*, 431 U.S. 678, 1977.

63. *Eisenstadt v Baird*, 405 U.S. 438, 1972; see also *McLaughlin v Florida*, 379 U.S. 184, 1964, which overturned a state law that banned sexual intercourse by single persons of different races.

64. Implicit in *Stanley v Georgia*, 394 U.S. 557, 1969.

65. *Roe v Wade*, 410 U.S. 113, 1973.

66. *Bowers v Hardwick*, 478 U.S. 186, 1986.

67. Eskridge, "Hardwick and Historiography," at 641.

NOTES TO CHAPTER 2

1. Vetri, "Almost Everything You Always Wanted to Know," at 45–46. It was extolled by some as the 1995 Term U.S. Supreme Court's "most important and symbolically momentous" opinion for the homosexual community. David J. Garrow. "The Rehnquist Reins," *The Sunday New York Times Magazine*, October 6, 1996, p. 82.

2. Hannon, "License to Oppress," at 515.

3. *Poe v Ullman*, 367 U.S. 541, 1962, Harlan, dissenting, at 553.

4. See Howard Ball and Philip Cooper, *Of Power and Right: Justices Hugo L. Black, William O. Douglas, and America's Constitutional Revolution*, New York: Oxford University Press, 1992.

5. 381 U.S. 479, 1964.

6. Ball and Cooper, *Of Power and Right*, p. 286.

7. The First Amendment states: "Congress shall make no law respecting an establishment of religion, or prohibiting the free exercise thereof; or abridging the freedom of speech, or of the press; or the right of the people peaceably to assemble, and to petition the Government for a redress of grievances."

8. Brennan wanted *Griswold* to reflect contemporary medical standards as well as address the right of privacy concept in a manner that would modify American constitutional law. When Douglas told Brennan that he was incorporating Bren-

nan's ideas directly into the Court's majority opinion, Brennan's clerk was ecstatic. "This is a signal victory [for you]. The penumbras stuff [accepted by Douglas, will] be explained as interpretation of the Amendments to include things not literally enumerated, to avoid attack by Justices Black and Stewart." This and other quotes in this segment of the chapter are from WJBP, LOC, Washington, DC.

9. *Griswold,* at 484.

10. *Griswold,* at 484.

11. Quoted in Roger K. Newman, *Hugo Black: A Biography,* New York: Pantheon, 1994, at 557.

12. See Howard Ball, *Hugo L. Black: Cold Steel Warrior,* New York: Oxford University Press, 1996.

13. Anne B. Brown, "The Evolving Definition of Marriage," 31 *Suffolk University Law Review* 917, 1998, at 917–918.

14. See, for example, *Zablocki v Redhail,* 434 U.S. 374, 1978, where the Court ruled that all state marital laws and regulations are subject to "strict scrutiny" by judges because marriage is a "fundamental" right. In *Zablocki,* the Court held unconstitutional a state statute that provided that a parent who failed to comply with child support orders was prohibited from marrying without court permission. The justices concluded that its decisions "made clear that the right to marry is of fundamental importance" for all individuals.

15. Webster's *New Collegiate Dictionary,* Ninth Edition, 1983, defines *homophobia* as the "irrational fear of homosexuality or homosexuals," at 578.

16. Kafahni Nkrumah, "The Defense of Marriage Act: Congress Re-Writes the Constitution to Pacify Its Fears," 23 *Thurgood Marshall Law Review* 513, Spring 1998, at 513.

17. Brown, "Evolving Definition," at 921.

18. See www.cornell.edu/topics

19. G. Kristian Miccio, "With All Due Deliberate Care," 29 *Columbia Human Rights Law Review* 641, Summer 1998, at 648–649.

20. 404 U.S. 71, 1971.

21. 411 U.S. 677, 1973. Having a "dependent" enabled the military person to receive increased housing quarters allowances and medical and dental benefits.

22. In a Memo to the Conference (MTTC), addressed to Brennan, Powell wrote that Brennan's position "would place the Court in the position of preempting the amendatory process initiated by the Congress.

I find the issue a difficult one. Women certainly have not been treated as being fungible with men (thank God!). Yet the reasons for different treatment have in no way resembled the purposeful and invidious discrimination directed against blacks and aliens. Nor may it be said any longer that, as a class, women are a discrete minority barred from effective participation in the political process. WJBP, LOC, Washington, DC.

23. 411 U.S. at 685.

24. Justice Blackmun wrote to Brennan: "After some struggle, I have now concluded that it is not advisable, and certainly not necessary, for us to reach out in this case and hold that sex, like race and national origin and alienage, is a suspect classification." In WJBP, LOC, Washington, DC.

25. WJBP, LOC, Washington, DC.

26. 440 U.S. 268, 1978.

27. Ibid. at 282, 283.

28. *Funk v U.S.*, 290 U.S. 371, 1933.

29. See Ball, *Hugo Black: Cold Steel Warrior,* at 20–22.

30. *Hawkins v U.S.*, 358 U.S. 74, 1958.

31. *Trammel v U.S.*, 445 U.S. 40, 1980.

32. *Evans v Tohono O'Odham Nation,* 528 U.S. 811, 1999, certiorari denied.

33. Vetri, "Almost Everything You Always Wanted to Know," at 49.

34. *Maynard v Hill,* 125 U.S. 190, 1888, at 205, 211.

35. Brown, "Evolving Definition," at 918. See, generally, Note, "Homosexuals Right to Marry: A Constitutional Test and a Legislative Solution," 128 *University of Pennsylvania Law Review* 193, 1979.

36. *Zablocki v Redhail,* 434 U.S. 374, 1978.

37. *Turner v Safley,* 482 U.S. 78, 1987.

38. Arland Thornton, "Comparative and Historical Perspectives on Marriage, Divorce, and Family Life," 1994 *Utah Law Review* 587, 1994, at 595ff.

39. In its entirety, the Tenth Amendment, known as the state "Police Powers" Amendment, says: "The powers not delegated to the United States by this Constitution, nor prohibited by it to the States, are reserved to the States respectively, or to the people."

40. *Loving v Virginia,* 388 U.S. 1, 1967, at 11–12.

41. 316 U.S. 535, 1942.

42. *Buck v Bell,* 274 U.S. 200, 1927, at 207.

43. William O. Douglas Papers (WODP), LOC, Washington, DC.

44. *Skinner,* at 538–539.

45. *Griswold v Connecticut,* 1965. An older (sixty-seven years of age), and soon to be married for a fourth time (to a twenty-one-year-old coed), Justice Douglas wrote the majority opinion for the U.S. Supreme Court in this case as well.

46. 83 U.S. 130, 1872. All the quotations in this section of the text are from this case.

47. 381 U.S. 479, 1965.

48. *Tileston v Ullman,* 318 U.S. 44, 1943, and *Poe v Ullman,* 367 U.S. 497, 1961.

49. Buxton was a litigant in the *Poe* case, not heard on the merits by the Court four years earlier. EWP, LOC, Washington, DC.

50. 381 U.S. 479, 1965.

51. See Lerner, *Nine Scorpions in a Bottle;* See also Philip J. Cooper, *Battles on the Bench: Conflict inside the Supreme Court,* Lawrence: University Press of Kansas, 1998, for a contemporary examination of the battles, personal and professional, that take place behind the velvet curtains of the Court.

52. Conference comments are from WJBP and Earl Warren Papers (EWP), LOC, Washington, DC.

53. The Chief joined this opinion even though he was told by his law clerk that the Goldberg opinion, "like Douglas' opinion, is *disturbingly unclear* as to the dimensions of the right which is being recognized." EWP, LOC, Washington, DC. However, Warren could not join White or Harlan and, because he was in the middle of a year-old battle with Douglas (in which the two did not speak to each other), he could not join that opinion. He was left with Goldberg's Ninth Amendment justification. See Ball and Cooper, *Of Power and Right.*

54. Miccio, "With All Due Deliberate Care," at 642. The author points out that "state inaction in the face of domestic violence contributes to the brutalization of three to four million women per year and an equal number of children. State failure to protect and prevent domestic violence contributes to the death of three to four thousand women and one to two thousand children annually." At 684.

55. Miccio noted that, in 1992, U.S. Surgeon General Antonia Novello cited intimate violence as the leading cause of injury to women—more than car accidents, muggings, occupational hazards, and cancer deaths combined. Miccio, "With All Due Deliberate Care," at 654. See also U.S. Senate Committee on the Judiciary, *Report on the Violence Against Women Act of 1991,* U.S. Senate Report No. 102-97, 102nd Congress, First Session, 1991.

56. U.S. Department of Justice, Bureau of Justice Statistics, Special Report 178247, *Intimate Partner Violence,* May 2000.

57. G. Kristian Miccio, "A Reasonable Battered Wife," 22 *Harvard Women's Law Journal* 89, Spring 1999, at 91.

58. Erica Goode, "Study Says 20% of Girls Reported Abuse by a Date," *The New York Times,* August 1, 2001, at A1.

59. 489 U.S. 189, 1988. Unless otherwise noted, all quotes in this section are from the U.S. Supreme Court opinion.

60. These were the opening words of Justice Blackmun's dissent: "Poor Joshua! Victim of repeated attacks by an irresponsible, bullying, cowardly, and intemperate father, and abandoned by the social services workers who placed him in a dangerous predicament and who knew or learned what was going on, and yet did essentially nothing. . . . It is a sad commentary upon American life."

61. Section 1983 of Title 42 of the USC is a major federal law that is used by persons who allege that their basic rights in the Constitution were infringed and ask the court to provide compensatory and punitive damages for the resultant injuries.

62. G. Kristian Miccio, "A Reasonable Battered Mother? Redefining, Reconstructing, and Recreating the Battered Mother in Child Protective Proceedings," 22 *Harvard Women's Law Journal* 89, Spring 1999, at 101.

63. Miccio, "A Reasonable Battered Mother," at 101–102.

64. *U.S. v Morrison*, 529 U.S. 598, 1999.

65. *Morrison*, Souter dissent, at 630.

66. Miccio, "A Reasonable Battered Wife," at 90, 91.

67. William Blackstone, *Commentaries on the Laws of England*, 1850, Chicago: University of Chicago Press, 1979, at 444.

68. Miccio, "With All Due Deliberate Care," at 648. Mississippi and other states, in the nineteenth century, "adopted the English common law position that a man was permitted to beat his wife as long as he used a 'rod not thicker than his thumb.'" Linda G. Mills, "Killing Her Softly: Intimate Abuse and the Violence of State Intervention," 113 *Harvard Law Review* 550, December 1999, at 557.

69. Reva B. Siegal, "The Rule of Love: Wife Beating as Prerogative," 105 *Yale Law Journal* 2117, June 1996, at 2119ff.

70. These were the congressional power to enforce the provisions of the Fourteenth Amendment (found in Section 5 of the Fourteenth Amendment) and the congressional power to regulate interstate commerce (found in Article I, Section 8, clause 3).

71. Sally F. Goldfarb, "Violence Against Women and the Persistence of Privacy," 61 *Ohio State Law Review* 1, 2000, at 6, 7.

72. Goldfarb, "Violence Against Women," at 9.

73. See, for example, the following cases where federal appeals courts validated the criminal provisions of the VAWA and the U.S. Supreme Court, in every case, denied certiorari, and thereby left standing the final judgments of these lower federal appellate courts. *U.S. v Gluzman*, 154 F 3rd 49 (2nd Cir. 1998); *U.S. v Bailey*, 112 F 3rd 758 (4th Cir. 1997); *U.S. v Wright*, 128 F 3rd 1274 (8th Cir. 1997).

74. *U.S. v Lankford*, 196 F 3rd 563 (5th Cir. 1999), at 571.

75. 529 U.S. 598, 2000.

76. Unless otherwise noted, all the quotes in this case study come from the opinions in *Morrison*.

77. Quotes from Joan Biskupic, "Sex-Assault Law under Scrutiny," *The Washington Post*, January 12, 2000, at A11.

78. Ibid.

79. *Lopez*, 514 U.S. at 557. In *Lopez*, the same Court majority invalidated a congressional statute, the Gun-Free School Zones Act of 1990, that made it a federal crime to "knowingly possess" a handgun in a school zone.

80. Christy Brzonkala never finished college. Her hoped-for career in sports nutrition evaporated. She overdosed on pills, When the decision was announced, she was working in a bar in Adams-Morgan. She said, about the opinion and her life: "I fell into a big black hole and this is where the rabbit ends up. It was disappointment

after disappointment." Quoted in Brooke A. Masters, "'No Winners' In Rape Lawsuit," *The Washington Post,* May 20, 2000, at B1.

81. Linda Greenhouse, "Battle on Federalism," *The New York Times,* May 17, 2000, at A1.

82. Joan Biskupic, "States' Role at Issue in Rape Suit," *The Washington Post,* January 10, 2000, at A17.

83. Ibid.

84. See, for example, the op-ed piece by Jack M. Balkin, "The Court Defers to a Racist Era," *The New York Times,* May 17, 2000, at A27.

85. AP, "Reno: Renew VAWA," *The New York Times,* May 18, 2000, at A1.

86. Joan Biskupic, "Justices Reject Lawsuits for Rape," *The Washington Post,* May 18, 2000, at A1.

87. Melissa A. Provost, "Disregarding the Constitution in the Name of Defending Marriage: The Unconstitutionality of the Defense of Marriage Act," 8 *Seton Hall Constitutional Law Journal* 157, Fall 1997, at 162ff.

88. Brown, "Evolving Definition," at 931.

89. *Baker v Nelson,* 191 N.W. 2nd 185 (Minnesota, 1971).

90. Lynne Marie Kohm, "Liberty and Marriage—*Baehr* and Beyond: Due Process in 1998," 12 *Brigham Young University Journal of Public Law* 253, 1998, at 254.

91. Brown, "Evolving Definition," at 917–918.

92. Richard A. Posner, *Sex and Reason,* Cambridge: Harvard University Press, 1992, at 313.

93. *Bowers,* 478 U.S. at 194.

94. 170 Vt 194, 1999.

95. Unless otherwise noted, all quotes in this case study are from the Amestoy opinion for the Vermont Supreme Court, 170 Vt 194, 1999.

96. Vermont Constitution, Chapter 1, Article 7.

97. Ibid. at 197–198.

98. Ibid. at 229.

99. See, for example, Debbie Howlett and Tony Mauro, "Into the Courts, Away from Congress," *USA Today,* September 11, 1996, polling results at 4A.

100. *Sutton v Lieb,* 342 U.S. 403, 1952.

101. Susan Summer, "The Full-Faith-And-Credit Clause: Its History," 34 *Oregon Law Review* 224, 1955, at 229.

102. *Fauntleroy v Lum,* 210 U.S. 230, 1908.

103. 80 Haw. 341, 1996; 92 Haw. 634, 1999.

104. HRS Section 572-1 defines the legal status of marriage as "the marital relation to a male and a female."

105. Kohm, "Liberty and Marriage," at 257–258.

106. *Brouse v Alaska Bureau of Vital Statistics,* No 3AN-956562 CI, 1998 WL 88743 (Alaska Superior Court, 1998), at 1.

107. See, generally, Evan Wolfson and Michael F. Melcher, "DOMA's House Divided: Why the Federal Anti-Gay, Anti-Marriage Law Is Unconstitutional," *The Federal Lawyer*, September 1997.

108. Quoted in Timothy J. Keefer, "DOMA as a Defensible Exercise of Congressional Power under the Full-Faith-And-Credit Clause," 54 *Washington and Lee Law Review* 1635, Fall 1997, at 163.

109. Wolfson and Melcher, "DOMA's House Divided," at 31.

110. 28 USC Section 1738 C. See Craig A. Bowman and Blake M. Cornish, "A More Perfect Union: A Legal and Social Analysis of Domestic Partnership Ordinances," 92 *Columbia Law Review* 1164, 1992. (In 1982, Berkeley, California, passed the first domestic partnership ordinance in the United States.)

111. Jennifer L. Heeb, "Homosexual Marriage, the Changing American Family, and the Heterosexual Right to Privacy," 24 *Seton Hall Law Review* 347, 1993, at 356–357.

112. Brown, "Evolving Definition," at 937.

113. 523 U.S. 75, 1998.

114. Quotes from Joan Biskupic, "Justices Hear Harassment Case," *The Washington Post*, December 4, 1997, at A25.

115. He gave as one example of "innocent man-to-man horseplay" a football coach "slapping the fanny" of a player who just made a great catch. "Nothing illegal there," he determined.

116. Richard Carelli, "Court: Same Sex Harassment Illegal," *The Washington Post*, March 4, 1998, at A1.

117. Kohm, "Liberty and Marriage," at 269.

NOTES TO CHAPTER 3

1. *Michael H. v Gerald D.*, 491 U.S. 110, 1989. Justice Brennan dissenting.

2. *Inez Moore v City of East Cleveland, Ohio*, 431 U.S. 494, 1976. The Burger Memo is in the TMP, LOC, Washington, DC.

3. Janet L. Dolgin, "Choice, Tradition, and the New Genetics: The Fragmentation of the Ideology of Family," 32 *Connecticut Law Review* 523, Winter 2000, at 524.

4. Quoted in Gustav Niebuhr, "Reporter's Notebook: Baptists Convene, and Turn to Family," *The New York Times*, June 14, 2001. at B5.

5. Quoted in editorial, "The Changing American Family," *The New York Times*, May 18, 2001, at A28.

6. Hutchinson, *The Man Who Once Was Whizzer White*, at 371.

7. *Michael H. v Gerald D.*, 491 U.S. 110, 1989, Brennan dissenting.

8. See U.S. Census Bureau, "Nation's Median Age Highest Ever," *U.S. Department of Commerce News*, May 15, 2001. One telling fact is that the number of families headed by women who have children, which are typically poorer than two-parent families, grew nearly five times faster in the 1990s than the number of married

couples with children. It is a small part of a trend "that some family experts and demographers described today as disturbing." Eric Schmitt, "For First Time, Nuclear Families Drop Below 25% of Households," *The New York Times*, May 15, 2001, at A1.

9. Hannon, "License to Oppress," at 511–512, 514.

10. Vetri, "Almost Everything You Always Wanted to Know," at p. 39.

11. Vetri, "Almost Everything You Always Wanted to Know," at 22, 28.

12. Howard Ball, *A Defiant Life: Thurgood Marshall and the Persistence of Racism in America*, New York: Random House, 1999.

13. *Inez Moore v East Cleveland, Ohio*, 431 U.S. 494, 1976.

14. TMP, LOC, Washington, DC.

15. Martha A. Fineman, "Privacy and the Family," 67 *George Washington Law Review* 1207, June/August 1999 at 217.

16. Jane Fritsch, "Aspirations: A Rise in Single Dads," *The New York Times*, May 20, 2001, at A1.

17. Jane Fritsch, "Matrimony: The Magic's Still Gone," *The New York Times*, May 20, 2001, at A1.

18. Adam Stern, "Single Dad: Popular But Misunderstood"; Joe Queenan, "Nuclear Dad: Last of My Kind"; Daniel Voll, "Unwed Dad: Marriage Is Just a Maybe," in "Sunday Styles" Section 9, at 1, 2, 8. *The New York Times*, June 17, 2001.

19. Carey Goldberg, "Single Dads Wage Revolution, One Bedtime Story at a Time," *The New York Times*, June 17, 2001, at A1, 14.

20. Goldberg, "Single Dads Wage Revolution," at 1.

21. Catharine MacKinnon, "Can Fatherhood Be Optional," *The New York Times*, June 17, 2001, Section 4, at 15.

22. Barbara Kantrowitz and Pat Wingart, "Unmarried, With Children," *Newsweek*, May 28, 2000, at 46–55.

23. *Village of Belle Terre v Boraas*, 416 U.S. 1, 1974

24. WJBP, LOC, Washington, DC.

25. TMP, LOC, Washington, DC.

26. Fineman, "Privacy and the Family," at 211ff.

27. Fineman, "Privacy and the Family," at 216–217.

28. 98 U.S. 145, 1878

29. Fineman, "Privacy and the Family," at 217.

30. Clare Dalton, "Deconstructing Contract Doctrine," 94 *Yale Law Journal* 997, 1985, at 1096–1113, passim.

31. Fineman, "Privacy and the Family," at 1207.

32. Edward Lazarus, *Closed Chambers: The Rise, Fall, and Future of the Modern Supreme Court*, New York: Penguin Books, 2001, at 388.

33. "The California statute that is the subject of this litigation is, in substance, more than a century old. California Code of Civ. Proc. § 1962(5), enacted in 1872, provided that "[t]he issue of a wife cohabiting with her husband, who is not impotent, is indisputably presumed to be legitimate."

34. Lazarus, *Closed Chambers,* at 388–404, passim.

35. Lazarus, *Closed Chambers,* at 389.

36. In 1955, it was also made into a Hollywood movie, starring Humphrey Bogart.

37. These and other quotes in this case study are taken from the papers of Justice William J. Brennan, WJBP, located in the Manuscript Division, LOC, Washington, DC.

38. The Fourth Amendment states, in part, that "the right of the people to be secure in their persons, houses, papers, and effects, against *unreasonable* searches and seizures, shall not be violated, and no warrants shall issue, but upon probable cause. . . .

39. See Ball, *Hugo Black,* at 194–195, passim.

40. WJBP, LOC, Washington, DC.

41. Hugo L. Black and Elizabeth Black, *Mr. Justice and Mrs. Black: The Memoirs of Hugo L. Black and Elizabeth Black,* New York: Random House, 1986, at 150, 153.

42. See Ball, *Hugo Black,* passim.

43. Fineman calls *Eisenstadt* a "radical departure because it takes the idea of marital privacy and expands constitutional protection beyond the common law limitations of the family relationship, at 1212–1213.

44. Quote is taken from the notes taken by Justice William O. Douglas, WODP, LOC, Washington, DC.

45. WJBP, LOC, Washington, DC.

46. Massachusetts General Laws Ann., c. 272, § 21, under which Baird was convicted, provides a maximum five-year term of imprisonment for "whoever . . . gives away . . . any drug, medicine, instrument or article whatever for the prevention of conception," except as authorized in § 21A. Under § 21A, "[a] registered physician may administer to or prescribe for any married person drugs or articles intended for the prevention of pregnancy or conception. [And a] registered pharmacist actually engaged in the business of pharmacy may furnish such drugs or articles to any married person presenting a prescription from a registered physician.

47. Tiffany Jones and Larry Peterman, "Whither the Family and Family Privacy?" 4 *Texas Review of Law and Politics* 193, Fall 1999, at 217–218.

48. Jones and Peterman, "Whither the Family," at 220.

49. *Roe v Wade,* 410 U.S. 113, 1972.

Notes to Chapter 4

1. HLBP, LOC, Washington, DC. Black received hundreds of letters from citizens voicing their views on abortion, all written before *Roe v Wade* came down in the Court's 1972 Term, more than a year after Black's death.

2. *Roe v Wade,* 1973.

3. Justice William Brennan to Justice William O. Douglas, June 1972, WJBP, LOC, Washington, DC.

4. WODP, LOC, Washington, DC.

5. Carl Rowan, *Dream Makers, Dream Breakers,* at 323.

6. Rowan, *Dream Makers,* at 325.

7. WJBP, LOC, Washington, DC.

8. President Nixon, as part of his announced "Southern" strategy, nominated Clement Haynsworth to replace the disgraced Fortas, the first U.S. Supreme Court justice forced into resignation because of scandal. Haynsworth, a Virginian, was a CA4 federal appeals judge at the time of his nomination. Labor and civil rights groups opposed him and, when ethical improprieties surfaced, the Senate defeated his nomination. He returned to the CA4 where he became Chief Judge of the circuit. Nixon then nominated a Floridian, G. Harrold Carswell, then a U.S. District Court judge. Carswell proved to be an even more controversial nominee. Civil rights groups campaigned successfully against him and the media discovered that, prior to his appointment to the federal bench, he was a very segregationist politician and lawyer. He was also the most overturned federal judge in the CA4, raising the question of his legal competence. Roman Hruska, the Republican Senator from Nebraska was his Senate "manager." He gave Carswell's candidacy the kiss of death when he uttered these memorable words: "What's wrong with being mediocre? A lot of people in America are mediocre and they need representation too. [Supreme Court Justices] cannot all be Brandeises, Cardozos, and Frankfurters!" (These three jurists were leading legal scholars and Justices of the U.S. Supreme Court. They were, too, Jewish jurists, which raised, probably unintentionally, the specter of anti-Semitism, for the disgraced Fortas was also Jewish.) Carswell was defeated in the Senate in early April 1970. He returned to the bench, left the federal court to run for a seat in the U.S. Senate and was unsuccessful. At last account, Carswell was arrested by police in a Florida public bathroom for exposing himself to another man. An angry, frustrated Nixon nominated federal appeals court judge Harry Blackmun, the new Chief's very close friend then sitting on the CA8. The Senate confirmed him, unanimously, in late May 1970.

9. James F. Simon, *The Center Holds: The Power Struggle inside the Rehnquist Court,* New York: Simon & Schuster, 1995, at 86.

10. Interview, James F. Simon with Harry A. Blackmun, May 7, 1991, quoted in Simon, *The Center Holds,* at 86.

11. All quotes taken from the WJBP and WODP, LOC, Washington, DC, and the LFPP, WL, Lexington, Virginia.

12. Barbara Craig and David O'Brien, *Abortion and American Politics,* Chatham, NJ: Chatham House, 1993, at 97–98.

13. 391 U.S. 68, 1968.

14. WJBP, LOC, Washington, DC.

15. See, for example, David J. Garrow, "Justice Powell's Forceful Role in *Roe*," *The Legal Times*, May 8, 2000, at 7–8.

16. LFPP, WL, Lexington, Virginia.

17. David O'Brien, *Constitutional Law and Politics, Volume II: Civil Rights and Liberties*, New York: Morrow, 1991, at 1153.

18. 448 U.S. 297, 1980.

19. After O'Connor was nominated, she received strong support from most conservative Republican quarters, except for the religious right. "The Reverend Jerry Falwell, the Moral Majority leader, called the O'Connor nomination a 'disaster' and John Wilkie, head of the National Coalition for the Right to Life, termed it a 'betrayal.'" Simon, *The Center Holds*, at 123.

20. TMP, LOC, Washington, DC.

21. Ball, *A Defiant Life*, at 371.

22. Quoted in Bernard Schwartz, *Decision: How the Supreme Court Decides Cases*, New York: Oxford University Press, 1996, at 12.

23. WJBP, LOC, Washington, DC.

24. WJBP, LOC, Washington, DC.

25. Jeffrey Toobin, "The Agonizer: Justice Kennedy," *The New Yorker*, Nov. 11, 1996, at 82, 86.

26. McDonagh, "My Body, My Consent," at 1060.

27. WJBP, LOC, Washington, DC.

28. TMP, LOC, Washington, DC.

29. 428 U.S. 52, 1976.

30. 428 U.S. at 69–70.

31. 428 U.S. at 71.

32. *Planned Parenthood of Southeastern Pennsylvania v Casey*, 505 U.S. 833, 1992.

33. Jeffrey Rosen, "The O'Connor Court: America's Most Powerful Jurist, *The New York Times Sunday Magazine*, June 3, 2001, at 38.

34. Rosen, "The O'Connor Court," at 41.

35. Quoted in Simon, *The Center Holds*, at 165.

36. Simon, *The Center Holds*, at 156.

37. Toobin, "Agonizer," at 87.

38. Toobin, "Agonizer," at 87.

39. O'Brien, *Constitutional Law and Politics*, at 1992.

40. Both quoted in Sean McCarthy, "Abortion's Empty Rhetoric," *Newsday*, July 1, 1992, at A8.

41. Both quoted in "The Conflict Continues: Differing Views of a Controversial Decision," *San Francisco Chronicle*, June 30, 1992, at A5.

42. Rosen, "The O'Connor Court," at 44.

43. Ironically, it was a 5:4 decision of the U.S. Supreme Court that led to Bush's victory, after the election was tossed in the air and into the state and federal courts

due to demands for a recount of votes in Florida. By one vote, the Court ended the presidential election of 2000 by overturning the Florida Supreme Court and ending the manual recounts of thousands of "undervotes" in the state. The Court determined that the mechanisms implemented to conduct the recount did not satisfy equal protection and that the Florida courts did not have the time to implement alternative means that would recount the votes in compliance with equal protection. Linda Greenhouse, the Pulitzer prize–winning *New York Times* reporter, wrote:

> In its quest to preserve an infinitesimal margin in Florida and win the state's decisive 25 electoral votes, the Bush campaign brought two cases to the Court, which decided them over an intense 18-day period culminating with the 5-to-4 ruling that determined the outcome of the election. The first case, *Bush v. Palm Beach County Canvassing Board,* was an appeal from the Florida Supreme Court's Nov. 21 decision that added 12 days to the deadline for certifying the vote. Argued on Dec. 1, this case resulted on Dec. 4 in a unanimous, unsigned and opaque opinion vacating the state court's decision and requesting clarification of the basis for it. Without answering the justices' questions, the Florida Supreme Court then turned to the Gore campaign's contest of the newly certified results and ordered a statewide manual recount of ballots that when counted by machine had not indicated a choice for president. The Bush campaign appealed immediately and, as the recount got under way, won a stay from the justices by a vote of 5 to 4.
>
> The court then heard the case, *Bush v. Gore,* on Dec. 11 and decided it the next day in an unsigned opinion that contained two conclusions: (1) the lack of uniform standards for the recount violated the 14th Amendment guarantee of equal protection, (2) there was no time for the state to fix the problem and keep the recount going. Thirty-six days after election day, the 2000 election, and the Supreme Court's role in it, were history. The election was over. The five in the majority were Chief Justice Rehnquist and Justices O'Connor, Kennedy, Scalia and Thomas.

Linda Greenhouse, "Supreme Court Term: Beyond Bush v Gore," *The New York Times,* July 2, 2001, at A1.

44. The eight years since Justice Breyer's appointment in 1994, is the longest such period without a change in the Supreme Court's membership since the 1820s. See Greenhouse, "The Supreme Court Term," at A1.

45. David G. Savage, *Turning Right: The Making of the Rehnquist Supreme Court,* New York: John Wiley and Sons, 1992, at 307–311, passim.

46. *Danforth,* 428 U.S. at 73.

47. *Danforth,* 428 U.S. at 74.

48. Jones and Peterman, "Whither," at 230.

49. Jones and Peterman, "Whither," at 229.

50. *Belotti v Baird,* 443 U.S. 622, 1979.

51. *Belotti,* 443 U.S. at 637.

52. *Belotti,* 443 U.S. at 647.

53. *Belotti,* 443 U.S. at 648. See also *H.L. v Matheson,* 450 U.S. 398, 1981, and *Hodgson v Minnesota,* 497 U.S. 417, 1990. In *Matheson,* Justice Marshall, dissenting, wrote: "Whatever its importance elsewhere, parental authority deserves *de minimis* legal reinforcement where the minor's exercise of a fundamental right is burdened." 497 U.S. at 449. In *Hodgson,* five members of the Court—Justices Stevens, Brennan, Marshall, Blackmun, and O'Connor—concluded that a Minnesota statute prohibiting a minor from having an abortion unless both parents were notified at least two days before the procedure was unconstitutional because "it does not reasonably further any legitimate state interest." 497 U.S. at 450.

54. Jones and Peterman, "Whither," at 232.

55. *Hodgson,* 497 U.S. at 501.

56. Joan Biskupic, "Court Takes Cases on Abortion, Gays," *The Washington Post,* January 15, 2000, at A1.

57. Alabama, Alaska, Arizona, Arkansas, Florida, Georgia, Idaho, Illinois, Indiana, Iowa, Kansas, Kentucky, Louisiana, Michigan, Mississippi, Missouri, Montana, Nebraska, New Jersey, North Dakota, Ohio, Oklahoma, Rhode Island, South Carolina, South Dakota, Tennessee, Utah, Virginia, West Virginia, and Wisconsin.

58. In 1992, the antiabortion National Right to Life Committee became aware of the gruesome nature of the partial birth abortion procedure and immediately began a campaign, complete with the bloody color photographs of the consequences of such a procedure. In less than a decade, thirty-one states passed legislation banning such a procedure.

59. Andrew D. Gough, "Banning Partial-Birth Abortion: A Constitutionally Acceptable Statute," 24 *Dayton Law Review* 187, Fall 1998, at 188,

60. 530 U.S. 94, 2000.

61. Quoted in Joan Biskupic, "A Divided High Court to Revisit Abortion," *The Washington Post,* April 23, 2000, at A3.

62. Joan Biskupic, "Abortion Argued at High Court," *The Washington Post,* April 26, 2000, at A1.

63. Ed Walsh and Amy Goldstein, "Supreme Court Upholds Two Key Abortion Rights," *The Washington Post,* June 29, 2000, at A1. The companion case, *Hill v Colorado,* involved a challenge to a state law that restricted antiabortion protesters outside abortion clinics. The law required demonstrators to stay at least eight feet away from persons entering a health care facility. The restriction applied within a hundred-foot radius around any clinic entrance. In a 6:3 vote, the Court upheld the state law. The three dissenters were Justices Scalia, Thomas, and Kennedy. The Chief Justice and Justice O'Connor joined the four moderates to validate the state law.

64. Quoted in Walsh and Goldstein, "Supreme Court Upholds," at A1.

65. Quoted in ibid.

66. *Plyler v Doe,* 457 U.S. 202, 1982. Texas refused to finance the costs to educate the U.S.–born children of illegal aliens in the United States. It authorized the local school districts to exclude them from the local public schools. Justice Brennan wrote the opinion for a five-person majority that overturned the law. The Fourteenth Amendment's Equal Protection Clause, which guarantees "any person within [the state's] jurisdiction the equal protection of the laws." Interpreted literally, "equal protection," Brennan wrote, was all-inclusive, regardless of citizenship or immigration status. Strict scrutiny was not the standard used because education was not a "fundamental" right and undocumented aliens were not considered a "suspect class." Instead, the intermediate standard, heightened scrutiny was employed, Chief Justice Burger dissented, joined by Justices O'Connor, Rehnquist, and White.

67. In 1968, the Court ruled that an illegitimate child is a "person" covered under the Fourteenth Amendment's Equal Protection Clause. Such persons can bring suits challenging state laws that discriminate against illegitimate children as a class as a denial of equal protection. *Levy v Louisiana,* 391 U.S. 68, 1968.

68. *Nguyen v. Immigration and Naturalization Service,* Nr. 99-2071, 2000, handed down on June 11, 2001. Consistent with the equal protection guarantee of the Fifth Amendment, the Court validated a citizenship law that treats children born out of wedlock to U.S. citizen mothers abroad differently than children born out of wedlock to U.S. citizen fathers abroad. The federal statute makes citizenship of the child automatic if the mother is a U.S. citizen but not automatic if the father of the child is a U.S. citizen. Joseph Boulais, an American citizen, fathered Tuan Anh Nguyan while he was in Vietnam. He was always involved, and when Tuan was five years old, the boy came to live with his father in Texas. Because the father did not officially "acknowledge" his relationship with his son before the child turned eighteen, Tuan was ordered deported after he was convicted of a crime. The disparate treatment based on sex is valid, said the Court, in a 5:4 decision, because of the differences in proving legitimate familial ties between a child and either parent. The rationale was a very traditional one: "[T]he mother's presence at birth provides a unique opportunity or potential to develop relationships that support citizenship, while biology gives a father, who may not even know his child was born, no such opportunity." See Catharine MacKinnon, "Can Fatherhood Be Optional?" *The New York Times,* June 17, 2001, at Section 4, p. 15.

69. See, for example, Nicole L. Cucci, "Constitutional Implications of In-Vitro Fertilization Procedures," 72 *St. John's Law Review* 417, Spring 1998; David Orentlicher, "Cloning and the Preservation of Family Integrity," 59 *Louisiana Law Review* 1019, Summer 1999; Lawrence Wu, "Family Planning Through Human Cloning: Is There a Fundamental Right?" 98 *Columbia Law Review* 1461, October 1998.

70. See Cucci, "Constitutional Implications of In-Vitro Fertilization Procedures," at 419–430, passim.

Notes to Chapter 5

1. "APA Report, Gary B. Melton, editor, *Adolescent Abortion: Psychological and Legal Issues*, 1986, at 21.

2. LFPP, WL, Lexington, Virginia. The case was *Parham v J.R.*, 442 U.S. 584, 1979, discussed in this chapter.

3. The great dissenter, Justice John M. Harlan, wrote: "It is the duty of all courts of justice to take care, for the general good of the community, that hard cases do not make bad law." *U.S. v Clark*, 96 U.S. 37, 1878, at 49.

4. Michelle Adams, "Knowing Your Place: Theorizing Sexual Harassment at Home," 40 *Arizona Law Review* 17, Spring 1998, at 24.

5. Adams, "Knowing Your Place," at 17.

6. Fineman, "Privacy and the Family," at 1215. Quote is from *Parham v J.R.*, 442 U.S. 584, 1979, at 602.

7. 405 U.S. 645, 1972.

8. Chief Justice Burger, dissenting, 405 U.S. 645, at 667.

9. Illinois Juvenile Court Act and the Illinois Paternity Act, Ill Rev. Stat C. 37, Sections 701–714 and 702–705 (1969).

10. Justices Black and Harlan had retired in September 1971 and their replacements, Justices Powell and Rehnquist, had not yet been confirmed when *Stanley* was decided.

11. TMP, LOC, Washington, DC.

12. Hutchinson, *The Man Who Once Was Whizzer White*, at 370.

13. Katheryn D. Katz, "The Pregnant Child's Right to Self-Determination," 62 *Albany Law Review* 1119, 1999, at 1128.

14. *Meyer v Nebraska*, 262 U.S. 390, 1923, at 399.

15. Meyer used a German Bible-history book as the text for his reading class.

16. 268 U.S. 510, 1925.

17. *Prince v Massachusetts*, 321 U.S. 158, 1944, at 166.

18. In a 1977 case, *Carey v. Population Services, International*, 431 U.S. 678, 1977, the Court majority said that a "parent may make, without unjustified governmental interference, decisions relating to child-rearing." At 684–685.

19. Justice Robert Jackson, joined by Justices Owen Roberts and Felix Frankfurter, after critiquing the Rutledge opinion, dissented "from the grounds of affirmance of a judgment I think was rightly decided, and upon right grounds, by the Supreme Judicial Court of Massachusetts."

20. *Prince v Massachusetts*, 321 U.S. at 167.

21. *Wisconsin v Yoder*, 406 U.S. 205, 1972, at 233–234.

22. WODP, LOC, Washington, DC. He recommended "grant," although Douglas scribbled "deny" on the memo. Douglas changed his mind and, a few weeks later, joined with five others to grant certiorari.

23. All quotes from WJBP and WODP, LOC, Washington, DC.

24. Hutchinson, *The Man Who Once Was Whizzer White*, at 371.

25. In an earlier draft, Burger went so far as to suggest that "parental direction" might be a "constitutional right." However, Justice Stewart wrote the Chief a sharp letter challenging such an assertion. "To be sure," Stewart wrote, "our society has long been organized in terms of the monogamous family structure, and this Court's cases make clear that the interests arising from that structure enjoy procedural due process as well as equal protection immunity from governmental interference. But it is something else to say that those interests are substantive constitutional rights. . . . I would hope that you could modify that language." The following day, Burger wrote: "[Y]our points give me no difficulty at all."

26. 519 U.S.102, 1996.

27. At 105ff.

28. *Cedar Rapids, Iowa Community School District v Garrret F.,a minor, by his mother and next friend, Charlene F.,* 119 SCt 902, 1999 (No. 96-1793).

29. All quotations from majority opinion of Justice Stevens in *Cedar Rapids,* unless otherwise indicated.

30. In another parent-child case involving the scope of the IDEA, the U.S. Supreme Court ruled, 5:4, that the federal funds could be used to provide a severely deaf high school student, Jim Zobrest, with a sign language interpreter, even though Jim was attending a Catholic high school. The family lived in Pennsylvania but moved to Arizona because Jim's parents found a school for their kindergartner to attend, the Arizona School for the Deaf and Blind. After five years he was mainstreamed but, because of his deafness (since infancy), Jim needed sign language help. When he was ready for high school, his parents enrolled him in Salpointe Catholic High School and asked the school district to use IDEA funds to cover the $7,000 annual costs for a sign language interpreter. However, the school district refused to provide a secular sign language interpreter to transmit religious views to a parochial school student. The family appealed the judgment all the way to the U.S. Supreme Court. And, in a 5:4 decision, written by Chief Justice Rehnquist, *Zobrest v Catalina, Arizona Foothills School District,* 509 U.S. 1, 1993, the Court concluded that IDEA funds could be used to provide the sign language interpreter. See also Aaron Epstein, "The Interpreter and the Establishment Clause," in Rodney A. Smolla, editor, *A Year in the Life of the Supreme Court,* Durham, N.C.: Duke University Press, 1995, at 126–140.

31. Stacy R. Walters, "Life-Sustaining Medical Decisions Involving Children: Father Knows Best," 15 *Thomas M. Cooley Law Review,* 115, 1998, at 127–130, passim.

32. 28 USC 1332, provides citizens residing in different states with a federal judicial forum to resolve civil disputes above $100,000. Carol Ankenbrandt lived in Missouri and her former husband, Jon Richards, lived in Louisiana. She brought suit in federal district court in Louisiana.

33. In the month prior to filing the federal lawsuit, a Louisiana juvenile court in Jefferson Parish, Louisiana, entered a judgment under the state's child protection

laws permanently terminating all of Richards's parental rights because of the physical and sexual abuses of his children. It also permanently enjoined him from any contact with them.

34. *Carol Ankenbrandt, as best friend and mother of L.R. and S.R., Petitioner v Jon Richards and Debra Kesler,* 504 U.S. 689, 1992.

35. The phrase was added to 29a in 1988, while Oakes's appeal was proceeding.

36. The only exception in 29A was if the photograph was taken "for a bona fide scientific or medical purpose, or for an educational or cultural purpose for a bona fide school, museum, or library."

37. *Massachusetts v Oakes,* 491 U.S. 576, 1989.

38. *Maryland v Craig,* 497 U.S. 836, 1990.

39. All quotations are from the majority opinion in *Maryland v Craig* unless otherwise noted.

40. The Sixth Amendment to the U.S. Constitution, ratified with nine other amendments in 1791, states: "In all criminal prosecutions, the accused shall enjoy the right to a speedy and public trial, by an impartial jury of the State and district wherein the crime shall have been committed, . . . and to be informed of the nature and cause of the accusation; *to be confronted with witnesses against him;* to have compulsory process for obtaining witnesses in his favor, and to have the Assistance of Counsel for his defence." (Italics added.)

41. At the time the case was in the Court, forty states had passed legislation similar to Maryland's statutory procedure.

42. 442 U.S. 584, 1979.

43. All quotes taken from majority opinion of CJ Burger, in *Parham,* unless otherwise noted.

44. Justice William H. Rehnquist, MTTC, May 24, 1977, in LFPP, WL, Lexington, Virginia.

45. Preliminary Bench Memo for LFP, June 15, 1976, in LFPP, WL, Lexington, Virginia. All quotes from LFPP unless otherwise noted.

46. LFPP, WL, Lexington, Virginia.

47. CJ Burger MTTC, December 15, 1977, in WJBP, LOC, Washington, DC.

48. Burger's draft opinion emphasized the "fractured family" and other findings in *Danforth* to the effect that "the family unit had already been severely damaged, if not destroyed, by the conflict between the parents and the child over the specific decision whether to obtain an abortion."

49. In a handwritten Memo, Powell's law clerk critically commented on Burger's second draft: "The manner in which he characterizes [*Danforth*] certainly seems to poison the well against the position I believe he (and, I *hope,* you!) will want to take in *Bellotti v Baird.*"

50. *Mathews v Eldridge,* 424 U.S. 319, 1976, at 335.

51. See, for example, how the brethren rewrote Burger's opinion in *Richard Nixon, President v United States,* 418 U.S. 683, 1974, in Howard Ball, *"We Have a*

Duty": The Supreme Court and the Watergate Tapes Litigation, Westport, CT: Greenwood Press, 1990.

52. 430 U.S. 651, 1977.

53. All quotes in this section from the majority opinion of the Court in *Ingraham,* written by Justice Powell, unless noted otherwise.

54. LFPP, WL. Justice White's dissent pointed out "that the record reveals that one student at Drew Junior High received 50 licks with a paddle for allegedly making an obscene phone call."

55. He did find a violation of the Florida law, which authorized "reasonable corporal punishment as a means of maintaining discipline." But such punishment may not be "degrading or unduly severe, and may be inflicted only after prior consultation with the school officials."

56. See *Goss v Lopez,* 419 U.S. 565 (1975), where the Court majority (with Powell among the dissenters) permitted a few minutes of "informal give-and-take between student and disciplinarian" before a student was suspended from school. At 583–584.

57. Quote from memo of Sam Estreicher to Powell during the *Parham* discussions, a year *after Ingraham,* dated December 5, 1977, LFPP, WL, Lexington, Virginia.

58. Powell's law clerk's recommendation was "possible grant. The result here, however, is incompatible with your views and given the unclarity of the CA5 opinion, you may want to deny." Powell wrote on the memo: "No good can come of a further [Court] intrusion into school discipline."

59. All quotations in this section from LFPP, WL, unless otherwise noted.

60. Announcing the decision from the bench, Powell said: "[W]e decline at this late date—and at a time when serious problems beset our schools—to impose an unnecessary restriction on all school teachers simply because of the misconduct of a few in one school in Florida."

61. Walters, "Life-Sustaining Medical Decisions," at 133.

62. Ibid. at 116.

63. Katz, "The Pregnant Child's Right to Self-Determination," at 1126–1127.

64. For example, when grandparents use their visitation right to "provide access to the father whose own visitation rights had been suspended by the Court, or who had threatened violence to the child and had agreed to stay away." Tom Eddy, "Grandparent Visitation Rights in Ohio When the Family Is Intact," 28 *Capital University Law Review* 197, 1999, at 198.

65. Eddy, "Grandparent Visitation Rights," at 198–199.

66. *Troxel v Grenville,* 530 U.S. 57, 2000.

67. Joan Biskupic, "Challenging Legal Notion of 'Family,'" *The Washington Post,* January 9, 2000, at A1.

68. Biskupic, "Challenging Legal Notion of 'Family,'" at A1.

69. Biskupic, "Challenging Legal Notion of 'Family,'" at A1. There are more than sixty million grandparents. Pressure groups such as the American Association of

Retired People (AARP) have weighed into the legal battle to support grandparent rights. The AARP and other governmental *amici curiae* argued in their briefs that government needs to be able to order third-party visitation to protect the welfare of children. Religious groups such as the Christian Legal Society have supported Tommie's position because they seek to support the traditional notion of family autonomy, and have been joined by liberal organizations such as the ACLU, who argue that the government has no right to dictate to parents who can visit with their children. Ibid.

70. Washington Revised Code Section 26.10.160 (3) permits "any person" to petition for visitation rights "at any time" and authorizes state superior courts to grant such rights whenever the visitation "may serve the child's best interest."

71. Biskupic, "Challenging Legal Notion of 'Family,'" at A1

72. Tony Mauro, "High Court Puts Parent's Rights First," *The Legal Times,* June 12, 2000, at 8. See also, for a view of the case from the gay and lesbian perspective, Patricia M. Logue and Ruth Harlow, "Family Fight," in *The Legal Times,* June 12, 2000, at 78.

73. Joan Biskupic, "Court Tackles Child Visitation Case," *The Washington Post,* January 13, 2000, at A3. Quotations in this segment from this Biskupic essay, unless otherwise indicated.

74. Seymour Moskowitz, "Saving Granny from the Wolf: Elder Abuse and Neglect—The Legal Framework," 31 *Connecticut Law Review* 77, Fall 1998.

75. Mistreatment includes physical and psychological, financial exploitation, and neglect of care-taking obligations. All are violations of the criminal law, including assault and battery, attempted murder, theft, larceny, and extortion.

76. Moskowitz, "Saving Granny from the Wolf," at 78–79.

77. Ibid. at 80.

78. See U.S. Senate Special Committee on Aging, 101st Congress, Report, *Aging America: Trends and Projections (Annotated).* Washington, DC: Government Printing Office, 1990, at 84–85.

NOTES TO CHAPTER 6

1. Conrad Rosenberg, "How Do I Sign?" 322 *New England Journal of Medicine* 1400, 1990, at 1400.

2. Francis J. Flaherty, "A 'Right-to-Die'?" *The National Law Journal,* January 14, 1985, at 1.

3. Kathleen M. Boozang, "An Intimate Passing: Restoring the Role of Family and Religion in Dying," 58 *University of Pittsburgh Law Review* 549, Spring 1997, at 553.

4. Thomas A. Preston, "Facing Death on Your Own Terms," *Newsweek,* May 22, 2000, at 82.

5. Sherwin B. Nuland, *How We Die: Reflections on Life's Final Chapter,* New York: Viking Press, 1993, at xvi.

6. Note, "How Technology Has Affected the Legal System: The Twilight Zone of Nancy Cruzan," 34 *Howard Law Journal* 201, 1991, at 201–202.

7. Paul Reidlinger, "Bouvia Finally Wins," 72 *American Bar Association Journal* 64, July 1, 1986, at 64.

8. Vicki Quade, "Lawscope: Death," 70 *American Bar Association Journal* 29, February 1984, at 30. In 1984, spurred on by right-to-life forces and the Reagan administration, Congress passed the Child Abuse Prevention and Treatment Act. It contained a strict standard for treatment of all impaired newborn babies; it called for "aggressive treatment" in virtually all "Baby Doe" cases, "regardless of the degree of suffering imposed and the burdens and risks involved. The federal rule evidences deep distrust of parental decision-making, relegating most parents to a non-participatory bystander role." Stephan A. Newman, "Baby Doe, Congress, and the States," 15 *American Journal of Law and Medicine* 1, 1989, at 1. In 1991, the Patient Self Determination Act took effect. The congressional statute required all patients admitted to hospitals and nursing homes to receive written information telling them of their right to make decisions concerning medical care, including the right to accept or refuse medical treatment.

9. PVS "describes a body which is functioning entirely in terms of its internal controls. It maintains temperature. It maintains heart beat and pulmonary ventilation. It maintains digestive activity. It maintains reflex activity of muscles and nerves for low level conditional responses. But there is no behavioral evidence of either self-awareness or awareness of the surroundings in a learned manner." *In Re Jobes,* 108 N.J. 394, 1987, at 403. (Statement of Dr. Fred Plum, Chair, Department of Neurology. Cornell University.) In a PVS, the patient's cognitive functions are totally and permanently lost, but the vegetative function remains.

10. In 1976, the Supreme Court denied certiorari in the headlines-producing tragedy that was taking place in New Jersey involving a young PVS patient, Karen Ann Quinlan. Her parents, devout Roman Catholics, wanted to remove her from life-support systems but the doctors refused, fearing criminal charges. *In Re Quinlan,* 70 N.J. 10, 1976; certiorari denied, 429 U.S. 922, 1976.

11. See, for example, Note, "How Technology Has Affected the Legal System."

12. *Nancy Cruzan v Director, Missouri Department of Health,* 497 U.S. 261,1990. See also Quade, "Lawscope: Death," at 29.

13. Boozang, "An Intimate Passing," at 566.

14. *Nancy Cruzan v Director, Missouri Department of Health,* 497 U.S. 261,1990.

15. *In Re Quinlan,* at 18.

16. Melvin I. Urofsky, *Lethal Judgments: Assisted Suicide and American Law,* Lawrence: University Press of Kansas, 2000, at 36.

17. *In Re Quinlan,* at 23.

18. *In Re Quinlan,* at 25.

19. *In Re Quinlan,* at 23.

20. *In Re Quinlan,* at 26–27.

21. Quoted in Dana Coleman, "Quinlan Attorney: A Leap to Fame," *New Jersey Lawyer*, April 8, 1996, at 1.

22. Urofsky, *Lethal Judgments*, at 37.

23. Ibid.

24. *In Re Quinlan*, at 27.

25. Quoted in Urofsky, *Lethal Judgments*, at 38.

26. Certiorari denied, 429 U.S. 922, 1976.

27. See Note, "How Technology Has Affected the Legal System," at 204–208. See also Urofsky, *Lethal Judgments*, at 39–57, passim. Some of the states that issued orders similar to New Jersey's Supreme Court were Arizona, Massachusetts, California, Maine, Connecticut, and Rhode Island. See *National Law Journal*, May 29, 1989, at 3.

28. Peter G. Filene, *In the Arms of Others: A Cultural History of the "Right-to-Die" in America*, Chicago: Ivan R. Dee Publisher, 1998, at xii.

29. Deborah Levy, "Euthanasia: The Lines Keep Shifting," *The Legal Times*, May 2, 1988, at 15. "But progress marches on. Since the *Quinlan* case, courts in New Jersey, California, and Massachusetts, have broken the feeding-tube barrier, finding the termination of artificial feeding the legal equivalent of the cutoff of other forms of life support, like respirators."

30. Levy, "Euthanasia," at 15.

31. John Cranford, "The Persistent Vegetative State: The Medical Reality," 18 *Hasting Center Report*, 27, 1988, at 32.

32. 497 U.S. 261, 1990

33. Since 1970, thirty-eight states have adopted a "brain death" standard, "which generally defines death as either the cessation of respiration and heartbeat—the traditional indicia of life—or the stoppage of all brain activity." Flaherty, "A 'Right-to-Die'?" at 1.

34. Urofsky, *Lethal Judgments*, at 58. See also *Cruzan*, at 266.

35. Quoted in *The New York Times*, December 29, 1990, at 8.

36. Quoted in *The Tallahassee, Florida, Democrat*, June 26, 1990, at A1.

37. Christopher Supernor, "Ignoring an Incompetent Person's Constitutional Right to Forgo Life-Sustaining Treatment," 19 *Florida State University Law Review* 209, Summer 1991, at 212.

38. *Cruzan*, at 264.

39. Louis Michael Seidman, "Confusion at the Border: *Cruzan*, the "Right-to-Die," and the Public/Private Distinction," in Dennis J. Hutchinson, et al., editors, *1991: The Supreme Court Review*, Chicago: University of Chicago Press, 1992, at 51–52.

40. Seidman, "Confusion at the Border," at 55.

41. *The New York Times*, December 29, 1990, at A1.

42. *The New York Times*, December 16, 1990, at 29.

43. Savage, *Turning Right*, at 342.

44. Quoted in Anna Fels, M.D., "An Escort into the Land of Sickness," *The New York Times*, July 31, 2001, at A1.

45. Dr. Jack Kevorkian, a retired medical pathologist who lived in Royal Oak, Michigan, is commonly referred to by the media as "Dr. Death." He helped more than 120 terminally ill patients commit suicide. In his first four trials he was acquitted. (See, for example, *People of Michigan v Kevorkian*, 447 Mich 436, 1994, and *Kevorkian v Thompson*, 96-CV-73777-DT, U.S. District Court, ED Michigan, 1997.) However, in 1999, he killed Thomas Youk, rather than assisting the suicide of Youk, a young man with Lou Gehrig's disease who could not turn the "death" machine on himself. This action was filmed and then shown on the CBS news show *60 Minutes*. Based on that evidence, he was charged with murder, tried, convicted, and, in April 1999, sentenced to ten to twenty-five years in prison for the mercy killing. For a supportive view of Kevorkian, see Joan Brovins and Thomas Oehmke, *Dr. Death: Dr. Jack Kevorkian's RX: Death*, Hollywood, FL: Lifetime Books, 1993.

46. Quoted in Laura Blumenfeld, "At Dawn, Activists Greet Matters of Death in Shades of Gray," *The Washington Post*, January 9, 1997 at A1.

47. 521 U.S. 702, 1996.

48. 521 U.S. 793, 1996.

49. Oregon, in 1997, became the first state to have a Death With Dignity statute. In 1994, the Hemlock Society was able to get Measure 16, a Death With Dignity act, on the Oregon ballot. It passed, 51 percent to 49 percent. Opponents challenged it in federal courts but the CA9 validated the measure. Another initiative, placed on the ballot by conservative religious organizations in 1997 to reject the statute was defeated by a wide margin. "Religion is fine," said taxi driver Lou Galaxy. "Believe what you want to believe, but don't shove your religion down my throat." Quoted in Urofsky, *Lethal Judgments*, at 104. On November 6, 2001, U.S. Attorney General John D. Ashcroft authorized federal drug agents (U.S. DEA) to identify and punish doctors who prescribe federally controlled drugs to help terminally ill patients commit suicide. It was an effort to effectively block implementation of Oregon's Death With Dignity law. His order called for the federal agents to revoke the drug licenses of Oregon doctors who help patients commit suicide. The following day four terminally ill Oregon patients joined the State's Attorney General Hardy Myers in his request in federal district court to impose a stay on Ashcroft's order. On November 8, 2001, U.S. District Court judge Robert Jones granted the temporary restraining order, effectively blocking the DEA from pursuing doctors in Oregon. The matter is still pending at this time.

50. See Susan Okie, "Country's Doctors Remain Divided Over Physician-Assisted Suicide," *The Washington Post*, January 8, 1997, at A15.

51. For an excellent summary of the arguments made by these amici, see Richard E. Coleson, "The Glucksberg and Quill Amicus Curiae Briefs: Verbatim Arguments Opposing Assisted Suicide," 13 *Issues in Law and Medicine*, Summer 1997, 3.

52. Quoted in Okie, "Country's Doctors Remain Divided," at 15.

53. Quoted in Okie, "Country's Doctors Remain Divided," at 15.

54. Quoted in Sedler, "Abortion, Physician-Assisted Suicide, and the Constitution," at 541.

55. Sedler, "Abortion, Physician-Assisted Suicide, and the Constitution," at 544–545.

56. Rothstein, Chief Judge, U.S. District Court in *Compassion in Dying v Washington*, 850 F Supp 1454, WD, Washingon, 1994.

57. Linda Greenhouse, "Clinton Administration Asks Supreme Court to Rule Against Assisted Suicide," *The New York Times*, November 13, 1997, at A10.

58. 505 U.S. 833, 1992.

59. 497 U.S. 261, 1990.

60. Quoted in Blumenfeld, "At Dawn, Activists Greet Matters of Death in Shades of Gray," at A1.

61. Joan Biskupic, ""Justices Skeptical of Assisted Suicide," *The Washington Post*, at A1.

62. Lawrence Baum, *The Supreme Court*, Washington, DC: The CQ Press, 7th edition, 2001, at 132.

63. Quoted in Baum, *Supreme Court*, at 130.

64. Quoted in Baum, *Supreme Court*, at 131.

65. All arguments quoted herein are from "Excerpts from the Supreme Court Oral Argument on Physician-Assisted Suicide," in *The Washington Post*, January 9, 1997, at A16.

66. At this point, Rehnquist enumerated the Constitution's fundamental rights and liberty interests that courts have acknowledged since the 1920s: marriage; having children; to direct their education and their upbringing; marital privacy; to use contraceptives; and to abortion. "We have assumed, and strongly suggested, that the Due Process Clause protects the traditional right to refuse unwanted lifesaving medical treatment." *Washington*, at 720.

67. She continued: "Every one of us at some point may be affected by our own or a family member's terminal illness. There is no reason to think the democratic process will not strike the proper balance between the interests of terminally ill, mentally competent individuals who would seek to end their suffering and the State's interests in protecting those who might seek to end life mistakenly or under pressure." *Washington*, at 737.

68. Joan Biskupic, "Unanimous Decision," *The Washington Post*, June 27, 1997, at A1.

69. Roberto Suro, "States to Become Forum," *The Washington Post*, June 27, 1997, at A19.

70. Amy Goldstein, "Court's Decision on Help with Suicide Leaves Doctors in a Gray Zone," *The Washington Post*, June 27, 2000, at A18.

71. Goldstein, "Court's Decision on Help with Suicide Leaves Doctors in a Gray Zone," at A18.

72. Gabrielle Degroot Redford, "Their Final Answers," *Modern Maturity,* September/October 2000, at 66.

73. Redford, "Their Final Answers," at 68. See also Denise Grady, "Planning for Death," and "Charting a Course of Comfort and Treatment at the End of Life," *The New York Times,* May 29, May 30, 2000, at A1.

Notes to Chapter 7

1. Tamara Lewin, "Father Owing Child Support Loses a Right to Procreate," *The New York Times,* July 12, 2001, at A1.

2. Lisa Belkin, "Watching Her Weight," *The New York Times Magazine,* Sunday, July 8, 2001, at 31.

3. Quoted in Belkin, "Watching Her Weight," at 32. Unless otherwise noted, all quotes in this segment from Belkin.

4. Alan B. Handler, "Individual Worth," 17 *Hofstra Law Review* 493, Spring 1989, at 495.

5. Robert S. Peck, "The Right to be Left Alone," 15 *Human Rights,* 26, 1987, at 27.

6. Thomas B. Kearns, "Technology and the Right to Privacy: The Convergence of Surveillance and Information Privacy Concerns," 7 *William and Mary Bill of Rights Journal* 975, April, 1999, at 986.

7. In *Silverman v U.S.,* 365 U.S. 505, 1961, the Court majority said that "at the very core" of the Fourth Amendment "stands the right of a man to retreat into his own home and there be free from unreasonable governmental intrusion." At 511. The case involved the use of a "spike mike" that was hammered into the wall of Silverman's house in order to eavesdrop on his conversations.

8. *Kyello v U.S.,* 121 SCT 2038, 2000, at . All quotes in this section, unless otherwise noted, are from the Court opinion.

9. In *Katz v U.S.,* 389 U.S. 347, 1967, the Court majority, in an opinion written by Justice Potter Stewart, concluded that the Fourth Amendment protects people, not places. Because Katz, a known bookie, "justifiably relied" upon the privacy of a public telephone booth (electronically bugged by the F.B.I.) law enforcement agents had to receive a search warrant before they could eavesdrop on his conversations. After 1967, then, physical trespass (*Silverman*) was replaced with the *Katz* standard: Did a person have a "reasonable expectation of privacy?" A Fourth Amendment "search occurs when the government violates a subjective expectation of privacy that society recognizes as reasonable."

10. Quoted in Charles Lane, "Justices Hear Oregon Case on High-Tech Surveillance," *The Washington Post,* February 21, 2001, at A3.

11. Lane, "Justices Hear Oregon Case," at A3.

12. Scalia pointed out that the thermal imager used in the *Kyello* case "might disclose, for example, at what hour each night the lady of the house takes her daily sauna and bath—a detail that many would consider 'intimate.'"

13. Linda Greenhouse, "As Crime Ebbs, Top Court's Privacy Rulings Flow," *The New York Times*, June 17, 2001, at A1.

14. Quoted in Jonathan Ringel, "A Check on Technology: Odd 5:4 Alliance Blocks Use of Heat Detector in Pot Prosecution," *The Legal Times*, June 18, 2001, at 9.

15. Quoted in Edward Walsh, "High-Tech Devices Require a Warrant," *The Washington Post*, June 12, 2001, at A1.

16. Quoted in Walsh, "High-Tech Devices," at A1.

17. 532 U.S. 483, 2001.

18. Nine states had "medical necessity" legislation on the books, allowing AIDS and cancer patients, among others, to purchase and use marijuana to alleviate their pain. They are Washington, Oregon, California, Nevada, Arizona, Colorado, Hawaii, Alaska, and Maine.

19. Charles Lane, "Court Rules Against 'Medical Marijuana,'" *The Washington Post*, May 15, 2001, at A1.

20. That same month, Arizona voters also voted for a similar measure.

21. Lane, "Court Rules Against 'Medical Marijuana,'" at A1.

22. Quoted in Roberto Suro, "U.S. Will Issue Warnings On Medical Marijuana Laws," *The Washington Post*, December 31, 1996, at A1.

23. Quoted in William Claiborne, "Four California Mayors Urge Clinton to Stop Lawsuits Against 'Cannabis Clubs,'" *The Washington Post*, March 19, 1998, at A10.

24. *U.S. v Oakland Cannabis Buyers' Cooperative*, 532 U.S. 483, 2001. Unless otherwise noted, all quotes in this section from the majority opinion.

25. Quoted Lane, "Court Rules Against 'Medical Marijuana,'" at A1

26. Lane, "Court Rules Against 'Medical Marijuana,'" at A1.

27. Jim Oliphant, "Seeking Shelter," *The Legal Times*, July 30, 2001, at 1.

28. Oliphant, "Seeking Shelter," at 14.

29. Quoted in Oliphant, "Seeking Shelter," at 14.

30. Handler, "Individual Worth," at 494. "What seems unusual about all of this is not the drama of these episodes, but that they have been produced and directed by courts."

31. See Walter F, Murphy's classic book, *Elements of Judicial Strategy*, Chicago: University of Chicago Press, 1960.

32. The U.S. Supreme Court has total discretion to create its docket of cases. Although the Justices received, in 2001, almost nine thousand petitions for certiorari and appeals (mostly certiorari petitions), they heard less than 1 percent of these cases. As noted, there must be a "vote of four" to grant certiorari. At the end of the

2000 Term of the Court, there were a total of eighty-seven plenary opinions handed down. See, generally, Cooper and Ball, *The U.S. Supreme Court*, and H. W. Perry, *Deciding to Decide*, Cambridge: Harvard University Press, 1992.

33. Murphy, *Elements of Judicial Strategy*, at 37–68, passim.

34. *Payne v Tennessee*, 501 U.S. 808, 1991.

35. *Regents of the University of California v Alan Bakke*, 438 U.S. 205, 1978.

36. See Howard Ball, *The Bakke Case: Race, Education, and Affirmative Action*, Lawrence: University Press of Kansas, 2000.

37. See *Shaw v Reno*, 509 U.S. 630, 1993; *Shaw v Hunt*, 517 U.S. 899, 1996; *Hunt v Cromartie*, 526 U.S. 541, 1999.

38. *Hunt v. Cromartie*, 532 U.S. 234, 2001.

39. See Thomas L. Thorson, *The Logic of Democracy*, New York: Holt, Rinehart and Winston, 1962, for a fascinating discussion of the *inevitability* of "fallibilism" in a democracy.

40. See Philip Cooper, *Battles on the Bench*, Lawrence: University Press of Kansas, 1998.

41. Justice Byron R. White, interview with author, November 18, 1986, Washington, DC.

42. Justice William J. Brennan, interview with author, November 1986; Harry Blackmun, interview with author, December, 1986, Washington, DC.

43. David J. Garrow, "The Rehnquist Reins," *The New York Times Sunday Magazine*, October 6, 1996, at 68–69.

44. Howard Ball and Philip Cooper, "Fighting Justices: Hugo L. Black and William O. Douglas and Supreme Court Conflict," 38 *The American Journal of Legal History* 1, January 1994.

45. Letter, Associate Justice David H. Souter to Howard Ball, April 29, 1996.

46. *Seminole Tribe of Florida v Florida*, 517 U.S. 44, 1996. Congress, in 1988, passed the Indian Gaming Regulatory Act, permitting Indian tribes to operate gambling casinos on their reservations and allowing tribes to file lawsuits in federal court when they claimed that the state failed to negotiate in good faith with them regarding what kinds of gambling activities would be allowed in the state. Florida's Governor was an opponent of casino gambling and refused to negotiate with the Seminole Indian tribe. The tribe took the Governor into federal court for failing to exercise good faith in not negotiating. The CA11 held that Congress lacked the authority to force the states to negotiate with Indian tribes because of the Eleventh Amendment, which did not extend "the judicial power" to "any suit in law and equity, commenced against one of the United States by citizens of another state, or by citizens or subjects of any foreign state." Florida could not be dragged into federal court, said the CA11, unless it gave its consent. From a gambling issue, the case became a federalism issue. The Clinton administration and the Seminole tribe argued that Congress had full authority, under the Indian Commerce Clause to pass the act. (Article I, Section 8: "Congress shall have power [clause 3] to regulate commerce

with foreign nations, and among the several states, and with the Indian Tribes.")
The Rehnquist majority opinion upheld the CA11, saying that the Eleventh Amendment restricted federal judicial power and that the Commerce Clause cannot be used to circumvent constitutional limits placed on the federal judiciary. Souter dissented, arguing that Congress had always believed that the states were subject to the jurisdiction of federal courts and that the Gaming Act was constitutional.

47. Justice Byron R. White, interview with author, November 18, 1986, Washington, DC.

Bibliography

Data from the papers and letters of a number of Justices of the U.S. Supreme Court have been used throughout the book. They are

Hugo L. Black papers, Library of Congress (LOC), Washington, DC.

William J. Brennan papers, LOC, Washington, DC.

Tom C. Clark papers, University of Texas Law Library, Austin, Texas.

William O. Douglas papers, LOC, Washington, DC.

John M. Harlan II papers, Mudd Memorial Library, Princeton University, Princeton, New Jersey.

Thurgood Marshall papers, LOC, Washington, DC.

Lewis F. Powell papers, Washington and Lee University Law Library Archives (WL), Lexington, Virginia.

Harlan Fiske Stone papers, LOC, Washington, DC.

Earl Warren Papers, LOC, Washington, DC.

Abraham, Henry J., *Justices, Presidents, and Senators: A History of the U.S. Supreme Court Appointments from Washington to Clinton.* New York: Rowman and Little-field Publishers, 1999.

Adams, Michelle, "Knowing Your Place: Theorizing Sexual Harassment at Home," 40 *Arizona Law Review* 17, Spring 1998.

AP, "Reno: Renew VAWA," *The New York Times,* May 18, 2000, at 27A.

Balkin, Jack M., "The Court Defers to a Racist Era," *The New York Times,* May 17, 2000.

Ball, Howard, *"We Have a Duty": The Supreme Court and the Watergate Tapes Litigation.* Westport, CT: Greenwood Press, 1990.

———, *Hugo Black: Cold Steel Warrior.* New York: Oxford University Press. 1996.

———, *A Defiant Life: Thurgood Marshall and the Persistence of Racism in America.* New York: Crown Publisher, 1999.

———, *The Bakke Case: Race, Education, and Affirmative Action.* Lawrence: University Press of Kansas, 2000.

Ball, Howard and Philip Cooper, *Of Power and Right: Justices Hugo L. Black, William O. Douglas, and America's Constitutional Revolution*. New York: Oxford University Press. 1992.

———, "Fighting Justices: Hugo L. Black and William O. Douglas and Supreme Court Conflict," 38 *The American Journal of Legal History* 1, January 1994.

Baum, Lawrence, *The Supreme Court*. Washington, DC: The CQ Press, 7th edition, 2001.

Belkin, Lisa, "Watching Her Weight," *The New York Times Magazine*, Sunday, July 8, 2001.

Biskupic, Joan, "Justices Skeptical of Assisted Suicide," *The Washington Post*, January 9, 1997.

———, "Unanimous Decision," *The Washington Post*, June 27, 1997.

———, "Justices Hear Harassment Case," *The Washington Post*, December 4, 1997, at A25.

———, "Challenging Legal Notion of 'Family,'" *The Washington Post*, January 9, 2000.

———, "States' Role at Issue in Rape Suit," *The Washington Post*, January 10, 2000.

———, "Sex-Assault Law Under Scrutiny," *The Washington Post*, January 12, 2000.

———, "Court Tackles Child Visitation Case," *The Washington Post*, January 13, 2000.

———, "Court Takes Cases on Abortion, Gays," *The Washington Post*, January 15, 2000.

———, "A Divided High Court to Revisit Abortion," *Washington Post*, April 23, 2000.

———, "Abortion Argued at High Court," *The Washington Post*, April 26, 2000.

———, "Justices Reject Lawsuits for Rape," *The Washington Post*, May 18, 2000.

Black, Hugo L. and Elizabeth Black, *Mr. Justice and Mrs. Black: The Memoirs of Hugo L. Black and Elizabeth Black*. New York: Random House, 1986.

Blackstone, William, *Commentaries on the Laws of England*, 1850. Chicago: University of Chicago Press, 1979.

Blumenfeld, Laura, "At Dawn, Activists Greet Matters of Death in Shades of Gray," *The Washington Post*, January 9, 1997.

Boozang, Kathleen M., "An Intimate Passing: Restoring the Role of Family and Religion in Dying," 58 *University of Pittsburgh Law Review* 549 Spring 1997.

Bowman, Craig A. and Blake M. Cornish, "A More Perfect Union: A Legal and Social Analysis of Domestic Partnership Ordinances," 92 *Columbia Law Review* 1164, 1992.

Brovins, Joan and Thomas Oehmke, *Dr. Death: Dr. Jack Kevorkian's RX: Death*. Hollywood, FL: Lifetime Books, 1993.

Brown, Anne B., "The Evolving Definition of Marriage," 31 *Suffolk University Law Review* 917, 1998.

Caplan, Lincoln, "The President's Lawyer, and the Court's," *The New York Times*, May 18, 2001, at A27.

Carelli, Richard, "Court: Same Sex Harassment Illegal," *The Washington Post*, March 4, 1998.

Claiborne, William, "Four California Mayors Urge Clinton to Stop Lawsuits Against 'Cannabis Clubs,'" *The Washington Post*, March 19, 1998.

Coleman, Dana, "Quinlan Attorney: A Leap to Fame," *New Jersey Lawyer*, April 8, 1996.

Coleson, Richard E., "The Glucksberg and Quill Amicus Curiae Briefs: Verbatim Arguments Opposing Assisted Suicide," 13 *Issues in Law and Medicine*, Summer 1997.

Cooper, Philip J., *Battles on the Bench: Conflict Inside the Supreme Court*. Lawrence: University Press of Kansas, 1998.

Cooper, Philip and Howard Ball, *The U.S. Supreme Court: From the Inside Out*. Englewood Cliffs, NJ: Prentice-Hall, 1996.

Craig, Barbara and David O'Brien, *Abortion and American Politics*. Chatham, NJ: Chatham House, 1993.

Cranford, John, "The Persistent Vegetative State: The Medical Reality," 18 *Hasting Center Report* 27, 1988.

Cucci, Nicole L., "Constitutional Implications of In-Vitro Fertilization Procedures," 72 *St. John's Law Review* 417, Spring 1998.

Cumming, Richard, editor, Max Lerner, *Nine Scorpions in a Bottle: Great Judges and Cases of the U.S. Supreme Court*. New York: Arcade Publishers, 1937, 1994.

Dalton, Clare, "Deconstructing Contract Doctrine," 94 *Yale Law Journal* 997, 1985.

Destro, Robert A., "*Loving v. Virginia* After 30 Years," 47 *Catholic University Law Review* 1207, Summer 1998.

Dolgin, Janet L., "Choice, Tradition, and the New Genetics: The Fragmentation of the Ideology of Family," 32 *Connecticut Law Review* 523, Winter 2000.

Eddy, Tom, "Grandparent Visitation Rights in Ohio When the Family Is Intact," 28 *Capital University Law Review* 197, 1999.

Epstein, Aaron, "The Interpreter and the Establishment Clause," in Rodney A. Smolla, editor, *A Year in the Life of the Supreme Court*. Durham, NC: Duke University Press, 1995.

Eskridge, William N., Jr., "*Hardwick* and Historiography," 1999 *University of Illinois Law Review* 631, 1999.

Fels, Anna, M.D., "An Escort into the Land of Sickness," *The New York Times*, July 31, 2001.

Filene, Peter G., *In the Arms of Others: A Cultural History of the "Right-to-Die" in America*. Chicago: Ivan R. Dee Publisher, 1998.

Fineman, Martha A., "Privacy and the Family," 67 *George Washington Law Review* 1207, June/August 1999.

Flaherty, Francis J., "A 'Right-to-Die'?" *The National Law Journal,* January 14, 1985.

Fritsch, Jane, "Aspirations: A Rise in Single Dads," *The New York Times,* May 20, 2001.

————, "Matrimony: The Magic's Still Gone," *The New York Times,* May 20, 2001.

Garrow, David J., "The Rehnquist Reins," *The New York Times Sunday Magazine,* October 6, 1996.

————, "Justice Powell's Forceful Role in *Roe,*" *The Legal Times,* May 8, 2000.

Goldberg, Carey, "Single Dads Wage Revolution, One Bedtime Story at a Time," *The New York Times,* June 17, 2001.

Goldfarb, Sally F., "Violence Against Women and the Persistence of Privacy," 61 *Ohio State Law Review* 1, 2000.

Goldstein, Amy, "Court's Decision on Help with Suicide Leaves Doctors in a Gray Zone," *The Washington Post,* June 27, 2000.

Goode, Erica, "Study Says 20% of Girls Reported Abuse by a Date," *The New York Times,* August 1, 2001.

Gough, Andrew D., "Banning Partial-Birth Abortion: A Constitutionally Acceptable Statute," 24 *Dayton Law Review* 187, Fall 1998.

Grady, Denise, "Planning for Death," and "Charting a Course of Comfort and Treatment at the End of Life," *The New York Times,* May 29, 30, 2000.

Greenhouse, Linda, "Clinton Administration Asks Supreme Court to Rule Against Assisted Suicide," *The New York Times,* November 13, 1997.

————, "Battle on Federalism," *The New York Times,* May 17, 2000.

————, "As Crime Ebbs, Top Court's Privacy Rulings Flow," *The New York Times,* June 17, 2001.

————, "The Supreme Court Term: Beyond Bush v. Gore," *The New York Times,* July 2, 2001.

Handler, Alan B., "Individual Worth," 17 *Hofstra Law Review* 493, Spring 1989.

Hannon, Sherene D., "License to Oppress: The Aftermath of *Bowers v. Hardwick,*" 19 *Pace Law Review* 507, Spring 1999.

Heeb, Jennifer L., "Homosexual Marriage, The Changing American Family, and the Heterosexual Right to Privacy," 24 *Seton Hall Law Review* 347, 1993.

Howard, J. Woodford, "On the Fluidity of Judicial Choice," 62 *American Political Science Review,* March 1968.

Howlett, Debbie and Tony Mauro, "Into the Courts, Away from Congress," *USA Today,* September 11, 1996.

Hutchinson, Dennis J., *The Man Who Once Was Whizzer White: A Portrait of Justice Byron R. White.* New York: The Free Press, 1998.

Irons, Peter, *The Courage of Their Convictions.* New York: Penguin Books, 1988.

————, *A People's History of the Supreme Court.* New York: Penguin Books, 1999.

Jeffries, John C., *Justice Lewis F. Powell, Jr.* New York: Scribner's, 1994.

Jones, Tiffany and Larry Peterman, "Whither the Family and Family Privacy?" 4 *Texas Review of Law and Politics* 193, Fall 1999.

Kantrowitz, Barbara and Pat Wingart, "Unmarried, With Children," *Newsweek*, May 28, 2000.

Katz, Katheryn D., "The Pregnant Child's Right to Self-Determination," 62 *Albany Law Review* 1119, 1999.

Kearns, Thomas B., "Technology and the Right to Privacy: The Convergence of Surveillance and Information Privacy Concerns," 7 *William and Mary Bill of Rights Journal* 975, April 1999.

Keefer, Timothy, "DOMA as a Defensible Exercise of Congressional Power Under the Full-Faith-and-Credit Clause," 54 *Washington and Lee Law Review* 1635, Fall 1997.

Kluger, Richard, *Simple Justice*. New York: Vintage Press, 1975.

Kohm, Lynne Marie, "Liberty and Marriage—*Baehr* and Beyond: Due Process in 1998," 12 *Brigham Young University Journal of Public Law* 253, 1998.

Lane, Charles, "Court Rules Against 'Medical Marijuana,'" *The Washington Post*, May 15, 2001.

———, "Justices Hear Oregon Case on High-Tech Surveillance," *The Washington Post*, February 21, 2001.

Lazarus, Edward, *Closed Chambers: The Rise, Fall, and Future of the Modern Supreme Court*. New York: Penguin Books, 1998.

Levy, Deborah, "Euthanasia: The Lines Keep Shifting," *The Legal Times*, May 2, 1998.

Lewin, Tamara, "Father Owing Child Support Loses a Right to Procreate," *The New York Times*, July 12, 2001.

Lewis, Kevin H., "Equal Protection After *Romer v Evans*: Implications for the Defense of Marriage Act and Other Laws," 49 *Hastings Law Journal* 175, November 1997.

Logue, Patricia M. and Ruth Harlow, "Family Fight," *The Legal Times*, June 12, 2000.

MacKinnon, Catharine, "Can Fatherhood Be Optional?" *The New York Times*, June 17, 2001.

Masters, Brooke A., "'No Winners' in Rape Lawsuit," *The Washington Post*, May 20, 2000.

Mauro, Tony, "High Court Puts Parent's Rights First," *The Legal Times*, June 12, 2000.

McCarthy, Sean, "Abortion's Empty Rhetoric," *Newsday*, July 1, 1992.

McDonaugh, Eileen L., "My Body, My Consent," 62 *Albany Law Review* 1057, 1999.

Miccio, G. Kristian, "With All Due Deliberate Care," 29 *Columbia Human Rights Law Review* 641, Summer 1998.

———, "A Reasonable Battered Mother? Redefining, Reconstructing, and Recreating the Battered Mother in Child Protective Proceedings," 22 *Harvard Women's Law Journal* 89, Spring 1999.

———, "A Reasonable Battered Wife," 22 *Harvard Women's Law Journal* 89, Spring 1999.

Mills, Linda G., "Killing Her Softly: Intimate Abuse and the Violence of State Intervention," 113 *Harvard Law Review* 550, December 1999.

Moskowitz, Seymour, "Saving Granny from the Wolf: Elder Abuse and Neglect—The Legal Framework," 31 *Connecticut Law Review* 77, Fall 1998.

Murdock, Joyce and Deb Price, *Courting Justice: Gay Men and Lesbians v. the Supreme Court.* New York: Basic Books, 2001.

Murphy, Walter F., *Elements of Judicial Strategy.* Chicago: University of Chicago Press, 1960.

Newman, Roger K., *Hugo Black: A Biography.* New York: Pantheon, 1994.

Newman, Stephan A., "Baby Doe, Congress, and the States," 15 *American Journal of Law and Medicine* 1, 1989.

Niebuhr, Gustav, "Reporter's Notebook: Baptists Convene, and Turn to Family," *The New York Times,* June 14, 2001.

Nkrumah, Kafahni, "The Defense of Marriage Act: Congress Re-Writes the Constitution to Pacify Its Fears," 23 *Thurgood Marshall Law Review* 513, Spring 1998.

Note, "Homosexuals Right to Marry: A Constitutional Test and a Legislative Solution," 128 *University of Pennsylvania Law Review* 193, 1979.

Note, "How Technology Has Affected the Legal System: The Twilight Zone of Nancy Cruzan," 34 *Howard Law Journal* 201, 1991.

Nuland, Sherwin B., *How We Die: Reflections on Life's Final Chapter.* New York: Viking Press, 1993.

O'Brien, David, *Constitutional Law and Politics, Volume II: Civil Rights and Liberties.* New York: Morrow, 1991.

Okie, Susan, "Country's Doctors Remain Divided Over Physician-Assisted Suicide," *The Washington Post,* January 8, 1997.

Oliphant, Jim, "Seeking Shelter," *The Legal Times,* July 30, 2001.

Orentlicher, David, "Cloning and the Preservation of Family Integrity," 59 *Louisiana Law Review* 1019, Summer 1999.

Peck, Robert S., "The Right to Be Left Alone," 15 *Human Rights,* 26, 1987.

Perry, H. W., *Deciding to Decide: Agenda-Setting in the U.S. Supreme Court.* Cambridge: Harvard University Press, 1992.

Polenberg, Richard. "Cardozo and the Criminal Law: *Palko v. Connecticut* Remembered," 1996 *Journal of Supreme Court History* 1996.

Posner, Richard A., *Cardozo: A Study in Reputation.* Chicago: University of Chicago Press, 1990.

———, *Sex and Reason.* Cambridge: Harvard University Press, 1992.

Preston, Thomas A., "Facing Death on Your Own Terms," *Newsweek,* May 22, 2000.

Provost, Melissa A., "Disregarding the Constitution in the Name of Defending Marriage: The Unconstitutionality of the Defense of Marriage Act," 8 *Seton Hall Constitutional Law Journal* 157, Fall 1997.

Quade, Vicki, "Lawscope: Death," 70 *American Bar Association Journal* 29, February 1984.

Redford, Gabrielle Degroot, "Their Final Answers," *Modern Maturity*, September/October 2000.

Reidlinger, Paul, "Bouvia Finally Wins," 72 *American Bar Association Journal* 64, July 1, 1986.

Ringel, Jonathan, "A Check on Technology: Odd 5:4 Alliance Blocks Use of Heat Detector in Pot Prosecution," *The Legal Times*, June 18, 2001.

Rivera, Rhonda R., "Our Straight-Laced Judges: The Legal Position of Homosexual Persons in the United States," 50 *Hastings Law Journal* 1015, April 1999.

Rosen, Jeffrey, "The O'Connor Court: America's Most Powerful Jurist," *The New York Times Sunday Magazine*, June 3, 2001.

Rosenberg, Conrad, "How Do I Sign?" 322 *New England Journal of Medicine* 1400, 1990.

Rowan, Carl T., *Dream Makers, Dream Breakers: The World of Justice Thurgood Marshall*. Boston: Little, Brown, 1993.

Savage, David G., *Turning Right: The Making of the Rehnquist Supreme Court*, New York: John Wiley and Sons, 1992.

Schmitt, Eric, "For First Time, Nuclear Families Drop Below 25% of Households," *The New York Times*, May 15, 2001.

Schwartz, Bernard, *The Super Chief: Earl Warren and His Supreme Court*. New York: Oxford University Press, 1986.

———, *Decision: How the Supreme Court Decides Cases*, New York: Oxford University Press, 1996.

Sedler, Robert A., "Abortion, Physician-Assisted Suicide and the Constitution: The View from Without and Within," 12 *Notre Dame Journal of Law, Ethics, and Public Policy* 529, 1998.

Seidman, Louis Michael, "Confusion at the Border: *Cruzan*, the "Right-to-Die," and the Public/Private Distinction," in Dennis J. Hutchinson et al. editors, *1991: The Supreme Court Review*. Chicago: University of Chicago Press, 1992.

Siegal, Reva B., "The Rule of Love: Wife Beating as Prerogative," 105 *Yale Law Journal* 2117, June 1996.

Simon, James F., *The Center Holds: The Power Struggle inside the Rehnquist Court*. New York: Simon & Schuster, 1995.

Stern, Adam, "Single Dad: Popular But Misunderstood"; Joe Queenan, "Nuclear Dad: Last of My Kind"; Daniel Voll, "Unwed Dad: Marriage Is Just a Maybe," in "Sunday Styles" Section 9, *The New York Times*, June 17, 2001.

Summer, Susan, "The Full-Faith-And-Credit Clause: Its History," 34 *Oregon Law Review* 224, 1955.

Supernor, Christopher, "Ignoring an Incompetent Person's Constitutional Right to Forgo Life-Sustaining Treatment," 19 *Florida State University Law Review* 209, Summer 1991.

Suro, Roberto, "U.S. Will Issue Warnings on Medical Marijuana Laws," *The Washington Post*, December 31, 1996.

Thornton, Arland, "Comparative and Historical Perspectives on Marriage, Divorce, and Family Life," 1994 *Utah Law Review* 587, 1994.

Thorson, Thomas L., *The Logic of Democracy.* New York: Holt, Rinehart, and Winston, 1962.

Toobin, Jeffrey, "The Agonizer: Justice Kennedy," *The New Yorker,* November 11, 1996.

U.S. Census Bureau, "Nation's Median Age Highest Ever," *U.S. Department of Commerce News,* May 15, 2001.

U.S. Department of Justice, Bureau of Justice Statistics, Special Report 178247, *Intimate Partner Violence,* May 2000.

U.S. Senate Special Committee on Aging, 101st Congress, Report, *Aging America: Trends and Projections (Annotated).* Washington, DC: Government Printing Office, 1990.

Urofsky, Melvin I., *Lethal Judgments: Assisted Suicide and American Law.* Lawrence: University Press of Kansas, 2000.

Vetri, Dominick, "Almost Everything You Always Wanted to Know About Lesbians and Gay Men, their Families, and the Law," 26 *Southern University Law Review* 1, Fall 1998.

Walsh, Edward, "An Activist Court Mixes Its High-Profile Messages," *The Washington Post,* July 2, 2000.

———, "High-Tech Devices Require a Warrant," *The Washington Post,* June 12, 2001.

Walsh, Edward and Amy Goldstein, "Supreme Court Upholds Two Key Abortion Rights," *The Washington Post,* June 29, 2000.

Walsh, Kenneth G., "Throwing Stones: Rational Basis Review Triumphs Over Homophobia," 27 *Seton Hall Law Review* 1064, 1997.

Walters, Stacy R., "Life-Sustaining Medical Decisions Involving Children: Father Knows Best," 15 *Thomas M. Cooley Law Review* 115, 1998.

Wolfson, Evan and Michael F. Melcher, "DOMA's House Divided: Why The Federal Anti-Gay, Anti-Marriage Law Is Unconstitutional," *The Federal Lawyer,* September 1997.

Woodward, C. Van, *The Strange Career of Jim Crow.* New York: Oxford University Press, 1955, 1974.

Wu, Lawrence, "Family Planning Through Human Cloning: Is There a Fundamental Right?" 98 *Columbia Law Review* 1461, October 1998.

Index

About the Author

Howard Ball is Professor of Political Science and University Scholar at the University of Vermont and Adjunct Professor of Law at Vermont Law School. He is the author of almost two dozen books on the U.S. Supreme Court and has written over three dozen articles in political science and law reviews and journals.